Germany on the Road to "Normalcy"

EUROPE IN TRANSITION: THE NYU EUROPEAN STUDIES SERIES

Germany on the Road to "Normalcy": Policies and Politics of the Red–Green Federal Government (1998–2002)

Edited by
Werner Reutter

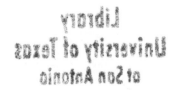

GERMANY ON THE ROAD TO 'NORMALCY'
© Werner Reutter, 2004

First published 2004 by
PALGRAVE MACMILLAN™
175 Fifth Avenue, New York, N.Y. 10010 and
Houndmills, Basingstoke, Hampshire, England RG21 6XS
Companies and representatives throughout the world

PALGRAVE MACMILLAN is the global academic imprint of the Palgrave Macmillan division of St. Martin's Press, LLC and of Palgrave Macmillan Ltd. Macmillan® is a registered trademark in the United States, United Kingdom and other countries. Palgrave is a registered trademark in the European Union and other countries.

ISBN 1–4039–6439–4 hardback

Library of Congress Cataloging-in-Publication Data
    Germany on the road to 'normalcy' : policies and politics of the
    Red-Green Federal government (1998–2002) / Werner Reutter (editor).
      p. cm.
    Includes bibliographical references and index.
    ISBN 1–4039–6439–4
      1. Political parties—Germany. 2. Coalition governments—Germany.
    3. Germany—Economic conditions. 4. Germany—Social conditions.
    5. Germany—Politics and government—1990– I. Reutter, Werner.

JN3971.A979G456 2004
320.943'09'049—dc22   2003058229

A catalogue record for this book is available from the British Library.

Design by Newgen Imaging Systems (P) Ltd., Chennai, India.

First edition: April, 2004
10 9 8 7 6 5 4 3 2 1

Printed in the United States of America.

Contents

Introduction

Part One   Institutional and Structural Dimensions: Parties, Coalition Government, and Chancellor Democracy

List of Tables

List of Figures

Abbreviations

ABM	Anti-Ballistic Missile
ALMP	Active Labor Market Policy
BDA	Bundesvereinigung der Deutschen Arbeitgeberverbände (Confederation of German Employers' Associations)
BDI	Bundesverband der Deutschen Industrie (Federation of German Industries)
BfV	Bundesamt für Verfassungsschutz (Federal Office for the Protection of the Constitution)
BGS	Bundesgrenzschutz (Federal Border Police)
BKA	Bundeskriminalamt (Federal Criminal Police Office)
BMAS	Bundesministerium für Arbeit und Sozialordnung (Federal Ministry of Labor and Social Affairs)
BMBF	Bundesministerium für Bildung und Forschung (Ministry of Education and Research)
BMF	Bundesministerium der Finanzen (Federal Ministry of Finance)
BMFSFJ	Bundesministerium für Frauen, Senioren, Familie und Jugend (Federal Ministry of Women, Elderly, Family, and Youth)
BMG	Bundesministerium für Gesundheit (Federal Ministry of Health)
BMI	Bundesministerium des Innern (Federal Ministry of the Interior)
BMU	Bundesministerium für Umwelt-, Naturschutz und Reaktorsicherheit (Federal Environmental Ministry)
BMWA	Bundesministerium für Wirtschaft und Arbeit (Federal Ministry of Economics and Labor)
BND	Bundesnachrichtendienst (Federal Intelligence Service)
BP	Bayernpartei (Bavarian Party)
BT-Drs.	Bundestags-Drucksache (Printed matter of the *Bundestag*)
BUND	Bund für Umwelt und Naturschutz Deutschland (Friends of the Earth)

BVerfGE	Entscheidungen des Bundesverfassungsgerichts (Decisions of the Federal Constitutional Court)
CAP	Common Agricultural Policy
CDU	Christlich Demokratische Union Deutschlands (Christian Democratic Union of Germany)
CEE	Central and Eastern Europe
CFSP	Common Foreign and Security Policy
CO_2	Carbon dioxide
CSU	Christlich Soziale Union in Bayern (Christian-Social Union in Bavaria)
DAG	Deutsche Angestellten-Gewerkschaft (Trade Union of Employees)
DGB	Deutscher Gewerkschaftsbund (German Confederation of Trade Unions)
DIW	Deutsches Institut für Wirtschaftsforschung (German Institute for Economic Research)
DKP/DRP	Deutsche Konservative Partei/Deutsche Rechtspartei (German Conservative Party/German Law Party)
DM	Deutsche Mark (German Mark)
DP	Deutsche Partei (German Party)
DPG	Deutsche Postgewerkschaft (Postal Workers' Union)
DVU	Deutsche Volksunion (German People Union)
EC	European Community
ECB	European Central Bank
ECOMOG	Economic Community of West African Monitoring Group
EFSP	European Foreign and Security Policy
EMS	European Monetary System
EP	European Parliament
EPC	European Political Cooperation
ESDI	European Security and Defense Identity
ESDP	European Security and Defense Policy
EU	European Union
FDP	Freie Demokratische Partei (Free Democratic Party)
FDP/DVP	Freie Demokratische Partei/Demokratische Volkspartei (Free Democratic Party/German People's Party)
GB-BHE	Gesamtdeutscher Block/Bund der Heimatvertriebenen und Entrechteten (Party of Expellees)
GDP	Gross Domestic Product
GDR	German Democratic Republic
GSG 9	Grenzschutzgruppe 9 (Anti-terror unit of BGS)

HBV	Gewerkschaft Handel, Banke, Versicherungen (Trade Union for Trade, Banking, and Insurance)
IEP	Institut für Europäische Politik (Institute of European Politics, Berlin)
IG BCE	Industriegewerkschaft Bergbau, Chemie, Energie (Trade Union for Mining, Chemicals, Energy)
IGC	Inter-Governmental Conference
IGM	Industriegewerkschaft Metall (Metalworkers' Union)
IG Medien	Industriegewerkschaft Medien (Trade Union for Media Workers)
ISAF	International Security Force in Afghanistan
KFOR	Kosovo Force
KPD	Kommunistische Partei Deutschlands (German Communist Party)
MAD	Militärischer Abschirmdienst (Military Counterintelligence Service)
MONUC	UN Mission in the Democratic Republic of Congo
MP	Member of Parliament
NATO	North Atlantic Treaty Organization
NGO	Non-Governmental Organization
NPD	Nationaldemokratische Partei Deutschlands (National Democratic Party of Germany)
OECD	Organization for Economic Cooperation and Development
OSCE	Organization for Security and Cooperation in Europe
ÖTV	Gewerkschaft Öffentliche Dienste, Transport und Verkehr (Trade Union for Public Services, Transport, and Communication)
PDS	Partei des Demokratischen Sozialismus (Party of Democratic Socialism)
PRO	Partei Rechtsstaatliche Offensive (Party for Rule-of-Law-Offensive)
RNE	Rat für Nachhaltige Entwicklung (Council for Sustainable Development)
RSF	Radikal-Soziale Freiheitspartei (Radical Liberty Party)
SDE	Social Democratic-led Economies
SED	Sozialistische Einheitspartei (Socialist Unity Party)
SFOR	Stabilization Force in Bosnia and Herzegovina
SGB	Sozialgesetzbuch (Law on Social Welfare)
SPD	Sozialdemokratische Partei Deutschlands (Socialdemocratic Party of Germany)

SRU	Rat von Sachverständigen für Umweltfragen (Council of Environmental Advisors)
SVR	Sachverständigenrat zur Begutachtung der gesamtwirtschaftlichen Entwicklung (Council of Economic Advisers)
TAFKO	Task Force Kosovo
UK	United Kingdom
UN	United Nations
UNAMSIL	United Nations Mission in Sierra Leone
UNIKOM	United Nations Iraq–Kuwait Observation Mission
UNMIBH	United Nations Mission in Bosnia and Herzegovina
UNMIK	United Nations Mission in Kosovo
UNOMIG	United Nations Observer Mission in Georgia
Ver.di	Vereinte Dienstleistungsgewerkschaft (United Services' Union)
WAV	Wirtschaftliche Aufbau Vereinigung (Economic Reconstruction League)
WZB	Wissenschaftszentrum Berlin für Sozialforschung (Social Science Research Center Berlin)
ZP	Zentrumspartei (Center Party)

Preface and Acknowledgments

Unification, it seemed, had solved the notorious "German Question" for good and put the country on the road to "normalcy"—whatever that means. Unification had created the first German nation-state satisfied with its external and internal settings. At the international level Germany had regained its full sovereignty, it was irreversibly integrated in the European Union and in the Western security system. Domestically the West German "model" has proved its superiority over the socialist experiment in the East. However, hardly a decade later, Germany, the former European star pupil, has been transformed into a problem child, and many hold the first Red–Green federal government responsible for the current "German malaise." This situation raises important questions about the performance of the Red–Green government and the political structure of the German polity after unification. The book analyzes these questions in detail. It draws an encompassing picture about the current state of affairs in Germany, puts the Red–Green government in a long-term perspective, and provides some conclusions about future developments.

Most of the contributions in this book were originally presented at a conference at the University of Minnesota on 26–29 September 2002, that is, shortly after the last federal election. It is, hence, my pleasure to thank all those who contributed to the conference and the book. First, I would like to thank John Freeman, Chair of the Department of Political Science at the University of Minnesota, Jack Zipes, Eric Weitz, and the Center for German and European Studies at the University of Minnesota. They supported the plan of a conference right from the beginning. I received helpful comments from Alison Alter, Stephen Feinstein, Bob Holt, Morris Kleiner, Simon Reich, Terry J. Roe, David J. Samuels, Joachim Savelsberg, Phil Shively, Klass Van der Sanden, and Gerhard Weiss. Special thanks go to Cheryl Olsen and Kristen Jones for their untiring administrative support. Kristen Jones and especially Angelica Fenner corrected and improved the style and language of most of the articles, and Ashley Biser compiled the index.

Everybody knows that the realization of this kind of project depends on institutions and organizations willing to finance scientific ideas. I am therefore especially grateful to the Washington Office of the Friedrich Ebert Foundation and its Director, Dr. Dieter Dettke, the German Academic Exchange Service, the Department of German Dutch and Scandinavian Studies, the College of Liberal Arts, and the Lippincott Fund of the Department of Political Science at the University of Minnesota.

Finally I would like to thank Michael and Ilana Favero. They literally made me feel "at home" in Minneapolis.

I dedicate the book to Susanne, my "significant other," as they say in the United States. Even though she had to bear all the negative side effects of this enterprise she never stopped supporting me.

Minneapolis and Berlin, May/June 2003
Werner Reutter

Notes on Contributors

GERT-JOACHIM GLAESSNER is Professor of Political Science at the Humboldt University in Berlin. He has published widely on problems of communist and postcommunist systems, German politics, and unification. Among his books are: *The German Unification Process* (1992); *Demokratie und Politik in Deutschland* (1999) and *Sicherheit in Freiheit. Die Schutzfunktion des demokratischen Staates und die Freiheit der Bürger* (forthcoming). E-mail: Gert-Joachim.Glaessner@rz.hu-berlin.de.

KURT HÜBNER is Professor of International Political Economy at the Berlin School of Economics, and Visiting Associate Professor at the Canadian Centre for German and European Studies, York University in Toronto, Canada. His main research fields are: currency regimes and global finance, Germany and the European Union. His latest books include: *Spiel mit Grenzen. Ökonomische Globalisierung und soziale Kohäsion* (2002) and *New Economy in Transatlantic Perspective* (forthcoming). E-mail: khuebner@YorkU.CA.

KRISTINE KERN is Senior Research Fellow at the Social Science Research Center, Berlin (WZB). Her research interests focus on governance of multilevel systems; globalization and transnational networks; policy diffusion and policy transfer; environmental policy and sustainable development. Her recent publications are: *Die Diffusion von Politikinnovation. Umweltpolitische Innovationen im Mehrebenensystem der USA* (2000) and *Zivilgesellschaft, Demokratie und Sozialkapital. Herausforderungen politischer und sozialer Integration* (2003, coeditor). E-mail: kern@wz-berlin.de.

STEPHANIE KOENEN received her graduate degree in Political Science from Berlin's Free University in June 2002. She currently works as a consultant for nonprofit management and as a project assistant in a European youth employment project. Her main research interest is in the influence of identity and culture on national foreign policy and their role in international relations. In this context, she has primarily worked on European integration and the development of a Common European Foreign and Security Policy. E-mail: steffi.koenen@web.de.

SABINE KROPP is Visiting Professor of Political Science and German Politics at the Faculty for Economics and Social Sciences, University of Potsdam. In 2000/2001 she was head of the Minister's Office in the Ministry for Housing, Urban Development and Transport in Saxony-Anhalt. Her publications include a number of books on decentralization in Russia, on coalition politics in Germany as well as in Western and Eastern Europe, such as: *Regieren in Koalitionen. Handlungsmuster und Entscheidungsbildung in deutschen Länderregierungen* (2001) and *Koalitionen in West- und Osteuropa* (2002, coeditor). E-mail: skropp@rz.uni-potsdam.de.

BARBARA LIPPERT is Deputy Director of the Institute of European Politics in Berlin (IEP), managing editor of the quarterly journal *integration* and Lecturer at Humboldt University Berlin. Her research fields include German EU policy, EU enlargement, relations between the EU and Central and Eastern European countries, and transformation of political systems in CEE. Publications include: *Auswärtige Kulturpolitik im Zeichen der Ostpolitik. Verhandlungen mit Moskau 1969–1990* (1996) and *Die Finanzierung der Osterweiterung der EU* (2002, coauthor). E-mail: blippert@iep-berlin.de.

TINA LÖFFELSEND graduated in Political Science from the Free University Berlin. She currently works as a Research Assistant at the Social Science Research Center Berlin (WZB) in projects on transnational environmental policy. Her main research interest is in the role and diffusion of norms in international relations and the concurrent change of governance in the international system. In this context, she has primarily focused on European integration and the human rights regime. E-mail: t.loeffelsend@web.de.

AUGUST PRADETTO is Professor of Political Science at the University of the Armed Forces Hamburg and holds the Chair for Foreign and International Policy of Central and Eastern European States. His main fields of interest are German and European foreign and security policy, international relations, foreign policy and security structures of Central and Eastern Europe and the Soviet Union since 1945, European integration, and transition processes in Central and Eastern Europe. Among his recent publications are: "Instrumenteller Multilateralismus und servile Rezeption: Der Irak, die USA und Europa," *Blätter für deutsche und internationale Politik* (no. 02, 2003) and *Internationale Reaktionen auf die Irak-Politik der USA. Studien zur Internationalen Politik* (2003, editor). E-mail: august.pradetto@unibw-hamburg.de.

WERNER REUTTER is Visiting Associate Professor of Political Science at the University of Minnesota. His research interests mainly focus on German and West European politics. He has published books and articles on interest groups, the international trade union movement, and on constitutional politics. Among his books are: *Möglichkeiten und Grenzen internationaler Gewerkschaftspolitik* (1998) and *Verbände und Verbandssysteme in Westeuropa* (2001, coeditor). E-mail: wreutter@polisci.umn.edu.

ROBERT ROHRSCHNEIDER is Professor of Political Science at Indiana University. His research interests center on comparative politics of advanced industrialized democracies with a concentration on Europe. He is especially interested in comparative public opinion, political parties, electoral behavior, democratization, environmentalism, and political culture. His publications include: *Learning Democracy. Democratic and Economic Values in Unified Germany (1999)*, which won the 1998 Stein Rokkan prize for Comparative Social Science Research. His research has also been published in such journals as the *American Journal of Political Science, American Political Science Review*, the *European Journal of Political Research, Comparative Political Studies*, and the *Journal of Politics*. E-mail: rrohrsch@indiana.edu

OLIVER SCHMIDTKE is Associate Professor at the University of Victoria (B.C., Canada). Among his recent publications are: *Politics of Identity. Ethnicity, Territory and the Political Opportunity Structure in Modern Italian Society* (1996) and *The Third Transformation of Social Democracy* (2002, editor). His areas of expertise include comparative European politics, EU integration, and political sociology. Presently his research interests focus on questions related to immigration, citizenship, ethnic conflict, and issues of multilevel governance. E-mail: oliver@uvic.ca

MARTIN SEELEIB-KAISER is Senior Research Fellow at the Centre for Social Policy Research, Bremen University. His research interests include: party politics, political economy, and comparative welfare state analysis. In addition to his recent publication entitled *Globalisierung und Sozialpolitik. Ein Vergleich der Diskurse und Wohlfahrtssysteme in Deutschland, Japan und den USA* (2001), he has published numerous articles in journals such as: *Czech Sociological Review, German Politics, Politische Vierteljahresschrift, Social Policy&Administration, Zeitschrift für Soziologie*, and *West European Politics*. E-mail: mseeleib@zes.uni-bremen.de.

BERNHARD WESSELS is Senior Researcher at the Social Science Research Center Berlin (WZB) and Lecturer of Political Science at the Free University of Berlin. His main fields of interest are: comparative politics, in particular electoral behavior and electoral systems, parliaments and political representation, and interest groups and interest intermediation. His recent book publications include: *The European Parliament, the National Parliaments, and European Integration* (1999, coeditor) and *Policy Representation in Western Democracies* (1999, coauthor). E-mail: wessels@wz-berlin.de.

MICHAEL WOLF is Assistant Professor of Political Science at Indiana University—Purdue University, Fort Wayne. His research concentrates on comparative and American political behavior, political parties, and dealignment. His current projects cover the responsiveness of different electoral groups to campaign cues in advanced industrial societies. E-mail: wolfm@ipfw.edu.

Introduction

CHAPTER 1

Germany on the Road to "Normalcy": Policies and Politics of the Red–Green Federal Government (1998–2002)

Werner Reutter

Gerhard Schröder started his campaign for reelection with a rally in his hometown of Hanover in Lower Saxony on 5 August 2002. He opened his speech with a phrase that was to become a major motif in the following weeks and months. Schröder declared that his government had set off "on our German way."[1] Albeit he may have intended to reference the domestic agenda and the *Modell Deutschland,* which Helmut Schmidt had introduced some 25 years earlier, Schröder surely knew that this allusion would evoke memories of the notorious pre- and interwar debates about a German *Sonderweg* and German exceptionalism. Schröder furthermore failed on this and other occasions to define (or perhaps deliberately avoided addressing) what he really meant by "our German way." Yet he did make clear that this formulation was not merely empty rhetoric. He justified his refusal to support the American policy toward Iraq by referring to national interests. Schröder criticized the American strategy and the threat to wage war on Iraq if it did not comply with international and American decisions. He refused to participate in any "adventure" and stated that the "checkbook diplomacy" of the Kohl era was over. Instead the new German security and foreign policy would be based on "self-conscious solidarity" and guided by the national interests of the German people (Schröder 2002a,d).

Notwithstanding Schröder's criticism of the Bush administration, which led to a postwar low in German–American relations, this speech did not amount to a major shift in Red–Green foreign policy. Both August Pradetto and Barbara Lippert show in their contributions to this volume (chapters 11 and 12) that the perspective briefly touched upon in Schröder's speech had already shaped foreign policy and the European politics of the first Red–Green government between 1998 and 2002. From the outset of his tenure, Schröder had stressed that his coalition would act in a different way than former governments, and kept emphasizing "national interests" in many speeches made during his term in office. This in itself seems justification enough to ask whether Germany is finally on the road to "normalcy."

Germany's Normalcy

Since 1949, the question of whether Germany[2] is on the road to "normalcy" has been repeatedly posed, in spite of the fact that the answers hardly vary and remain overwhelmingly positive. Even after unification there was no doubt that Germany would remain firmly integrated into international and European organizations and be part of the "West," that relations to the United States especially would remain close and amicable, and that former *Machtpolitik*, power politics, had been resolutely rejected and replaced with an unwavering commitment to democracy and the precedence of international over national interests. The "greatest political achievement" of the postwar period, "the unconditional opening of the Federal Republic to the political culture of the West," as Jürgen Habermas (1993: 43) expressed it during the *Historikerstreit*, was not in jeopardy. The "German question" appeared solved for good. However, the subtlety of the "German question" rests not in the answer. The question itself is intriguing, necessarily implying that Germany's domestic and foreign policy can only be understood in the light of its history and that this history was and still is overshadowed by the Third Reich and the Holocaust. This historical legacy has very much shaped and influenced Germany's domestic developments, international relations, and the perceptions of Germany from abroad (Markovits and Reich 1997).

But it would be misleading to assume that this historical legacy is a sort of unwavering national constant or a fixture that remains unchanged over time and across generations. On the contrary, since 1949, three periods can be distinguished, each characterized by a specific way of registering the recent past in the national collective memory of Germany. The period of *Beschweigen* of the Holocaust (a sort of "deliberative and intended silence") in the 1950s and 1960s by the generation of the perpetrators, bystanders, and even many victims, was followed by a phase of *Vergangenheitsbewältigung* during the 1970s and 1980s, that is, public and political attempts to actively come to terms with the past. The contemporary generation seems to regard history in more pragmatic terms. This attitude does not downplay or deny the significance of the Holocaust and respects the responsibilities accruing from history. But because its representatives lack any personal experience with the Third Reich, they approach history in a more distant and ritualized manner, grounded in the mostly intellectual appropriation of the recent German past through the process of *Vergangenheitsbewältigung*. Some even claim that German's current politics is shaped by a sort of *Geschichtsvergessenheit*, of ignorance about Germany's past—not without reason at least as far as Gerhard Schröder is concerned (see also Lippert, chapter 12 in this volume). In line with this shift in attitude, history, the Third Reich, and Auschwitz are regarded as having a less formative impact on contemporary youth than 20 or 30 years ago (Deutsche Shell 2002).

Every generation deals with this historical legacy in its own way, and this is, of course, also true for the Red–Green coalition, whose members were mostly "sixty-eighters." Even before representatives of this generation came to power, Andrei S. Markovits and Simon Reich (1997) predicted that Germany's perception of itself, its power, and its foreign policy would witness significant changes, recognizing that future political elites would lack first-hand experience with the Third Reich and, thus, treat this historical legacy in a different way. From this perspective, the shaping of the elites by postmaterial values, their political socialization in the 1960s and 1970s, and the transformations taking place in the economy will necessarily have repercussions for national identity.

From a sociological point of view, the first Red–Green coalition was the first truly postwar government. In 2002 the members of the government were on average about 56 years old. Most of them were born in the early 1940s or after the end of World War II. Gerhard Schröder, for example, was born in 1944 and Joschka Fischer, the foreign minister, in 1948. Consequently, most members of this government lacked any personal experience with the war or with the Third Reich. Once in office this surely made it easier for them to speak more freely about "national interests" and redefine Germany's role in international politics.

In addition, most members of the former government were very much involved in the student movement of the 1960s and in social movements in the 1970s and 1980s. Gerhard Schröder, who is a trained lawyer, defended activists against nuclear power plants in the 1970s. Otto Schily, minister of the interior, had also been a practicing lawyer and defended members of the terrorist Red-Army Faction in the 1970s. Joschka Fischer, one of the founders of the Green party, similarly belonged to some leftist groups and even had to admit in 2000/2001 that he had attacked a policeman during one of the demonstrations in which he participated in the mid-1970s. It is worth pointing out that all this happened when the Social Democratic Party of Germany (SPD) was in power. It can be regarded as one of the great ironies of history that when in office, the very same people who had fought against Helmut Schmidt's policies in the 1970s had to make decisions they would have bitterly opposed and fiercely criticized some 25 years ago.

In combination with German unification, these generational changes had to have some impact on German political culture. Before 1989/90 the political culture in West Germany was very much shaped by an anti-totalitarian consensus grounded in the dual stances of anticommunism and antifascism. Of course, democracy always excludes communism and fascism. But in Germany the constitutional interpretation and its politics, the political culture, and the development of the welfare state cannot fully be understood without referring to the historical legacies of the Third Reich and to the socialist experiment in East Germany (Merkl 1965; Niclauß 1998). This also created the basis for playing down nationalism and replacing it by a sort of *Verfassungspatriotismus*, constitutional patriotism, albeit this remained a rather intellectual and elitist concept. The concept of *Verfassungspatriotismus* was first introduced by Dolf Sternberger (1990)[3] and was popularized by Jürgen Habermas during the *Historikerstreit* and the unification process (Habermas 1990, 1993). It basically rests on the assumption that after the catastrophe of the Third Reich the "nation" could no longer be a focal point for the affective integration of the German political community. It was to be replaced by a sort of enlightened patriotism that should rest on the Basic Law and the successful West German development after 1949. This aspect of national self-identification was reconfirmed in the mid-1980s during the *Historikerstreit*, and unification did not immediately affect this basis for (West-)Germany's self-understanding. On the contrary, Kohl and his two post-unification governments guaranteed a high degree of continuity within (West-)German identity. Perhaps no other German politician than Helmut Kohl could have so perfectly symbolized the illusion that nothing would change in West Germany after unification.

However, many observed a shift in national identity between 1998 and 2002. In retrospect, Martin Walser's notorious speech on 11 October 1998, shortly after the federal elections, somehow seems like the resurfacing and long-awaited prelude to a debate about collective memory, historical guilt, and national identity. In his speech, Martin Walser (1998) characterized Auschwitz and the Holocaust as a "moral cudgel" (*Moralkeule*) used in an illegitimate way to constrain modern Germany and prevent it from developing a new national identity. Although Gerhard Schröder neither positively nor negatively commented on this speech, he agreed readily enough to participate in a public debate with Walser on the state of the German nation as his first tenure was drawing to an end. This debate, which was organized by the SPD, took place on 8 May 2002, that is, on the anniversary of the German capitulation at the end of World War II. While the event was much less interesting than expected, it reinforced Schröder's claim to represent the *Neue Mitte*, the new political Center in Germany, by appealing to national sentiments. The aforementioned political discourse about "enlightened national interests" was, hence, interfaced by and linked with corresponding cultural debates. It goes without saying that the conservative parties did not want to stand back. With their notorious debate about a German *Leitkultur*, they attempted to attract the very same constituency as Schröder (see also Schmidtke, chapter 9 in this volume). It fits perfectly well with these developments that the last election campaign witnessed attempts to exploit national sentiments in a populist way as well.

Probably the most notorious example of this was provided by Jürgen W. Möllemann, who was one of the deputy chairmen of the FDP and head of the most important party's state organization in North Rhine Westphalia. He was a well-known politician, a former federal minister, and had a huge influence in the liberal party. Möllemann played a populist card in the last election campaign in order to realize one of the electoral goals of the FDP, namely, to win 18 percent of the votes and to transform the FDP into a liberal "catch-all-party." In order to achieve this goal he sharply criticized Israel's and Ariel Scharon's policy in the occupied territories and in the Middle East, he claimed that statements by representatives of the German Jewish community justified the resentment of Germans toward the Jews, and he attempted to exploit undercurrent nationalistic and anti-Semitic sentiments in Germany.[4]

Albeit many of the aforementioned examples remained at the level of rhetoric or symbolic politics and did not find an echo in radically new political strategies, they nevertheless indicate that German political culture is shifting. Of course, it would be ridiculous to assume that these examples are a sort of prelude for a new nationalist Germany. August Pradetto and Barbara Lippert both make it clear in their contributions (chapters 11 and 12) that Germany's foreign policy is still guided by the very same principles—even though some important changes have taken place. But the combination of generational changes, shifts in public discourses, and a different stance toward the nation and national interests indicate that the German *Verfassungspolitik* has adopted tender nationalist colors. In this respect Germany has become as "normal" as this country could possibly get 50 years after the end of World War II. The oxymoron "Germany's Normalcy" points to this state of affairs.

The German "Semisovereign State" in Action: Policies and Politics of the Red–Green Government (1998–2002)

As already mentioned, Gerhard Schröder's allusions to "our German way" not only fueled debates about a new national identity, they also touched upon a concept first successfully employed in 1976 by Helmut Schmidt, the former SPD chancellor, which came to be known as the "German model." Until a few years ago, many scholars were very much intrigued by the lasting and ongoing success of the "German model" (Pulzer 1996; Paterson and Smith 1981; Markovits 1982). Referring to Germany's postwar success, Peter Katzenstein (1987) labeled Germany a "semisovereign" state, that is, one whose sovereignty is limited and whose structure is dispersed and fragmented. Albeit Katzenstein did not rule out that "bold policy change" (Katzenstein 1987: 385) might occur in Germany, he regarded this as an unlikely result of the political process. Due to the institutional structure of the German polity, radical reforms require a broad consensus and demand compromises that rarely lead to far-reaching changes, but rather, to the "policy of the middle way," which was so characteristic of the German "Grand Coalition State" (Schmidt 1987, 1996; cf. also Holtman and Voelzkow 2000).

As the contributions to this volume show, the first Red–Green federal government seems a most promising case with which to answer the question as to whether the German "semisovereign state" still leads to the aforementioned results. In fact, at the outset there were great expectations of the previous government regarding "bold policy change" and for dissolving the notorious *Reformstau* of the Kohl era. The two parties had ousted Helmut Kohl out of office after 16 years of rule and the Red–Green coalition was the first government composed of the SPD and Alliance '90/The Greens. Many studies in the same vein addressed the question of whether this Day of Judgment in 1998[5] had marked the end of an era, herein already insinuating that a new era was about to begin (Padgett and Saalfeld 2000; Conradt et al. 2000). So the expectation that the alternation in government was going to make a difference and that the Red–Green coalition would initiate overdue reforms seemed high in 1998, although it was already being claimed that the new government lacked a clear agenda and an encompassing program (e.g., Habermas 2001: 11–24).

Table 1.1 gives an overview of the policy fields covered in this volume. It categorizes and differentiates these policy fields according to three dimensions, which are analyzed in more detail in part 1 of this book and which refer to the institutional and structural preconditions. The first dimension indicates whether in the respective policy field the *Bundesrat* or the Federal Constitutional Court had direct restraining

Table 1.1 Policies of the Red–Green government

	Role of veto-players (Bundesrat *and* Constitutional Court) *(polity)*	*Policies and programs (policies)*	*Coalition politics and party conflicts (politics)*	*Output*
Alliance for Jobs	Without direct effects	Old Politics (Third Way)	Conflicts between "old" and "new" Left	Poor, mostly failure
Economic policy	Without direct effects	Old Politics (Third Way)	Conflicts between "old" and "new" Left	Poor, failure
Social policy	Without direct effects	Old Politics (Third Way)	Highly controversial, "old" and "new" Left	Reforms, continuity
Domestic security	Without direct effects	Ad hoc (Old Politics)	Hardly restraining	Modest reforms
Immigration	Partly important (invalidation of law on immigration)	New Politics	SPD cautioned on immigration and citizenship	Modest, reforms
Environmental policy	Without direct effects	New Politics	SPD partly restraining	Mixed, partly successful
Foreign policy	Without direct effects	Unspecific, ambiguous	Partly controversial, conflicts	Partly "paradigm shift"
European politics	Without direct effects	Unspecific, ambiguous	Consensus	Mainly continuity, new rhetoric

effects either by vetoing bills or by invalidating them. The second dimension classifies the policy field either as "Old" or "New Politics" (Baker et al. 1981: 136–62). "Old Politics" is based on the traditional cleavage structure (see Wessels, chapter 3 in this volume) notably between capital and labor and addresses mostly materialist issues. These policy areas (like social policy, labor market policy, economics) are highly organized with established party structures, trade unions, employer organizations, and the like (see part 2 in this volume). "New Politics" rests on postmaterialist values (Inglehart 1997) and is most prominently represented by the Green party and new social movements (see part 3, Schmidtke, and Kern et al., chapters 9 and 10 in this volume). It covers environmental matters, as well as immigration, and includes new forms of political participation. Rather difficult to classify, however, is internal security (see Glaessner, chapter 8 in this volume). Because it was mainly developed on an ad hoc basis after the terrorist attacks in New York and Washington, it was included in part 3. Germany's foreign policy and European politics are difficult to classify as well. Even though some aspects (like the human rights perspective, which Joschka Fischer in particular had developed as a major motif for his policies) point to "New" rather than to "Old Politics," Schröder's *leitmotiv* of "national interests" does not fit into this picture. The fourth column indicates whether party competition and coalition politics played a significant role for decision-making and the output in the policy areas. The final column tries to summarize how "successfully" the Red–Green government performed in the respective policy field. It goes without saying that the contributions to this volume arrive at varied and detailed results. They also make clear that the equation, "change means success," when applied to a government, is far too superficial. Seeleib-Kaiser (chapter 7) for example, shows that the social policy was an "overall success" not only because it put into practice most of the respective stipulations in the coalition agreement, but because it continued the "dual transformation" of the German welfare state already set in motion in former legislative terms—notwithstanding the fact that these reforms failed to solve the current problems of the German social security system.

It is striking that, contrary to the views of many critics, significant "successes" have been achieved in some areas. As already mentioned, the social policy was an "overall success" (Martin Seeleib-Kaiser, chapter 7); Kristine Kern, Stephanie Koenen, and Tina Löffelsend (chapter 10) report that the environmental policy is regarded as one of the "few success stories" of the last government, despite a few setbacks; and

August Pradetto (chapter 11) partly identifies a "paradigm shift" in foreign policy and concludes that Germany is changing from a "tamed" to a "normal" power. Comparatively modest reforms took place in the areas of domestic security (Gert-Joachim Glaessner, chapter 8), in immigration policy (Oliver Schmidtke, chapter 9), and in European politics (Barbara Lippert, chapter 12). Hardly any changes were witnessed in the two areas that ranked highest as voter concerns in opinion polls: labor market policy (Werner Reutter, chapter 5) and economic policy (Kurt Hübner, chapter 6). They have to be characterized as "policy failures."

This mixed record foregrounds the fact that, in some areas, the last coalition did far better than many were ready to admit. But it also raises questions about the grounds for the differences and policy failures. The contributions to this volume refer to three highly interrelated factors in order to explain changes and/or failed reforms in the various policy areas: the program and the agenda in the respective policy field, the constraints set by party politics and coalition government, and finally the institutional framework that structures the decision-making process and limits the output. In addition, external shocks, unforeseen events, and both global and European developments played important roles in different policy areas (environmental policy, foreign policy, European politics, economic policy, labor market policy, and domestic security).

Comparative studies point out that institutional path dependency can be more important than converging programmatic forces. However this must not be interpreted in a deterministic way. As Sabine Kropp concludes in her convincing and subtle analysis (chapter 4), the output of political decision-making very much depended on the capacity of the chancellor and the cabinet to manage different arenas. Between 1998 and 2002, political decision-making was, therefore, a highly contingent process; further, the major domestic veto-players, the Federal Constitutional Court and the *Bundesrat*, have not blocked any major reform bills during the last four years—apart from the Law on Immigration, which was invalidated as unconstitutional in December 2002. Also the *Bundesrat* only partly functioned as an effective veto-player, even after the Red–Green coalition lost its majority in the upper house in February 1999.

By the end of the fourteenth legislative term, the *Bundesrat* had vetoed 19 bills, a figure well above the average of 10.7 vetoes per term (Bundesrat 2002). Yet, in these four years the *Bundesrat* ultimately denied approval for only seven bills. These figures are in similar ranges with other periods when there was a divided government, that is, when the government had no majority in the upper house. As in former periods, between 1998 and 2002 the opposition parties also tried to use the *Bundesrat* as an "instrument of blockage." However, it has to be stressed that no important bill was blocked due to the missing approval of the *Bundesrat* between 1998 and 2002. This raises the question of why, in contrast to earlier periods, most notably the Christian Democratic Union of Germany (CDU) more or less failed to transform its potential influence in the upper house into an effective veto-position.

While I may risk stretching the point too far, I would assume that these developments were not only attributable to *fortuna* or to Gerhard Schröder's exceptional *virtú*, to invoke the terms used by Niccolò Machiavelli (1983) to describe techniques and morality of ruling. To be sure, Schröder had *fortuna* when Helmut Kohl had to admit in December 1999 that he had misused donations and party funds and had violated the Law on Parties (*Parteiengesetz*) as well as Art. 21 of the German constitution. These and other acts of financial fraud committed by the CDU weakened the opposition for nearly two years, and Angela Merkel, the current chairwoman of the party, is still struggling to assert her position as leader of the party. It speaks in favor of Schröder's political talent and *virtú* that he knew how to capitalize on this weakness. However, there were also some structural shifts which may alter the decision-making process in Germany in a more profound and lasting way. Sabine Kropp (chapter 4) offers an important and interesting approach with which to examine these changes. She links the constitutionally defined structure of the political system with elements focusing on the party system and the logic of coalition government.

This link between the constitutional structure, on the one hand, and the functioning of the party system and party competition, on the other, is mostly regarded as a problematic one. It was Gerhard Lehmbruch (2000)[6] who first theorized that party competition and cooperative federalism function to create a structural contradiction or, as he later called it, a tension. While cooperative federalism requires compromises, negotiations, and consensus, the party system is based on competition, conflict, and majoritarian decision-making. Notwithstanding the fact that the implicit crisis assumption in his book turned out to be exaggerated, it still is a highly productive approach for analyzing the last coalition. However, it must be taken into account that the party system has experienced important changes as elaborated by Robert Rohrschneider and Michael Wolf and Bernhard Wessels (chapters 2 and 3).

Three aspects are most important in this regard: the party system has become more fragmented, there is a general tendency toward regionalization, and coalition building at the state level offers a variety of options. In his highly interesting analysis, Wessels stresses the point that there are in fact "three" party systems in Germany: a West German, an East German, and a Bavarian. This intensifies the conflict between responsiveness and governability, and also creates a special problem for the SPD. In a similar fashion, Robert Rohrschneider and Michael Wolf examine the differences between the East and West German electorates. Again, this created a "quandary" most particularly for the SPD, which can neither move to the Left without losing voters to the CDU, nor move to the Right without indirectly benefiting the Greens in the West and the Party of Democratic Socialism (PDS) in the East. Hence, it comes as no surprise that the Red–Green coalition could only return to office by dint of exceptional circumstances (i.e., the flooding in East Germany and the American threat to wage war on Iraq).

Both contributions confirm that in the last two decades the German party system witnessed important processes of differentiation and fragmentation, which were redirected and transformed by German unification in 1990. These changes were accompanied by a tendency toward regionalization. *Länder*-specific issues and interests became more prominent and determined the policies of the parties in the different states (Jeffery 1999).

However, the revaluation of local or state interests can improve the chances for federal governments to establish compromises across party borders. Coalition building at state levels has also become more heterogeneous. During the SPD/FDP (Free Democratic Party) governments between 1969 and 1982 there was no great coalition whatsoever at the state level and the FDP only very rarely formed a coalition with the CDU.[7] As a result, the structure of the federal party competition was mirrored and supported at the state level. In addition, during the period of the first Left of Center government in Germany between 1969 and 1982, party discipline assumed clear precedence over local or regional interests (Sturm 1999).

As table 1.2 shows, the situation was different between 1998 and 2002. Following the federal election in September 1998, the SPD and the Greens lost nearly all state elections in 1999 (apart from Bremen), and it was only the financial scandal of the CDU that halted and partly averted this downward trend. At the same time, all kinds of coalitions were formed during this period—although with some important exceptions. Berlin, Brandenburg, and Bremen had great coalitions, the Social–Liberal government returned to office in Rhineland Palatinate, in Saxony-Anhalt the SPD formed a minority government tolerated by the PDS, and in Mecklenburg-West Pomerania, and Berlin, the SPD

Table 1.2   State elections, state governments, and *Bundesrat* (1998–2002)

Länder (seats in Bundesrat)	Date of state election	Gain (+)/loss (−) (in %) in state elections for		State government before election 2002[a]	State government after state election[a]	SPD/Greens sympathetic votes in Bundesrat
		SPD	Greens			
Hesse (5)	02/07/99	+1.4	−4.0	*SPD/Greens*	CDU/FDP	33
Bremen (3)	06/06/99	+9.2	−4.2	SPD/CDU	SPD/CDU	33
Brandenburg (4)	09/05/99	−14.8	−1.0	*SPD*	SPD/CDU	29
Saarland (3)	09/05/99	−5.0	−2.3	*SPD*	CDU	26
Thuringia (4)	09/12/99	−11.1	−2.6	CDU/SPD	CDU	26
Saxony (4)	09/19/99	−5.9	−1.5	CDU	CDU	26
Berlin (4)	10/10/99	−1.2	−3.3	CDU/SPD	CDU/SPD	26
Schleswig-Holstein (4)	02/27/00	+3.3	−1.9	*SPD/Greens*	*SPD/Greens*	26
North Rhine-Westphalia (6)	05/14/00	−3.2	−2.9	*SPD/Greens*	*SPD/Greens*	26
Rhineland Palatinate (6)	03/25/01	+4.9	−1.7	SPD/FDP	SPD/FDP	26
Baden-Württemberg (6)	03/25/01	+8.2	−4.4	CDU/FDP	CDU/FDP	26
Hamburg (3)	09/23/01	+0.3	−5.3	*SPD/Greens*	CDU/PRO/FDP	23
Berlin (4)	10/21/01	+7.3	−0.8	*SPD/Greens*	*SPD/PDS*	22
Saxony-Anhalt[b] (4)	04/21/02	−15.9	−1.2	*SPD*	CDU/FDP	19
Mecklenburg-West Pomerania (3)	09/22/02	+6.3	−0.1	*SPD/PDS*	*SPD/PDS*	19
Lower Saxony[c] (6)	—	—	—	*SPD*	*SPD*	22
Bavaria[c] (6)	—	—	—	CSU	CSU	22

[a] Underlined: SPD and Greens or PDS form state government; regular = state government has at least one opposition party (i.e. CDU, CSU, or FDP). The PDS, opposition party in the *Bundestag*, is counted as sympathetic to the Red–Green government.
[b] Between 1998 and 2002 the SPD formed a minority government that was tolerated by the PDS.
[c] There were no state elections between September 1998 and September 2002 in Bavaria and in Lower Saxony. However, on 2 February 2003 the SPD lost the state election in Lower Saxony.

and the PDS finally entered formal coalitions. But it should be pointed out that there were no coalitions between the CDU and the Greens, not to mention the PDS. This is worth noting because it provided the SPD with the strategic advantage of different options, while the Greens could only form a coalition with the SPD. Furthermore, the participation of the SPD in governments in which either the CDU or the FDP were involved proved to be of special relevance in political decision-making (see Kropp, chapter 4 in this volume). It was precisely these mixed governments that were the prime addressees for horse-trading or other forms of compromise when a bill needed the approval of the *Bundesrat*.

Especially when it came to important bills, Gerhard Schröder used the means the German constitution had placed at his disposal either to outplay the *Bundesrat* or to secure a majority by some sort of horse-trading or package deal. As a result the institutional structure of the political system maintained its constraining influence, but between 1998 and 2002 it was far from being overdetermined. In areas where the government maintained a comparatively clear agenda and the political will to push through decisions, the institutional framework was never a hindrance to reforms or the passage of bills.

Conclusion

German unification in 1990 has created a sovereign nation-state, which for the first time in its history is territorially satisfied and surrounded by friends. But, in some regards, this historical event had minimal impact upon the identity of West Germany. The majority of adjustments and transformations were made by people in East Germany. This reality is perhaps most evidently symbolized in the figure of Helmut Kohl, the "Unification Chancellor" (*Kanzler der Einheit*), who represented continuity and West German tradition rather than radical change. Concomitantly, a number of studies highlighted amazing continuities between the "Bonn" and the "Berlin Republic." The Red–Green government acted very much in the same vein, and Gerhard Schröder's often quoted remark in the election campaign of 1998, that he did not want to make everything different, but most things better, reflects this in a very blunt way. However, at the beginning of the second term in power it seems that the Red–Green government eventually took into consideration that unification, European integration, and the globalization of the economy require far-reaching and structural reforms in important policy areas. Against this background the question about the future of the "German model" and a "German normalcy" refers to the "external" as well as to the "internal" setting of the unified country.

As far as foreign policy was concerned the Red–Green government made pivotal decisions. Surely, the Red–Green government paved the way for a more active foreign and security policy. Even though institutionalization and codification of international politics remained primary goals in foreign policy, the Red–Green government made it clear that in the future Germany would rely more on national interests and acknowledge its military forces. In this respect the notorious German "political dwarf" in international politics has grown up. It is still an open question as to what the results of these changes will be. But Germany has become aware that it has to play a different role in world politics. The generational and value changes, as well as the public discourses that took place during Schröder's first tenure, underpin this new German "normalcy" with regard to at least the external setting. Notwithstanding the disastrous impact the policy of Gerhard Schröder had on transatlantic relations and NATO it is safe to predict that there is no way back to a pre-unification position.

The other side of the "semisovereign state," the internal setting, witnessed some important reforms as well, but they were surely less deep and not as far-reaching. Nevertheless they already indicate that the Berlin Republic will ultimately be quite different from the Bonn Republic. Important features of the "German model" are in jeopardy. Even though the contributions to this volume reveal a mixed record, there are important areas that were crucial for the "Rhenish Capitalism" and in which the Red–Green government was not able to embark on structural reforms and initiate long-overdue changes. The Labor market and economic policy especially lacked a clear agenda and programmatic perspectives. This also holds true for other areas, where the Red–Green coalition just continued with the famous "policy of the middle way." It seems therefore most telling that areas belonging to "New Politics" were those that witnessed more radical changes. This points once again to the fact that the major deficit of the Red–Green government was that it failed to define a long-term perspective and to develop consistent agendas in the different policy fields. Of course, as former governments, the Red–Green coalition was restrained by the institutional structure of the German political system as it tried to address new challenges and problems. But the changes initiated prove that if there is a clear agenda and the political will to transform this agenda into decisions "bold policy change" is possible in Germany.

Today, Germany seems to be at a crossroads. Simple continuity of policies is not sufficient. In this respect, the first Red–Green coalition can be regarded as a transitory government: sociologically, ideologically, and politically it represented the "old" postwar (West)Germany, which did not yet grasp that the end of the GDR, unification, European integration, and globalization also necessarily involved a sort of second foundation of the FRG. Germany has yet to find a proper response to these challenges.

Notes

1. The opening sentence of his speech was: "Es ist wahr, wir haben uns auf den Weg gemacht, auf unseren deutschen Weg, . . ." (Schröder 2002d: 2).

2. If not indicated otherwise I only refer to West or to united Germany in this introduction.
3. Sternberger developed this concept first in an article in the *Frankfurter Allgemeine Zeitung* in 1979.
4. Cf. e.g. Leinemann 2002. After the election Mölleman who had distributed an illegally financed flyer left the FDP; he died in 2003.
5. Karl Popper (1988) qualified election days as Days of Judgment—if there is a plurality electoral system and a two-party system.
6. Lehmbruch's seminal study on "Parteienwettbewerb und Bundesstaat" was first published in 1976.
7. The CDU/FDP coalition in Lower Saxony existed between January 1977 and July 1978, and in Saarland the Christian–Liberal government lasted from 1977 until 1985 (Schindler 1999: 1451–56).

Institutional and Structural Dimensions: Parties, Coalition Government, and Chancellor Democracy

CHAPTER 2

One Electorate? Social Policy Views and Voters' Choice in Unified Germany Since 1990

Robert Rohrschneider and Michael Wolf

The 2002 federal election illustrates the wide regional divide between the East and the West. Despite the virtual tie in vote shares for the two largest parties, the SPD gained a substantial number of voters in the East compared to 1998, and lost significantly in the West. Further illustrating the regional character of German electoral politics is the fact that the CDU/CSU gained most of its increase in Bavaria, where the CSU (Christian Social Union in Bavaria) won nearly 1 million more voters than in 1998 (Rohrschneider and Dalton 2003).

This chapter analyzes the forces affecting voters in the East and the West. We pay particular attention to the question of whether the East and the West constitute two electorates (Dalton and Bürklin 1995; Rohrschneider and Fuchs 1995). Our chapter focuses on eastern and western Germany, whereas Wessels's study in this volume (chapter 3) examines the degree to which Bavaria constitutes a separate "electorate." We begin by discussing the basic forces defining the competitive framework in the unified electorate. Our central argument is that unified Germany actually consists of two separate electorates. We then examine the influence of the social policy dimension on voters' choice. As we will explain here, this policy domain is well suited to document the different strategic contexts in which parties have to operate across the East–West divide.

The Two Electorates

Creating a competitive party system in eastern Germany after unification looked deceptively simple. With few exceptions, the same parties—CDU, FDP, and the SPD—merely seemed to extend their reach to the former GDR. Only the successor to the Socialist Unity Party (SED)—the PDS—and the Alliance '90 had their origins in eastern German society. Indeed, after the western Greens merged with the Alliance '90, the PDS remains as the only party that has a distinct eastern German origin.

However, this overt simplicity masks several differences in the party systems across the former East–West divide. For example, in the initial elections in unified Germany, movements between parties were considerably larger in the East (7.5 percent between 1994 and 1998) than the West (2.3 percent) (Emmert et al. 2002; Schoen and Falter 2002). Further, in the 1998 election, the SPD was considerably stronger in the East, whereas the CDU and the Greens[1] were stronger in the West. And the PDS's appeal is largely limited to eastern voters: 19.5 percent supported it in the 1998 federal election, whereas a miniscule 1.1 percent of the western population supported the post-communist party.

In order to understand the forces explaining these East–West differences, it is instructive to apply a heuristic framework that first considers the electoral developments in western Germany up to unification. We then highlight what is known about the eastern electorate, after which we examine whether unification reinforces or modifies preexisting trends in the larger and older western German electorate.

The Western Electorate

The long-term dynamic of the western electorate can be captured by three basic characteristics: the role of social cleavages, the slow, but steady, weakening of socio-structural predictors on vote choice, and the evolution of postmaterial values, as exemplified by the strong environmental movement in the West.[2]

Lipset and Rokkan's (1967) seminal work traces the evolution of class and religious differences to the national and industrial revolutions that divided European societies into various sectors. These sectors, or pillars, separated societies on the basis of identity-related values (ethnic, religious, and regional values) and ideological positions (socialist versus market-based ideologies). However, more than just defining different interests, these value-based interests were stabilized by a host of affiliated organizations, such as churches (in the religious domain) or unions and employers' associations in the industrial sector. When party systems formed at the turn of the nineteenth century, political elites mobilized their constituencies along predefined sectoral and organizational lines, which provided considerable stability to these cleavages.

Despite the disruption of society during the Nazi era, the cleavage framework goes a long way in explaining the formation of the western electorate after the western Allies established a parliamentary democracy in 1949. The SPD primarily mobilized the working class, whereas the Center-conservative party appealed mainly to the middle-class, economic Center–Right voters, as well as religious Protestants and Catholics (Pappi 1977). In election campaigns up to the late 1960s, parties designed campaign platforms that mainly center on economic issues, the welfare state, and security issues (Budge et al. 2001). In short, the social cleavage model provides a good framework for understanding the electoral behavior in western Germany's postwar elections.

From the early 1970s onward, however, there were growing signs that the tranquility of previous decades would give way to a more volatile electorate in Western Europe (Dalton and Wattenberg 2000). Inter-election volatility increased slowly but steadily; voters became more issue-oriented; vote decisions were made later and later during the campaign—in short, the stability of party alignments began to erode. This was also reflected in the election campaigns themselves, which tended to become increasingly personality-centered (Brettschneider 2002).

The Green party, which after a failed initial run in 1980 passed the 5 percent threshold to enter the West German parliament in 1983, became a visible manifestation of the party system's volatility. The Greens symbolize the changing nature of West German society as it represents a new generation of citizens who do not automatically accept the economic policy priorities of the West German party system (Inglehart 1977, 1997). Rather, for reasons rooted in the affluence and modernity of West Germany, postwar cohorts possess postmaterialist value priorities, that tend to fuel policy interests in such nonmaterial issue areas as the environment or gender equality.

Naturally, this short synopsis necessarily omits other important developments. However, it does highlight the fact that by the time Germany unified, class and religious cleavages at least had begun to erode if not were fully eroded as a predictor of electoral choice; issue voting became more important to citizens, and postmaterial value priorities increasingly shaped the issues and party preferences of a significant portion of the electorate. Consequently, the SPD moderated its leftist issue stances by championing programs that clashed with the interests of their working-class base that could threaten industrial jobs. The CDU also had to appeal to centrists without dismantling the welfare state. And, where parties ignored voters' preferences, activists such as the Greens took it upon themselves to represent their interests in the West German parliament.

The Eastern Electorate

Naturally, the eastern German electorate does not share the societal characteristics that promoted many of the changes in the West. First, eastern Germans did not vote freely between January 1933, when Hitler was appointed to the chancellor's office, and March 1990, when eastern Germans elected the short-lived eastern German parliament (*Volkskammer*). Further, the level of modernity and affluence in the East was substantially lower than in the West. With an economic and political system ostensibly designed to defeat class and religious distinctions, many socio-structural characteristics that define western German society were eradicated during the 40-year reign of the SED. Given these socio-structural differences, eastern voters do not neatly fit into the campaign mold of western German parties.

This has several consequences. For one, eastern Germans are considerably more volatile because they have not developed habitual party preferences based on prior elections (Kaase and Klingemann 1994). Further, socio-demographic characteristics—especially voters' middle-class status—affect vote choice in ways that are inconsistent with the cleavage framework. For example, the working class disproportionately supported the CDU during the 1990 and 1994 elections (Rohrschneider and Fuchs 1995). The novelty of the party system thus explains several of the initial characteristics of the eastern electorate, including its greater volatility, and the reversed class-vote linkage observed particularly during the 1990 and 1994 federal elections (Dalton and Bürklin 1995), though workers were more likely to support the SPD in the 1998 election, just as their western counterpart (Gibowski 1999). A similar pattern emerged in the 2002 election campaign (Rohrschneider and Dalton 2003).

Another variation concerns the different levels of economic and social-structural affluence. While western German society reached a level of affluence that topped that of the most advanced industrial societies (e.g., wealth; educational attainment; size of the service sector), eastern Germany lacked these qualities. Consequently, it would be inaccurate to assume that the consequences of postindustrial society had transformed the electorate in eastern Germany.

Finally, a third important difference concerns the presence of the PDS. As the only "homegrown" eastern party, it draws on a diverse group of voters. For one, it disproportionately attracts voters who are dissatisfied with the social and economic status quo. As we will discuss in the following, a large majority in eastern Germany continues to support socialist ideals and favors an extensive welfare net—a constituency that the PDS is well suited to attract. Moreover, the PDS also appeals to voters who are dissatisfied with the manner in which unification proceeded; or who suffered the economic consequences of the near collapse of the eastern industry (Pollack 1997)—voters who are unlikely to reward the western parties with their vote.

The Unified Electorate

When we consider the merged electorate, we think it likely that at least two important consequences follow from the East–West variations. First, we expect that voters in the unified electorate increasingly base their party choice on policy concerns and are less driven by socio-structural (cleavage) characteristics. While the partisan dealignment began in western Germany during the 1980s, the near-absence of socio-structural influences on vote choice will no doubt accentuate the role of policy issues in determining one's party preferences. Thus, the unified electorate, as a whole, is expected to be especially volatile, and their vote choice increasingly determined by short-term issues and campaign efforts.

Second, and relatedly, we expect that the nature of eastern German society, combined with the enormous costs of unification, should shift voters' attention away from postmaterial issues such as environmental protection, to more fundamental economic concerns (Roller 1998). For instance, the *Politbarometer* series regularly asks respondents in an open-ended question about the most important problem. In 1989, a majority of western voters mention environmental protection as the most important problem (16.9 percent), closely followed by unemployment (16.2 percent).[3] In 1998, in contrast, unemployment has become the front-runner, with 77.1 percent of western voters (!) mentioning it, whereas environmental protection virtually vanished from the agenda (1 percent). Not surprisingly, eastern voters are even more concerned with unemployment (85.7 percent) whereas environmental protection does not loom large on the minds of eastern voters (.5 percent). Similarly, in 2002, about 70 percent in the West and 78 percent in the East view unemployment as the most important problem.[4]

Third, the fact that a substantial proportion of the unified electorate has been born and raised in a socialist system, adds a social-egalitarian policy dimension to the unified electorate. While most western Germans accept the idea of a welfare state, eastern Germans demand more extensive government services, based on their socialization experience in the former GDR (Fuchs 1999; Rohrschneider 1999).

These changes have important consequences for parties' ability to mobilize their constituencies and to cover the range of voters from the Left to the conservative end of the electorate. First, all parties have to deal with a more mobile electorate. While partisan dealignments occur in most advanced democracies (Dalton and Wattenberg 2000), the volatile eastern electorate jolted the otherwise slow pace of dealignments. Thus, unification both increased the number of noncommitted voters through the addition of the entire East, while further upsetting the issue alignments of western parties. All parties must now try to attract a larger number of floating voters who bring very different and conflicting issue concerns to the table.

At the same time, we would argue that the strategic quandary of the SPD is especially severe. This results from the SPD's pivotal position at the Center–Left point in Germany's party system. The SPD must cater to centrist voters in order to compete for potential CDU/CSU support, while simultaneously making appeals to their working-class base. The challenges to bridging this broad span has become even more daunting with the need to attract the Left spectrum of the eastern party system in order to compete with the PDS. In addition, it also has to vie programmatically with the Greens over environmental and, to a lesser degree, social-egalitarian issues in the West. Thus, the competitive situation between the Center and Left requires a programmatic "split" from the SPD. The strategic position of the CDU/CSU is more comfortable: it must appeal primarily to centrist voters, but it currently does not have to be concerned with a strong right-wing competitor. While the SPD seems to have ceded the postmaterial spectrum to the Greens—and the Greens, in turn, have become more pragmatic while in government—it cannot relinquish the Left-end to the PDS as long as it is committed not to form a coalition with the former communist party.[5]

In sum, parties must face a new electorate in the East, while still trying to come to grips with the changes that the western party system had already faced. This combined with the fact that the party systems vary across the East–West divide, both in terms of the number of parties (PDS in the East) and the nature of the same parties (e.g., Greens) entail that electoral competition has become considerably more complex in unified Germany.

Social Policy and Party Competition

The social policy dimension represents a good policy domain to examine the extent to which the thesis that there are two distinct electorates in unified Germany is accurate. It structures party competition in western democracies between Left-of-Center parties, usually some major social democratic party, and Center-conservative party (Pappi 1977). If the presence of the PDS, for instance, introduces an element of party competition to the Left of the SPD in the East, as we argue, then this should be reflected in different effects of the social dimension on party support across the East–West divide.

Three Dimensions of Social Policy

We distinguish between three dimensions of the social policy domain (Roller 1999b). Each successive dimension implies a larger role of government involvement in procuring social equality in Germany. First, we examine the extent to which attitudes about a minimalist welfare state affect party support. Most western and eastern Germans favor a society in which the needy are supported by government services during times of emergencies (Roller 1992, 1999a,b). As we will show in the following, there is virtually a consensus over the desirability of some form of government support for those struck by personal disasters; what differs is the precise extent to which a government ought to help its citizens (called the *welfare* factor).

Second, beyond this minimalist view, a broader view directly reflects the egalitarian tradition of social democracy by asking citizens to evaluate whether the current status differences among various groups as unjust. This dimension represents a generalized performance assessment of how well a regime manages to achieve a subjective standard of social fairness. It is linked to the programmatic legacy of social democratic parties and typically reflects a preference for an egalitarian distribution of material and social goods (Dahl 1989; Fuchs 1997). We will refer to this as the *status* factor.

Finally, at the broadest, normative level, we examine whether individuals' views about general socialist norms affect their party support. This dimension (called the *socialist* factor) goes beyond the welfare and status factors in its normative focus on a sociopolitical alternative to the extant liberal-representative democracy and market economy. For individuals evaluate whether they find socialism in principle a desirable form of government.

How does each dimension affect voters' partisanship? As the demands for government provision of equality move from the welfare factor, to the status factor, and finally to the socialist factor, does the competitive quandary for the SPD grow?

The welfare factor and party support

Before we discuss the relationship between welfare views and party support, note first that most respondents support some form of social-welfare service. For example, when asked in 1984 whether the state should care for the needy (e.g., in times of sickness, unemployment, and retirement), 56 percent of western Germans strongly agree and 35 percent agree; a miniscule minority (7 percent) opposes this notion.[6] By 2000, there is some erosion in this consensus: 37 percent strongly support this policy, and 47 percent agree with it, whereas about 15 percent of the West German public oppose an active welfare state. The East German public provides even more lopsided support for the welfare state: only 1 percent reject it in 1991; and this proportion increases to about 7 percent in 2000. Thus, over 90 percent in the East support a welfare state, thus boosting the pro-welfare sentiments in unified Germany.

Accordingly, most of the variation over this basic welfare aspect occurs over the degree to which the state should engage in welfare policies, not over whether such policies are desirable in the first place. We do note some movement away from an unqualified position of endorsement for the welfare state; western Germans in particular become slightly more equivocal over time. These patterns no doubt partly reflect, partly drive, public controversies started during the 1980s by the CDU/CSU government over cuts in welfare services; a development that has received some support from the centrist forces within the SPD-led government since 1998.

Do welfare views affect the partisan preferences of voters? Table 2.1 shows the relationship between the welfare factor and respondents' intended vote if there were an election next Sunday. The two indicators are available for four time points, including 1984 which provides us with a baseline of the "normal" pre-unification politics. We are thus able to examine whether the overall relationship changes, and the specific locus of any modification in the German party system.

Let us begin with the time point 1984 in the West. In overall terms, the relationship is quite modest (Cramer's $V = .13$), suggesting that the discriminating effect of welfare views has been limited for nearly two decades. Still, we observe the predictable effect of welfare views on vote

Table 2.1 Party preference and respondents' opinions on the welfare state[a]

	1984			1991			1994			2000		
	Strongly agree	Agree somewhat	Disagree	Strongly agree	Agree somewhat	Disagree	Strongly agree	Agree somewhat	Disagree	Strongly agree	Agree somewhat	Disagree
West												
CDU/CSU	38.4	49.2	62.4	29.9	36.3	42.3	30.2	38.5	46.4	37.9	34.3	43.0
FDP	3.9	5.6	8.3	11.1	11.1	17.1	8.7	8.0	13.8	8.6	11.5	15.5
SPD	45.7	35.8	22.2	49.7	44.8	32.4	44.9	38.5	27.6	43.8	42.7	33.3
Greens	11.9	9.5	7.2	9.3	7.8	8.1	16.2	15.1	12.2	9.8	11.5	8.5
(N)	(1214)	(771)	(194)	(549)	(442)	(111)	(679)	(598)	(196)	(420)	(574)	(200)
Cramer's V	.13			0.08			.10			.08		
East												
CDU/CSU				22.7	24.6	7.8	21.8	27.9	21.7	26.4	24.0	34.5
FDP				12.9	18.5	23.1	9.7	6.4	21.7	3.9	2.0	5.5
SPD				47.6	40.0	61.5	38.5	33.6	43.5	37.4	46.7	30.9
Greens				10.6	13.3	7.7	11.7	19.3	8.7	3.9	6.1	5.5
PDS				6.2	3.4	0.0	18.4	12.9	4.4	28.4	21.1	23.6
(N)				(796)	(195)	(13)	(528)	(140)	(23)	(356)	(246)	(55)
Cramer's V				.08			.11			.10		

[a] "The state should take care of the needy and unemployed." Response categories range from "agree" (strongly (1) or somewhat (2)) to "disagree" (strongly (3) or somewhat (4)).

choice, especially among the major parties. Take the CDU/CSU, for example. While a substantial proportion of citizens who strongly support a welfare system are willing to support the Center–Right party (38.4 percent), it is considerably more likely to attract opponents to the welfare state (62.4 percent). However, given the large number of welfare supporters, and the small proportion of opponents, the CDU/CSU has not been able to ignore these policies and endorses some degree of welfare service in order to remain viable.

In fact, a comparison to the SPD constituency suggests that this classical social-democratic domain hardly benefits the worker's party—the proportion of welfare advocates supporting the SPD is only marginally larger (45.7) than that voting for the CDU/CSU (38.4 percent). Even in 1984, then, when the comparatively tranquil welfare policies appeared to have established clear markers between the SPD and CDU/CSU, the influence of these views on party support are surprisingly modest.

The relationship becomes even weaker by 2000. The change occurs because opponents to the welfare state are increasingly willing to support the SPD. That is, the change occurs not because supporters switch their party support, but because opponents to welfare policies find the SPD increasingly acceptable. Consequently, the overall relationship between welfare policies and vote choice weakens, to the point where the difference between the two major parties has nearly vanished! This no doubt results from the fact that both major parties support the welfare state to a considerable degree, but also because of the growing willingness of the SPD to curtail welfare benefits. These developments clearly reduce the need for supporters or opponents to select one party over another if the welfare dimension is deemed important.

It is more difficult to trace these developments over time in the East. The shorter time period covered by these surveys and the unique circumstances of the 1990 "unification election" entail that we have at best two time points available (1994 and 2000). Generally, by the latest available survey (2000), the link between welfare views and partisanship is quite weak, just as in the West. This too suggests that parties' position on the welfare dimension has a fairly weak influence on voters' party preference among eastern voters.

Social status differences
Does the weakening effect of the welfare dimension also appear regarding the other dimensions? In addition to providing basic services to lower classes, the program of the worker's movement envisions a more egalitarian, fair, and just society. This heritage provides a vision of a

society where basic needs are met, the distribution of resources is considered fair, and where differences among various social groups and classes are reduced to acceptable proportions. While the SPD, like many other Left parties in Europe, has been transformed throughout the twentieth century from a mainly leftist party advocating the rights of workers to a moderate Left-of-Center party (Baker et al. 1981), it continues to lay claim to be the main agent for a more just society.

In light of the finding that the SPD does not hold a distinct partisan advantage over the CDU/CSU in the welfare domain, it is important to know whether we find a similar pattern concerning the broader, normatively rooted principles of social democracy. If the SPD does not have a competitive edge in *these* domains, it would be difficult for Social Democrats to claim to remain the main representative of the working class. On the other hand, if the SPD becomes attractive to those who favor a less active state, then it may enhance its attractiveness among opponents to social democratic programs. Such a pattern would signal its continuing move toward the programmatic center.

In 1984 in the West, 41 percent perceived social status differences as unjust, whereas 37 percent considered these differences acceptable, with about 21 percent being undecided.[7] By the year 2000, however, 32 percent considered the status quo unjust, whereas over 41 percent deemed social status differences acceptable. This means that the core constituency of traditional social democratic programs has been reduced by nearly 10 percent.[8]

Do these views structure voters' party choice? The answer is affirmative (table 2.2). Let us, again, begin with the western part of the electorate. In 1984, of those who deem status differences unjust, a little over one-fifth of voters support the CDU/CSU (27.4 percent), whereas nearly half (49.5 percent) side with the SPD. The reverse pattern emerges for voters who consider the status quo just; here the CDU/CSU is the clear front-runner with 59.7 percent compared to 30.8 percent supporting the SPD. Just as one would expect it on the basis of Lipset and Rokkan's cleavage theory, attitudes about status differences align with party support in predictable fashion—the Right benefits from perceptions that no change is needed; the Left benefits from perceptions that the status quo is unjust.

By 2000, however, the relationship has changed, particularly regarding the ability of the SPD to attract those voters who consider the status quo acceptable. That is, as in the welfare domain, the SPD is making inroads into the camp of opponents to a more egalitarian society—usually the domain of the CDU/CSU—by increasing its share of opponents to the egalitarian vision (44.9 percent for the CDU/CSU as

Table 2.2 Party preference and respondents' opinions on whether social status differences are just[a]

	1984			1991			1994			2000		
	Unjust	*Middle*	*Just*	*Unjust*	*Middle*	*Just*	*Unjust*	*Middle*	*Just*	*Unjust*	*Middle*	*Just*
West												
CDU/CSU	27.4	45.0	59.7	18.3	34.5	48.9	20.2	30.7	50.8	22.3	38.4	44.9
FDP	3.3	5.8	6.2	10.0	9.5	15.9	7.2	11.5	9.6	10.6	14.2	10.2
SPD	49.5	40.9	30.8	56.6	49.2	31.5	48.0	42.3	31.8	47.4	36.1	40.9
Greens	19.8	8.4	3.4	15.2	6.7	3.6	24.5	15.3	7.8	19.7	11.3	4.0
(N)	(814)	(416)	(796)	(389)	(252)	(384)	(498)	(339)	(553)	(340)	(302)	(501)
Cramer's V		.24			.24			.23			.19	
East												
CDU/CSU				17.6	24.2	37.9	18.4	24.8	34.0	20.6	30.2	36.1
FDP				10.6	20.2	17.4	9.2	12.0	9.6	1.9	6.4	5.0
SPD				50.9	42.2	37.9	37.4	39.0	38.3	39.3	40.3	41.2
Greens				14.2	8.1	6.2	14.7	12.0	9.6	6.0	3.8	3.4
PDS				6.7	5.4	0.6	20.4	12.0	8.5	32.1	18.9	14.3
(N)				(564)	(223)	(161)	(436)	(133)	(94)	(364)	(159)	(119)
Cramer's V					.18			.13			.16	

[a] Social status is an additive index of answers to these statements: "Differences between people in terms of their social standing are acceptable because they reflect individuals' accomplishments"; and "Differences in social status are just." Responses range from agree to disagree with "strongly" or "somewhat" as categories for both. Additive indicators range from 2 (reject current status) to 8 (accept) with "unjust" (2–4), "middle" (5), and "just" (6–8).

against 40.9 percent for the SPD). Viewed from this perspective, the SPD has been quite successful in increasing its appeal to voters who are in the Center–Right ideological camp.[9]

But this comes at a cost. Those parts of the labor movement who oppose centrist policies may become disillusioned with the SPD and abstain from voting. And the PDS is not really a viable alternative to voters in the West given that it is closely rooted in the history of the GDR.

In the East, however, such centrist policies put the SPD in a strategically disadvantageous position vis-à-vis the PDS. Note that, with the exception of 1991, easterners who view status differences as just are *more* likely to support the SPD (41.2 percent in 2000, e.g.) than those who consider it unjust (39.3 percent). Of course, the percentage differences are miniscule and statistically insignificant. Substantively, however, this pattern exemplifies the strategic quandary of the SPD regarding the egalitarian dimension. It is the communist successor party—the PDS—which primarily attracts supporters of an egalitarian vision, not the SPD. The PDS steadily increased its share of voters among egalitarian proponents from 6.7 percent in 1991 to 32.1 percent in 2000. This increase no doubt results from the fact that after the initial euphoria and its accompanying rejection of the communist successor party to the SED, the PDS had established itself as an agent of interest representation for citizens who continue to adhere to socialist-egalitarian ideals.

Socialism as an ideal

While the first section focuses on a specific welfare policy and the second examines one performance-based aspect of socialist theory, this last section uses the broadest measure of leftist attitudes: one's support for socialism. Respondents were asked whether they agree (strongly, somewhat) or disagree (strongly, somewhat) with the following statement: "Socialism is a good idea that was poorly implemented." Typically, about 75 percent of eastern Germans agreed with this statement in 2000, whereas about half the respondents in the West endorsed this sentiment; and these proportions have remained essentially unchanged since 1991 (Rohrschneider and Schmitt-Beck 2002).

Despite the broad nature of the indicator, its relationship to voters' party preferences, with few exceptions, mirrors that of the status indicator (table 2.3). In the West, the SPD loses somewhat among those who support the statement; and the Greens gain. But, in general terms, the relationship by 2000 is weak in light of the historical origins of the SPD; a pattern that roughly parallels that of the influence of the welfare and status indicators on party preferences.

Table 2.3 Party preference and respondents' opinions on whether socialism is a good idea[a]

	1991		1994		2000	
	Agree	Disagree	Agree	Disagree	Agree	Disagree
West						
CDU/CSU	21.7	40.7	24.0	42.7	29.7	41.6
FDP	9.7	14.3	9.1	9.3	8.8	12.3
SPD	55.9	38.7	46.1	35.8	46.9	37.5
Greens	17.7	6.2	20.8	12.1	14.5	8.6
(N)	(411)	(594)	(562)	(805)	(262)	(269)
Cramer's V	.24		.21		.16	
East						
CDU/CSU	15.8	42.9	20.0	34.9	22.3	34.2
FDP	12.1	17.7	8.0	16.7	1.7	7.9
SPD	51.9	31.0	38.6	31.2	38.0	46.1
Greens	12.5	8.3	12.6	14.3	6.6	7.9
PDS	7.8	0.0	20.1	2.4	31.4	3.9
(N)	(704)	(242)	(550)	(126)	(242)	(61)
Cramer's V	.32		.24		.30	

[a] "Socialism is a good idea that was poorly implemented." Response categories range from "agree" (strongly (1) or somewhat (2)) to "disagree" (strongly (3) or somewhat (4)).

In the East, the patterns also parallel that of the other two indicators. The CDU is preferred by respondents who view socialist ideals with skepticism. Similarly, by a slim margin, a greater proportion of opponents to socialist ideals support the SPD than adherents of socialist ideals—a pattern that also emerged regarding the citizens' views about status differences. In turn, the PDS has established itself as the party of social-egalitarian views. It is nearly as likely as the SPD to draw on socialist sentiments in eastern Germany—and this group is quite large as we noted earlier. It thus occupies an electoral niche that, in the West, is covered by the SPD and, to a lesser degree, the Green party.

Welfare Policies and Party Competency

Up to this point, we examined whether voters' positions on social policy affect party preferences. In light of the weakening relationships, we also would like to have a sense of whether voters' perceive diminishing differences among parties to address issues in this policy domain. We use one indicator which has been asked over time in the West: which government would be best able to secure pensions? Despite the changes in question wording over time (see the appendix), we believe that the relative position of parties permits us to glean whether the SPD lacks a clear advantage as our previous arguments suggest.

Indeed, the public does not necessarily see the SPD as best able to handle specific social dimension issues (table 2.4). Given that the SPD historically has championed such issues, the SPD has had an advantage at times. As others have noted, it took the SPD a while before it was seen to be a realistic alternative to the Union following the SPD's shift from leftists to Left–Center party in the 1959 Bad Godesberg conference (Baker et al. 1981). This probably explains why the public viewed the CDU as best able to handle old-age security. Nevertheless, the SPD soon dominated on this issue and did so for 20 years. However, just as the German public realigned, the western public actually perceived that a Union-led government would best secure pensions during most of the 1980s, and the large fluctuations and lack of any consistent trend are telling. The public does not perceive consistently that the SPD best handles an issue that it should naturally own. Further, while the SPD has an advantage over the CDU, the answer that "neither" party could best handle the issue had doubled by the late 1990s over its average level in the 1980s and had become the modal response.

There are two possible reasons for this, or perhaps a combination of them. First, despite its ownership of the issue and the advantage the

Table 2.4 Which party best deals with old-age security or which party best secures pensions (in percent)

	SPD or SPD-led government	CDU or CDU-led government	Both	Neither
1961	47.7	52.3	—	—
1969	62.4	37.6	—	—
1972	46.8	27.6	24.0	2.0
1976	70.0	27.4	—	11.7
1980	36.8	28.8	29.0	5.0
1982	29.4	35.9	26.3	8.3
1984	25.7	31.7	28.9	13.7
1985	29.6	31.5	19.8	19.1
1986	28.4	39.0	19.6	13.0
1987	28.9	32.7	24.9	13.4
1988	29.4	30.0	23.4	17.2
1989	42.0	32.7	15.0	10.3
1990	41.6	34.4	19.1	5.0
1997	32.5	16.5	17.0	34.0
1998	30.1	18.7	20.4	30.8

Source: German National Election Studies (until 1980); *Politbarometer*.

public gives to it at times, western voters do not perceive the SPD (or any party) as significantly more able to handle this issue. Second, the western public may not view this issue as very salient. Compared to unification and economic issues, the problem has become less salient over time.[10] The SPD's move toward the Center may match the decline of this dimension, but it also leads the public to claim that "neither"— rather than the SPD or even "both" parties—are particularly able to handle the issue. Not only is the SPD unable to separate itself in the public's mind on broader assessments of the social dimension such as the safety net, equality, and the socialist ideal, but the party is also unable (and/or unwilling) to find an advantage on specific issues related to this dimension. This conclusion matches a detailed analyses of party competency scores by Pappi and Shikano who conclude that during the 1998 elections, differences between the main parties in terms of the "economic and social policy competency are small" (Pappi and Shikano 2002).

Summary

From a competitive vantage point, this situation defines a delicate context for the SPD. Supporting a centrist program increases the odds that the traditional constituency abstains. If, on the other hand, the SPD tries to cater to the PDS constituency, it may lose its appeal to centrist voters in the West. To juggle these competing incentives and to package them in a platform with broad appeal requires finely honed and well-balanced campaign messages.

The CDU/CSU faces a different set of incentives. It is clearly the party of the status quo as far as the egalitarian dimension is concerned. At the same time, it is not supported in substantial numbers by opponents to basic welfare policies. Thus, its successful electoral formula lies in modest support for the welfare state, couched in an economic vision that emphasizes tempered market forces as the main economic incentives. While this also requires a balancing act, the CDU/CSU does not have to deal with a party that is economically more conservative; the main goal is to balance support for basic welfare services with a moderate vision of a market economy.

The smaller parties, except for the PDS in the East and, to a lesser degree, the Greens in the West, do not benefit substantially from the various welfare dimensions. The PDS, for reasons just mentioned, is clearly the beneficiary of the SPD's strategic quandary in the eastern electorate. In the West, the Greens do appear to attract a share of egalitarian opponents, but this proportion is smaller than that going to the CDU/CSU.[11]

Multivariate Analyses

Do these relationships hold up when we control for other traditional predictors of citizens' vote choice? It is plausible to expect that the link between various welfare dimensions and electoral choice be partly affected by respondents' perceptions of the economy. Respondents who assess the state of the economy negatively, for instance, all else being equal may support extensive welfare services. In order to assess the net effect of the various welfare dimensions on vote choice, we estimated their effect on party support controlling for the following predictors:

- *present and future economic perceptions (Rattinger and Faas 2002);[12]
- *postmaterial values (Inglehart 1977);
- *religiosity (Pappi 1977);
- *age and education.

Thus, we estimate the following model:

Vote Choice = Constant + State provide for needy + Status is unjust + Socialism is good + Postmaterialism + Religiosity + Evals of current economy + Evals of future economy + Age + Education + e

We estimated the model separately for western and eastern Germany. Given the nominal nature of the dependent variable, we used multinominal logit to estimate the coefficients.[13] For the West, the dependent variable is the party choice between the CDU/CSU, FDP, SPD, and the Greens; in the East, we added the PDS as a fifth party group.

Since logit coefficients are difficult to interpret, table 2.5, which contains the results for western Germany, displays the change in party support as one moves from the minimum of a predictor to its maximum, keeping constant all other variables at their mean (Long 1997). For example, in 1991, the likelihood that the CDU/CSU is supported decreases by 23 percent as one moves from respondents who strongly reject a welfare state to those who strongly support it. Conversely, support for the SPD increases by 25 percent in 1991 as one moves across the entire spectrum of this welfare factor. Thus, in 1991, the SPD benefits to some degree from the welfare dimension.

By 2000, however, there is a substantial drop in support for the SPD as one moves across the entire range of this variable (14 percent, down from 25 percent in 1991). Furthermore, the odds of supporting the

Table 2.5 Predicting party preferences: West Germany[a]

	1991				1994				2000			
	CDU/CSU	FDP	SPD	Greens	CDU/CSU	FDP	SPD	Greens	CDU/CSU	FDP	SPD	Greens
State should help needy	-23	-1	25	-1	-18	-6	22	2	-8	-12	14	6
Status differences unjust	-47	-12	48	11	-36	-8	28	16	-36	-1	18	19
Socialism is good	-27	0	20	7	-22	1	14	7	-11	-5	10	6
Postmaterialism	-20	-2	6	16	-32	4	12	17	-24	2	11	11
Religiosity	44	-4	-39	1	46	-5	-30	-11	52	-7	-39	-6
Present economy good	9	9	-13	-5	21	1	-18	-4	-6	-4	3	7
Future economy good	16	-6	1	-11	8	-5	-6	3	-25	-4	30	1
Age	20	8	-13	-14	14	-1	4	-17	0	17	-8	-8
Education	2	23	-27	2	2	6	-22	14	19	9	-38	11

[a] Entries reflect changes in predicted probabilities as one moves from the minimum to the maximum of a variable, keeping all other variables at their mean. Probabilities are generated by multinomial logistic regression using the mlogit command in Stata 7.

CDU are not decreased by as much (an 8 percent decline). Just as the bivariate analysis of these indicators suggests (table 2.1), the SPD is substantially less likely to attract voters in its traditional policy domain in 2000.

Indeed, even these patterns tend to overly emphasize the extent to which the SPD remains attractive to its core clientele because they are computed by moving across the entire range of the welfare indicator. However, our earlier discussion suggests that about 90 percent of voters either "strongly agree" or "agree" with this policy. If one looks at these two response categories only, then the odds of supporting the SPD in the West increase by 9 percent in 1991 and a mere 4 percent in 2000 as one moves from the "agree" to "strongly agree;" the figures for the CDU/CSU are 7 and 3 percent, respectively. For all practical purposes, then, this basic welfare dimension, which is closely connected to the SPD's programmatic legacy, has hardly any discernable advantage for the SPD!

Regarding the other social dimensions, the SPD fares a little better. Those who perceive status differences as unjust or consider socialism a good idea are more likely to support the SPD than opponents to these policy positions. Even here, however, we note a substantial decline in relative advantage for the SPD. While the coefficients remain statistically significant, the SPD's partisan advantage is cut by about half (for the socialism indicator) and even more for the status indicator. All of this points to the growing irrelevance of the social dimension as a determinant of voters' choice.

The most important predictors in the western electorate, by 2000, are voters' religiosity and their expectations about the future economy. Religious respondents are substantially more likely to support the CDU/CSU. The CDU/CSU, however, cannot rely on this loyal group of voters alone as fewer than 20 percent are attending church regularly on at least a monthly basis.

Economic perceptions, in turn, substantially favor the incumbent government in the West (the SPD/Greens coalition at the time of the 2000 survey) if the economy is perceived positively; if not, voters tend to side with the opposition party. Given that a substantial percentage of voters are ambivalent about the economy—almost all respondents fall into the three middle categories on the five-point indicator—changes can occur fairly easily and thus substantially affect the outcome of an election. The predicted vote choice for the SPD and CDU/CSU, respectively, for respondents who believe the economy is rather good are 53 and 28 percent. Moving from the "rather good" category via undecided voters to the "rather bad" category, changes the predicted percentages to 38 and 42 percent for the SPD and CDU/CSU, respectively. Thus, the SPD loses 15 percent and the CDU/CSU gains 14 percent. Given that subjective economic assessments tend to react fairly quickly around the Center categories, such shifts in the end contributed to the victory of the Red-Green coalition in 2002 (Rohrschneider and Dalton 2003).

In the East, the patterns differ in important respects, especially after the party system became more familiar to eastern voters (table 2.6). Beginning with 1991, note that the social security predictor favors the SPD (17 percent), not relative to the CDU/CSU (8 percent), but compared to the FDP (−24 percent). In contrast, the PDS does not benefit from this factor because most eastern voters did not support the successor party to the SED shortly after the communist regime collapsed. In contrast, views about status differences and socialism produce substantial partisan advantages for the SPD, disadvantages for the CDU/CSU, and no effect on the PDS.

These results are atypical, however, because the euphoria over Germany's unification and the novelty of the party system clearly structured the tenuous link between voters and parties. By 2000 if not already by 1994, the partisan advantage of the SPD in the social domains vanishes nearly entirely. For instance, the welfare factor produces no partisan distinction at all between the various parties. This, no doubt reflects the consensus over this issue in the East where about 92 percent consider it an obligation of the state to take care of the needy and unemployed.

But we also find that views about status differences and a socialist utopia affect benefit the SPD. Among those who support socialist ideals (about 75 percent in the East), the SPD's partisan advantage *declines* by 30 percent, whereas the CDU's advantage declines by 10 percent. In contrast, the PDS strongly benefits from the status factor (30 percent increase) and, especially, the socialism predictor (42 percent). Thus, the SPD is basically unable to attract its traditional core constituency among eastern voters where the PDS has established itself as the main party of a social-egalitarian utopia.

Finally, note that while the SPD benefits from positive economic perceptions in 2000 (21 percent) so does the CDU/CSU (19 percent). Thus, positive economic assessments do not produce a distinct partisan advantage for the SPD relative to the CDU. In contrast, the PDS is the main beneficiary of negative economic assessments. Regarding the social dimension, eastern voters seem to perceive greater similarities between the CDU and SPD than the SPD and PDS.

Table 2.6 Predicting party preferences: East Germany[a]

	1991					1994					2000				
	CDU/CSU	FDP	SPD	Greens	PDS	CDU/CSU	FDP	SPD	Greens	PDS	CDU/CSU	FDP	SPD	Greens	PDS
State should help needy	8	−24	17	−2	1	2	1	−3	1	−1	−3	−1	1	0	3
Status differences unjust	−21	−19	25	14	1	−24	−1	4	9	12	−39	−4	11	2	30
Socialism is good	−31	−7	30	4	4	−15	−8	2	1	20	−10	−1	−30	0	42
Postmaterialism	−11	4	1	4	2	−15	−6	11	10	0	−8	−2	1	−2	11
Religiosity	43	1	−39	−1	−4	26	7	−20	−3	−16	60	0	−40	7	−27
Present economy good	15	−9	−10	8	−4	18	5	−2	−7	−14	19	2	21	4	−47
Future economy good	21	7	2	−21	−9	22	−3	−6	−11	−15	−11	−2	2	−2	17
Age	−4	10	9	−17	2	14	−10	10	−13	−1	−18	−9	33	−20	14
Education	−14	3	1	9	1	−2	−3	−24	9	20	−37	3	18	13	3

[a] Entries reflect changes in predicted probabilities as one moves from the minimum to the maximum of a variable, keeping all other variables at their mean. Probabilities are generated by multinomial logistic regression using the mlogit command in Stata 7.

Discussion and Conclusion

There are, of course, a myriad of detailed patterns in these analyses, so let us highlight the central findings. First, the SPD does not enjoy a clear partisan advantage in the West regarding the welfare factor. While the SPD continues to lead by a substantial margin among those who endorse a vision of a more egalitarian society, at least in the West, most election campaigns focus on more concrete welfare policies—and here the SPD no longer holds a substantial advantage.

Second, the SPD is not the main beneficiary of *any* of the three social dimensions among eastern voters. Instead, to the degree that this dimension structures eastern voters' party support, the PDS benefits. Thus, this illustrates the thesis that there are two electorates in Germany and means that the SPD has to cover the moderate Center and, simultaneously, compete with the PDS over socialist ideals.

Overall, based on this logic, we would expect the SPD to be successful when two factors coincide: (1) it has the ability to cover the Center to the Left policy spectrum in terms of the social dimensions; (2) the issue context is favorable, such that economic conditions are positive when the SPD is the incumbent party or negative when the Social Democrats are in the opposition. For "performance" issues, such as political shocks and negative economic conditions and perception, are often the downfall of government parties and a windfall to opposition parties. In this way the SPD's competitive situation is not unique. What makes both factors particularly acute for the SPD, however, is that they must coincide. For example, in 1998 the economy favored the then-opposition SPD, and the SPD also supplied the ideological breadth to cater to its various constituencies.

The context of the 2002 election, however, was less favorable for the SPD. First, high unemployment rates dominated the news about the economy throughout 2002. Accordingly, for most of the 2002 election year, voters were quite pessimistic about economic conditions.[14] Since incumbent governments are usually penalized for poor economic conditions, the economy established an unfavorable policy climate for the SPD in this arena. Add to this Chancellor Schröder's promise—made shortly after his victorious campaign in 1998—to evaluate his performance on the basis of how much his government would reduce unemployment rates and his party faced an uphill battle in the election.

In addition, the SPD did not succeed in developing a campaign theme that could appeal and mobilize the left-leaning elements in the West and the East. Our study shows that the welfare dimension does not attract voters, in part because the SPD is not seen as the main guarantor of the welfare dimension. The CDU is viewed by voters to be as appealing as the SPD. Furthermore, it appears that the SPD is not able to mobilize its followers on the basis of more extensive social policy dimensions. All in all, economic problems, along with the reduced capacity of the SPD to benefit from the social policy dimension, provided an unfavorable backdrop for the SPD during the 2002 election campaign.

But the SPD did not lose. This is due, in large part, to the fact that the SPD was helped by two issues that it had little control over (Rohrschneider and Fuchs 2003). For one, the unprecedented flood in eastern Germany bolstered the SPD's opportunities to win the election. Schröder garnered credit for his acumen in handling this crisis. His ability to quickly dispense aid to victims with little red tape, convene European Union (EU) leaders to lead continentally, as well as to highlight the environmental issues associated with the problem meant that the public viewed the government as an effective handler of a crisis. It also propelled environmental issues back onto the political agenda, to the delight of the Green campaign manager.[15]

The other event that has helped the SPD is the public controversy over the question of whether German troops should help the United States to invade Iraq. Chancellor Schröder's decision to oppose an invasion under any circumstances was very popular with voters in the East and the West, especially those who lacked firm party ties (Rohrschneider and Fuchs 2003).

However, the unique conditions of this may also highlight the precarious electoral condition in which the SPD finds itself. After all, such a 500-year flood cannot buoy the SPD every election cycle. And it cannot count again that an international issue helps to sway undecided voters to support the SPD. Just how the SPD managed to pull even with the CDU/CSU in 2002 may turn out to be a symbol of the growing irrelevance of the welfare dimension for the SPD.

Appendix: Measurement

Welfare: "The state should take care of citizens when they get sick, experience an emergency, during unemployment, and when they are old." Response categories range from agree (strongly or somewhat [1, 2]) to disagree (strongly or somewhat [3, 4]).
Social status: An additive indicator based on two questions: "Differences between people in terms of their social standing are acceptable because

they reflect individuals' accomplishments." And: "Differences in social status are just." Response categories range from agree (strongly or somewhat to disagree (strongly or somewhat). We created an additive indicator, ranging from 2 (reject current status) to 8 (accept current status). For the purpose of table 2.2, we collapsed the indicator into three categories: reject status as just (2, 3, 4); undecided (5); and accept status as just (6, 7, 8).

Socialism: "Socialism is a good idea that was poorly implemented." Response categories range from agree (strongly or somewhat [1, 2]) to disagree (strongly or somewhat [3, 4]).

Party Competency Scores on Securing Pensions:

Before 1984 the sources are various German election studies:

1961 And which of the two large parties can best deal with the following problem—the SPD or the CDU/CSU? Old-age security?

1969 Old-age security—which party do you think can best deal with this problem?

1972 Old-age security—which party is best able to deal with this problem?

1976 Which party is best able to deal with securing pensions?

1980 Secure pensions—who is more qualified to deal with this problem?

Beginning with 1984, *Politbarometer* surveys are used:

• Between 1984 and 1988, the question wording is: "Who is best qualified to solve the following problem to your satisfaction?" Secure pensions.

• In 1989: the question wording is: "Who in your view is best qualified to secure pensions?"

• After 1989, the question wording is: "In your view, who is most likely to secure pensions?"

Party Support: "If there were an election next Sunday, whom would you vote for?"

Economic Perceptions: Do respondents believe the present/future economy to improve or to get worse?

Religiosity: Frequency of Church attendance.

Age: In years.

Education: Years of schooling.

Notes

We would like to thank Dieter Fuchs, Edeltraud Roller, and Bernhard Wessels for many useful discussions about the analyses presented in this essay. Roller also provided an insightful critique of an earlier version of this chapter.

1. Technically, the Greens are called the Alliance '90/Greens, signifying that the western German Greens merged with the eastern Alliance '90.
2. Much of the discussion in this section relies on ideas developed elsewhere (Rohrschneider and Fuchs 1995).
3. See the cumulative *Politbarometer*, available from the ICPSR.
4. This information is gleaned from the Forschungsgruppe Wahlen, Blitzumfrage, 9-16/9-20, 2002.
5. Another East–West difference concerns the absence of a strong Green party in eastern Germany. Relatedly, the type of voters for the Greens tends to vary: in the West, its voters are primarily the younger, better-educated, postmaterial citizens; in the East, its main base is rooted in the opposition to the GDR. Finally, the FDP is considerably weaker in the East than the West.
6. Data are from Allbus, the German version of the General Social Surveys. We used *Allbus* surveys conducted between 1984 and 2000.
7. *Allbus* surveys, various years.
8. The intervening years, for which these indicators are available, show a slow and steady reduction in size of the group believing that social status differences are unjust. The only exception is in the year 1998 when about the same proportion as in 1984 consider differences unacceptable.
9. To some degree, this moderation is related to the greater moderation of voters. Supporters of a more egalitarian society constituted the modal group in 1984, with 40.2% claiming such status differences are unjust. By 2000, this group is reduced to 29.8% and not even close to being the modal group. Thus, in one sense the SPD had to move toward centrist appeals because its core constituency is decreasing.
10. This is assessed with the "most important issue" and second most important issue questions in *Politbarometer* studies over the same time period.
11. The multivariate analyses discussed in the next section will confirm that the broader status measure significantly discriminates between the SPD and Green voters.
12. Earlier models also considered respondents' personal financial situation. Because these variables are mostly insignificant, we excluded them from the final model in the interest of ease of presentation.
13. All analyses were conducted using Stata 7.0.
14. This is borne out by the data published by the *Forschungsgruppe Wahlen* and Forsa.
15. Meeting with a Green campaign strategist, 18 September 2002.

CHAPTER 3

The German Party System: Developments After Unification

Bernhard Wessels

T he German party system has changed considerably during recent years. It still seems to be in a flux, given the volatile situation particularly in the new *Länder*. Some changes have been very noticeable, especially the differentiation of the parliamentary party system. Not so obvious, though significant, is the enormous extension of the supply side, that is, more party lists are running in federal elections. This indicates that political entrepreneurs in the 1990s have increasingly regarded successful strategic entry as more likely than they did in the 1980s.

In contrast to the last decade, the party system of the FRG had been regarded as "super-stable" for a long time. After concentration and consolidation in the 1950s, very little change took place until the 1980s. Not everybody shared the view that this was a positive feature of the German system. Political observers criticized the cartel of the established parties and the impermeability of the German electoral system. However, in 1983 the Greens were successful in federal elections for the first time, a possibility not anticipated, given the 5-percent threshold of the electoral system. This change in the party system demonstrated that new interests, reaching a critical mass, could gain political representation. The interpretation from a system-theoretical perspective was straightforward: integration through differentiation. Whereas positive positions toward this change of the party system prevailed in the 1980s, the discussion takes a different route today. There are warnings about the danger of too much fractionalization of the party system and of too much volatility that might bring about the danger of successful populist mobilization.

Against this background, an attempt is made here to shed some light on the most recent developments and to answer the question whether the German institutional solution, quite often cited as a blueprint for a stable party system with the "best of both worlds" solution (Shugart and Wattenberg 2001) for the trade-off of representation and governance, has lost the capacity to integrate the differentiation between interests and changing demands.

It is a commonplace that in political terms unified Germany is still divided. With regard to the party system, since unification there are supposed to be two: one in the West and one in the East (see Rohrschneider and Wolf, chapter 2 in this volume). Here, we go one step further. The general hypothesis to be evaluated is that following unification one should not talk of one federal party system, but of three. We follow here an observation made by Pappi and Shikano (2001).

In a first step, the development of the German party system over the entire postwar period is briefly evaluated to gain a yardstick for measuring how much change really did take place after 1990. In a second step, the 1990s plus the years until 2002 are studied in more detail, restricting analysis to the period 1994–2002. The election of 1990 is excluded because it is a deviating, though important case: in 1990 the electoral system was different, for the threshold was applied to the two regions separately. This was the stepping-stone for the success of the PDS, the post-communist party, and the starting point for an East–West divide in the party system. The degree to which the hypothesis of a divided party system holds up is investigated by studying the electoral districts in the regions by means of analysis of variance. This step will concentrate on the formal characteristics of the party system(s), that is, fractionalization, asymmetry, and the like. Thereafter, a brief comparison of the political center of gravity in the three regions (East Germany, Bavaria, remaining West Germany) is made. The last part of the essay includes some speculation about the consequences of the findings.

The General Background

According to Sartori's theory of party systems, Germany can be characterized as a system of moderate pluralism where three to five relevant parties with coalescent behavior tend to form bipolar, Center–Right versus Center–Left governmental coalitions of two or three parties (Sartori 1976). Almost all parties are potential coalition partners. The electorate's preferences are, generally speaking, centrist and party competition is centripetal. This is at least true for the time after the immediate postwar period. Generally, the history of the German party system after 1945 is divided into four phases of evolution (Rudzio 2000: 136–55): the setup period (1945–1951), the concentration period (1952–1961), the consolidated party system (1961–1982), the period of differentiation and regionalization (from 1983 until today)—some, however, differentiate between the period before and after unification. There is good reason for this further differentiation as will be demonstrated. In the following, a brief description of the cleavage system that the German party system rests upon and a description of the development of the party system in terms of formal characteristics, that is, the number of electoral and parliamentary parties, volatility, and political competition, will be presented.

Party System Concentration

In the initial and the concentration periods, the German party system was quite fragmented. During these periods, postwar problems ranked quite high on the agenda and some parties concerned with the issues of expellees (Party of Expellees [GB-BHE]), some with regional interests (Bavarian Party [BP]) as well as some Left and Right parties tried their luck. Altogether, 13 parties made it into parliament, of which six formed pairwise electoral alliances (CDU/CSU, SPD, Liberals, and German Peoples Party [FDP/DVP], Communists [KPD], BP, German Party [DP], Center Party [ZP], Economic Reconstruction League [WAV], German Conservative Party/German Law Party [DKP/DRP], and Radical Liberty Party [RSF]). DP, KPD, and BP did not make it in 1953, and the ZP did so only by electoral alliance with the CDU. GB/BHE was successful in 1953 but dropped out again in 1961. With this development, the basic structure of the German party system, resting on class and religious cleavages, was settled for the next 20 years (figure 3.1).

Political cleavages are, as Lipset and Rokkan (1967) pointed out, the central features organizing the structure of party systems. Basic conflicts rooting in different historical periods (state–church conflict and center–periphery conflict arising with nation-building, capital–labor conflict arising with the Industrial Revolution, e.g.) are reflected and taken up by various interest organizations and parties, which in turn mobilize on the respective issues. Cleavages are based on structural

Character		Traditional			New	
Dimension		Socioeconomic		Religion/denomination	Cultural	East/West
Content Basis		Labour	Capital			
Party system		(SPD) Social Democrats	(FDP, CDU/CSU) Liberals, Christian Democrats	(CDU/CSU) Christian Democrats	"New Politics"/ ecology	(PDS) Post communists
Interest groups and movements		Labour unions	Employer's and business associations	Christian churches	Greens	
Social structure		Blue/white collar	Old middle classes, self-employed	Christian social setting (milieus)	Environmental interest groups	?
Value structure		Unionized economic ideology	Consensus about growth and technological progress, economic individualism	Religious traditionalism	Postmaterial movement milieus	Eastern regional provenance
					Post materialism	Socialist democracy

Figure 3.1 Structure and institutionalization of political cleavages in Germany

Source: Taken from Wessels (1991) and modified.

conflict of interest, reproduced and strengthened by party politics. Therefore, cleavages can be regarded as politicized social structures (Pappi 1977) organizing voter alignments (social alliances between voters and organizations/elite groups) and respective coalitions between political or organizational elites (Stinchcombe 1975). As in most western European societies, the major division lines in Germany are the religious and the class cleavages. These two have structured the German party system for almost three decades.

Since 1961 at the latest, social alliances between the electorate and the parties have been very stable, elite coalitions had been established even earlier. The party system is not a totally symmetric reflection of the cleavage structure, given the double role of the Christian Democrats. They represent at least partly the pro-business pole on the class dimension as well as the Christian or religious pole on the religious dimension. In the class cleavage, the Social Democrats traditionally represent the opposite pole. The religious dimension is to some degree asymmetric in itself, since a clear opponent is missing here, although the Liberals and parts of the Social Democrats and the Greens display laicistic attitudes. Today, the religious cleavage dimension is hardly ever based on denomination. The important characteristic is religiosity and participation or abstention from religious service. The social alliances on which the cleavages and the party systems rest are (or at least have been) very firm. Pappi (1973, 1979, 1986, 1990) has demonstrated again and again the explanatory power of the respective social characteristics for voting behavior. This relevance of social group differences to voting behavior has persisted more or less until today. The tremendous change is not in the social group influence but in the composition of the electorate. The size of the social core groups of political parties (workers and union members in case of the Social Democrats, Catholics and churchgoers in case of the Christian Democrats) has declined dramatically. Whereas in the 1950s roughly 35 percent of the voters of the two big parties belonged to the respective social core groups, this portion has decreased to about 15 percent in the 1990s due to social change and secularization (Wessels 2000b).

The concentration of the party system on nationwide relevant cleavages was facilitated by a change in the electoral system. Of the ten parties and alliances that made it into the *Bundestag* in 1949, only the KPD received more than 5 percent nationwide besides the three traditional parliamentary parties (CDU/CSU, SPD, FDP); in 1953, this was the case only for the GB/BHE. The development of the parliamentary party system in connection with the changes in electoral law is depicted

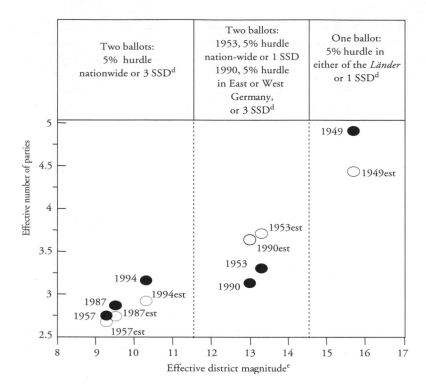

Figure 3.2 Electoral system change[a] and the number of parties[b] in Germany[c]

[a] Filled dot, empirical value; empty dot, estimated value.
[b] Effective number of parties (N_{Eff}):
$N_{Eff} = 1/HH = 1/\text{sum } (p_i^2)$; where p is the fractional share of parties.
[c] Regression equation
$N_{Eff} = 0.24 + 0.27(M_{Eff}) + e$
$R^2 = 0.74$; SE B 0.08.
[d] SSD: single seat district.
[e] Effective district magnitude (M_{Eff}):

  (1) Seats/districts; where districts is calculated as the sum of SSD and the number of *Länder*-based multi-seat districts.
  (2) Effective threshold = 50%/legal threshold (5%) (Taagepera and Shugart 1989: 135).
  (3) Seat threshold = 50%/SSD-seats/seat threshold*100).
  (4) M_{Eff} = geometric mean of the three measures, i.e., (1*2*3) exp 1/3.

in figure 3.2 (see also Klingemann and Wessels 2001). It demonstrates a close relationship between the changes in the threshold and the effective number of parliamentary parties. However, it would be a fault to regard party system change as a pure product of the change of the rules of the game. Rather, the development indicates that institutional change went together perfectly with social change.

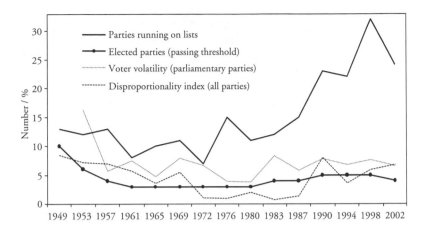

Figure 3.3 Running and elected parties (1949–2002)

In formal terms, that is, fragmentation, asymmetry, and concentration of votes, the party system was stable between 1957 and 1983 (Niedermayer 1997, 2000). Data in figure 3.3 confirms stability. It can also be seen that this situation of no change came to an end in 1983 with regard to three aspects: first, the number of parties in parliament increased by one due to the success of the Greens; second, volatility increased and stayed at a higher level the years afterward; third, the number of party lists running in the *Bundestag* election exceeded all previous numbers in 1987, rose steeply to a maximum in 1998, and dropped a little in 2002. Although the electoral system seems to be an effective buffer against a steady increase of fractionalization, it is interesting enough to notice that political entrepreneurs obviously see a chance for new political offers. Until now, strategic entry (Cox 1997) has not been successful. The question is whether this is a guarantee for the future. What these observations neglect, however, is the regional split in the party system (and cleavage structure), which arose with German unification.

The Regionally Divided Party System in the 1990s

The most obvious fact pointing to a regionally differentiated party system is the success of the PDS, the post-communist party in the new *Länder*, its failure in the West, and the poor results of the Liberals (FDP) and Greens in the East after 1990. They gained less than 5 percent of the votes until the 2002 federal elections when Liberals almost doubled their result of 1998 (6.4 percent) and when the Greens were able to get a little more than 5 percent. Whereas the western *Länder's* party system is quite the same as before unification, the eastern *Länder's* party system is very different. If there had been a separate election with a 5 percent hurdle in the East, only SPD, CDU, and PDS would have made it into the parliament after 1990 and until 2002 (tables 3.1 and 3.2).

Unification has put the German polity under quite some stress in many respects. The challenges that had and in some respects still have to be faced are economic transformation in the new *Länder*, transfer of West German political institutions and organizations, including parties and interest groups, and the mutual recognition of similarities and differences in history, culture, and interests.

It was not helpful that in contrast to the expectations of the "Unification Chancellor," Helmut Kohl, economic success and well-being has not developed well in East Germany. Growth rates in the new *Länder* are lower than in the West, unemployment rates much higher due to de-industrialization, lower growth, and a traditionally higher labor market participation in particular of women. The problem is not so much the pure material situation. Social transfers guarantee that household income is not lower than in times of the German Democratic Republic (GDR). But compared to expectations and even more important to the situation in West Germany, many people in the new *Länder* see good reason to feel relatively deprived and to develop some regional identity on this basis.

However, this is not the whole story. There are also considerable differences in political culture and the approach to politics. The most obvious discrepancy is related to the expectations about the role of the state, resulting in quite diverse normative conceptions of democracy in East and West. Roller has shown that the expectations concerning welfare state functions are much higher in the East, both in terms of extensity and intensity (Roller 1999a,b).

Fuchs (1999, 2000) has demonstrated that attitudes toward the role of the state and participatory demands merge into a prevailing vision of democracy in the East that he has labeled *socialist democracy*, whereas in the West liberal democracy is most strongly supported. Rohrschneider and Wolf (chapter 2, in this volume) and Fuchs and Rohrschneider come to the conclusion that the German electorate is divided along these lines in attitudes and in political behavior (Rohrschneider and Fuchs 1995; Fuchs and Rohrschneider 2001).

Following Pappi and Shikano (2001), there is good reason to regionally differentiate even further and to separate Bavaria from the rest of the western *Länder*. The argument in this regard, however, is totally

Table 3.1 Distribution of list votes in *Bundestag* elections (1949–2002)

Year	Turnout	Percent list votes						Concentration (CDU/CSU+SPD)		Volatility
		CDU/CSU	SPD	FDP[a]	Greens[b]	PDS[c]	Others[d]	List vote	Seats	
1949	78.5	31.0	29.2	11.9			27.9	60.2	67.2	
1953	86.0	45.2	28.8	9.5			16.5	74.0	80.9	14.2
1957	87.8	50.2	31.8	7.7			10.3	82.0	88.3	8.0
1961	87.7	45.3	36.2	12.8			5.7	81.5	86.6	9.5
1965	86.8	47.6	39.3	9.5			3.6	86.9	90.1	5.4
1969	86.7	46.1	42.7	5.8			5.4	88.8	94.0	5.2
1972	91.1	44.9	45.8	8.4			1.0	90.7	91.7	5.7
1976	90.7	48.6	42.6	7.9			0.9	91.2	92.1	3.8
1980	88.6	44.5	42.9	10.6	1.5		0.5	87.4	89.3	4.5
1983	89.1	48.8	38.2	7.0	5.6		0.5	87.0	87.8	8.4
1987	84.4	44.3	37.0	9.1	8.3		1.4	81.3	82.3	5.7
1990	77.8	43.8	33.5	11.0	5.0	2.4	4.2	77.3	84.3	7.2
1994	79.0	41.5	36.4	6.9	7.3	4.4	3.5	77.9	81.3	7.2
1998	82.2	35.1	40.9	6.2	6.7	5.1	5.9	76.0	81.2	7.7
2002	79.1	38.5	38.5	7.4	8.6	4.0	3.0	77.0	82.7	6.5
Mean	*85.0*	*43.7*	*37.6*	*8.8*	*6.1*	*4.0*	*6.0*	*81.3*	*85.3*	*7.1*

[a] 1949 and 1953, FDP and DVP.

[b] 1990 and 1994, *Bündnis '90/Die Grünen*.

[c] 1990, PDS/*Linke Liste*.

[d] 1949, in % of eligible voters: KPD 5.7; BP 4.2; DP 4.0; ZP 3.1; WAV 2.9; others 5.1; 1953, in % of eligible voters: GB/BHE 5.9; DP 3.3; *Zentrum* 0.8; 1957, in % of eligible voters: DP 3.5.

Source: Wahlstatistik des Statistischen Bundesamtes.

Table 3.2 Distribution of list votes in *Bundestag* elections (East and West Germany, 1990–2002)

Year	Turnout	Percent list votes						Concentration (CDU/CSU +SPD)	Volatility
		CDU/ CSU	SPD	FDP	Greens[a]	PDS[b]	Others	List vote	
1990									
New BL	74.5	41.8	24.3	12.9	6.1	11.1	3.8	66.1	
Old BL	78.4	44.1	35.9	10.6	4.7	0.3	4.3	80.0	
1994									
New BL	72.9	38.5	31.5	3.5	4.3	19.8	2.4	70.0	15.9
Old BL	80.6	42.1	37.5	7.7	8.4	1.0	3.8	79.6	5.7
1998									
New BL	80.0	27.3	35.1	3.3	4.1	21.6	8.6	62.4	11.6
Old BL	82.8	37.0	42.3	7.0	7.3	1.2	5.2	79.3	6.7
2002									
New BL	72.8	28.2	39.7	6.4	5.1	16.7	4.0	67.9	9.6
Old BL	80.6	40.9	38.3	7.6	9.4	1.1	2.8	79.2	6.6

New BL, New *Bundesländer* (East Germany); Old BL, Old *Bundesländer* (West Germany).
[a] 1990 and 1994, Bündnis '90/Die Grünen.
[b] 1990, PDS/Linke Liste.
Source: Wahlstatistik des Statistischen Bundesamtes.

different than in the case of East–West differentiation. One formal point is very clear: voters face a different decision situation since the CDU is not running in Bavaria and the CSU not in the other *Länder*. But there is more to it. Pappi and Shikano found out that the tandem supply of chancellor candidate and party does not work with regard to the vote decision for the CSU whereas it does for the CDU. This implies that voters in Bavaria do not regard "their" CSU and a chancellor candidate of the sister party CDU as one package. This is different, of course, if the chancellor candidate comes from the CSU like Franz Josef Strauß in 1980 and Edmund Stoiber in 2002. Thus it seems legitimate to assume or at least to pursue the hypothesis of a separate decision situation, if not a different party system. In the following, the hypothesis of three different party systems is investigated using electoral districts as units of analysis. Analysis will be restricted to the period 1994–2002, since in 1990 conditions of competition were different due to the unusual circumstances of this particular election (see earlier, figure 3.2).

Criteria

The most common criteria used to characterize a party system are of a more or less formal nature and try to capture with parsimonious measures "the set of political parties operating within a nation in an organized pattern . . ."—the latter is the definition of a party system by Lane and Ersson (1994: 175). The measures must provide information about the competition situation of every single party. Obviously, the number and the political profile of competitors are of crucial importance. It is still an open debate as to which measures best capture these two dimensions.

Niedermayer (2000) has proposed to use the following measures for Germany: fragmentation, asymmetry, polarization, and segmentation. Fragmentation characterizes the viable number of competitors. This is not just the number of parties, but also the so-called effective number of parties, an index proposed by Taagepera (1997). It accounts for the strength of the parties, thus providing a measure of the realistic intensity of competition and number of competitors. Asymmetry is a measure that tries to capture whether there is equilibrium of strength between the two biggest parties and therefore a chance of alternating government. Polarization and segmentation concern the relationship of party profiles. Polarization refers to the range of political supply in programmatic terms utilizing the Left–Right dimension, segmentation to the degree to which parties are separated so strongly from another that they would never form a coalition, measured as the proportion of politically realistic coalitions of theoretically possible coalitions.

Since in this section we are interested in the question as to which degree the German party system is regionally divided, polarization and segmentation are of no interest. They are constants for the party system on the whole and not for separate regions. But the differences between regions with regard to the political center of gravity are important. That is, whether the electorates in the regions are at different centers in the Left–Right dimension. Thus, in the following, the regional party systems are first described in terms of fragmentation and asymmetry as well as in terms of volatility because this is of particular interest with regard to East–West differences and can also shape party competition; second, it will be investigated whether regional difference holds up looking into the variation within regions and between regions; third, the differences between regions will be investigated, holding socio-demographic characteristics of the districts constant. Finally, the political centers of gravity in the regions will be determined.

The Significance of Regional Differences

A first, though important, observation can be made by looking at election results. They reveal typical differences between the regions. In table 3.3, the important dissimilarities are in italics there is a typical discrepancy in Social Democratic vote share between Bavaria and the remaining old *Länder*; it is relatively low in the first and much stronger in the second region. Another characteristic of Bavaria is the extraordinary strength of the CSU. Both regions contrast sharply with East Germany, where Greens and Liberals were not able to get even 5 percent of the votes in 1994 and 1998 and where the PDS is very strong with about one-fifth of the votes.

This translates directly into differences in the effective number of electoral parties: the figure is lowest in Bavaria, quite closely followed by the rest of West Germany, and highest in East Germany. This rank order applies both to list and nominal votes. Note that these and the following figures are mean differences calculated from district distributions (table 3.3).

If each region would form a government on the basis of the regional vote distribution, Bavaria would come first with regard to asymmetry. Particularly in 2002, asymmetry of list votes reached a high level not observed in the 1990s. Alternation of government in Germany would not be very likely if the federal distribution of votes looked similar in this

Table 3.3 Election results in three German regions[a] (1994, 1998, and 2002)

	SPD		CDU		CSU		Greens		FDP		PDS	
	N^b	L^b	N	L	N	L	N	L	N	L	N	L
1994												
WGE	*42.0*	*39.5*	44.0	39.8	—	—	7.3	8.3	3.4	7.9	0.5	1.1
Bav.	31.0	29.9	—	—	*54.5*	*51.0*	6.0	6.3	3.1	6.4	0.2	0.6
EGE	31.9	31.5	40.4	38.8	—	—	*3.7*	*4.3*	3.0	3.5	*20.1*	*19.5*
1998												
WGE	*47.7*	*44.4*	39.4	34.4	—	—	5.6	7.6	3.1	7.3	0.9	1.3
Bav.	36.0	34.7	—	—	*51.5*	*47.4*	4.6	6.0	2.6	5.1	0.3	0.7
EGE	38.0	35.2	29.8	27.4	—	—	*3.3*	*4.1*	2.8	3.3	*22.2*	*21.5*
2002												
WGE	*45.7*	*41.1*	40.0	36.7	—	—	6.0	9.8	6.1	8.3	1.1	1.2
Bav.	29.1	26.3	—	—	*59.0*	*58.6*	5.9	7.5	4.1	4.5	0.6	0.7
EGE	39.1	39.8	30.2	28.2	—	—	*4.0*	*5.0*	6.0	6.4	*19.0*	*16.7*

[a] Bav., Bavaria; WGE, West Germany, Bavaria excluded; EGE, East Germany.

[b] N = Nominal votes, L = List votes.

region. Least asymmetry can be found in West Germany. Between 1994 and 1998, volatility was highest in the East, and a little higher in West Germany than in Bavaria. Comparing 1998 and 2002, Bavaria and West Germany changed places due to the extraordinary success of the CSU.

In general, it can be concluded that competition is strongest in the regional party systems and most variable in East Germany; it is the least strongest and least volatile in Bavaria.

A crucial question is, however, whether these regions really form units that can be significantly separated from each other. Aggregate observations may hide huge variations within regions and suggest an unrealistic assumption of clear boundaries between them. To test this, analyses of variance have been performed using the reported party system characteristics at the district level as units. By this approach it can be checked whether within-region homogeneity is high enough to differentiate between regions, that is, within-region variance is significantly smaller than between-region variance. For this purpose, not just a test of significance of mean differences has been performed but a comparison of every region with each other. To confirm the hypothesis of three different party systems, analysis must confirm the significance of between-region differences against within-region differences. A measure for this is the Duncan index. It is provided in the right column of table 3.4.

Concerning differences of the effective number of parties, regional differences for three of four measures (list and nominal vote, 1994, 1998, and 2002) seem to be significant. For nominal vote in 1998, only the difference between East Germany and the other two regions is significant, but not between the latter two. Asymmetry shows significant regional differences in 1994, in 1998 and 2002 it is significant only for Bavaria against the other two regions. Volatility differs consistently and significantly between the three regions, regardless of nominal or list vote.

These results strongly confirm that the party system in the East is different and that Bavaria differs from the remaining *Länder* in the West in this regard. However, sufficient homogeneity within regions to differentiate them from each other may be due to a socio-structural composition effect. It is possible, though not very likely, that the electorates differ strongly in social characteristics. This would still mean that there are different party systems, but the reason would lie in the social structure and not in the region, whatever that may encompass (history, legacy, culture, values, etc.). In order to test for this possibility, regression analyses have been performed, using socio-demographic characteristics as independent ("explanatory") variables of vote choice. The assumption behind this

Table 3.4 Effective number of parties, asymmetry, and volatility: variance analytic comparisons between regions[a,b]

Year	Vote type	No. of districts	Bav.	WGE	EGE	eta^2	Pairwise group comparison,[c] Duncan < 0.05
Effective number of parties[d]							
1994	list votes	328	2.8	3.0	3.3	0.21	All
1998	list votes	328	2.8	3.0	3.9	0.59	All
1998	list votes	299	2.8	3.0	3.9	0.56	All
2002	list votes	299	2.4	3.0	3.6	0.56	All
1994	nominal votes	328	2.5	2.6	3.0	0.40	All
1998	nominal votes	328	2.5	2.5	3.3	0.66	EGE : Bav., WGE
1998	nominal votes	299	2.5	2.5	3.4	0.67	EGE : Bav., WGE
2002	nominal votes	299	2.2	2.6	3.4	0.72	All
Asymmetry[e]							
1994	list votes	328	21.1	0.2	7.0	0.22	All
1998	list votes	328	12.7	−10.1	−8.0	0.29	Bav. : WGE, EGE
1998	list votes	299	13.0	−9.1	−8.4	0.30	Bav. : WGE, EGE
2002	list votes	299	32.3	−4.5	−11.6	0.54	All
1994	nominal votes	328	23.5	1.9	8.2	0.20	All
1998	nominal votes	328	15.5	−8.2	−8.6	0.27	Bav. : WGE, EGE
1998	nominal votes	299	15.9	−7.3	−8.9	0.29	Bav. : WGE, EGE
2002	nominal votes	299	29.6	−5.8	−9.0	0.46	Bav. : WGE, EGE
Volatility[f]							
1994/1998	list votes	328	5.2	6.0	9.7	0.41	All
1998/2002	list votes	299	10.8	4.3	7.2	0.67	All
1994/1998	nominal votes	328	5.3	6.5	11.0	0.33	All
1998/2002	nominal votes	299	8.4	4.1	6.2	0.36	All

[a] Based on 328 districts in 1994 and 1998, 299 districts in 2002, and 1998 redistricted to 2002.

[b] Bav., Bavaria; WGE, West Germany, Bavaria excluded; EGE, East Germany.

[c] Pairwise group comparison: "all" indicates that differences are significant at 0.05 between any pair of regions (i.e., Bavaria vs. West Germany; Bavaria vs. East Germany; West Germany vs. East Germany); other entries indicate which region differs significantly from the other two.

[d] Effective number of electoral parties: according to Taagepera's (1997) measure no. 1.

[e] Asymmetry: CDU/CSU share minus SPD share.

[f] Volatility: sum of absolute changes of parliamentary parties in vote share divided by two.

follows very much the individual-level socio-structural approach to explain vote choice. With the ecological approach, we cannot claim to investigate individual-level relationships. But we know that there exists a relationship between population characteristics and election outcomes, resulting from individual-level relationships.

The variety of available socio-demographic characteristics is limited. But we have access to data on population density, age distribution, change in population, unemployment rate, and employment rates in different sectors. With these variables, characterizing the social composition and situation of a district, we can quite sufficiently predict the electoral outcome for the parties. The portion of explained variance in all three elections is about 30 percent or higher for the SPD (33 percent on average), for the CDU/CSU 37 percent in 1994, over 50 in 1998 and 2002 (50 percent on average), almost 75 percent for the Greens in 1994 and 1998 (69 percent on average), roughly 50 percent for the Liberals in 1994 and 1998, but only 14 percent in 2002 (46 percent on average), and over 70 percent for the PDS (80 percent on average).

The question to be answered is the following: what are the differences in the electoral fortune of the parties in the regions, if controlled for the socio-demographic characteristics of the districts? The resulting figure gives us the net impact of region above social structure. In table 3.5 the results are presented and interpretation is straightforward: if the

Table 3.5 Effects of regions[a] on election results[b] (list votes), controlled for demographic characteristics[c] of districts

| | 1994 % in districts | | | | 1998 % in districts | | | |
| | EGE | | Bav. | | Increase in R-square | EGE | | Bav. | | Increase in R-square |
	Estim.	(real)	Estim.	(real)		Estim.	(real)	Estim.	(real)	
SPD	−19,70	(−8,0)	−5,73	(−9,6)	0,20	−21,51	(−9,2)	−5,66	(−9,7)	0,24
CDU/CSU	7,52	(−1,0)	8,97	(11,2)	0,15	1,60	(−7,0)	10,51	(13,0)	0,16
Greens	−1,36	(−4,0)	−2,41	(−2,0)	0,07	−0,61	(3,5)	−2,07	(−1,6)	0,04
FDP	−1,98	(−3,4)	−2,38	(−1,5)	0,11	−1,11	(4,0)	−3,06	(−2,2)	0,19
PDS	14,71	(18,4)	−0,41	(−0,5)	0,08	15,89	(20,2)	−0,38	(−0,6)	0,09

	1998 % in districts					2002 % in districts				
SPD	−15.78	(−8.6)	−5.71	(−11.3)	0.14	−8.62	(−1.3)	−11.44	(−14.8)	0.22
CDU/CSU	−3.87	(−7.9)	10.74	(12.8)	0.17	−3.48	(−8.8)	19.11	(19.9)	0.30
Greens	−2.17	(−3.1)	−2.04	(−1.7)	0.06	−3.31	(−4.8)	−2.57	(−2.1)	0.06
FDP	−1.70	(−4.1)	−3.06	(−2.4)	0.20	−0.50	(−1.9)	−3.96	(−3.8)	0.45
PDS	19.78	(16.1)	−0.51	(−0.7)	0.13	14.89	(15.5)	−0.51	(−0.6)	0.13

[a] Region of reference: West Germany without Bavaria.

[b] Based on 328 districts in 1994 and 1998, 299 districts in 2002, and 1998 redistricted to 2002.

[c] Demographic characteristics controlled for: population density; four portions of age distribution (percent of population between 18–24 years, 24–34, 35–59, and 60 and older); population change per 1,000 inhabitants; unemployment rate; three portions of sector employment (percent employed in agriculture, production, and service). Complete regression tables are available from the author on request (wessels@wz-berlin.de) or can be downloaded from http://www.wz-berlin.de/~wessels/BWDownloads.de.htm.

socio-demographic structure in East Germany would be the same as in West Germany, Bavaria excluded, the Social Democrats would have received even less votes in East Germany in all three investigated elections than they did, even though their real vote share is already much lower than in the West. Christian Democrats, Greens, and Liberals would have gained a little more votes than in reality. The marked difference of a much higher vote share of the PDS in the East than in the West would remain the same or even be somewhat bigger if social composition of the districts would be the same in the whole of Germany. The differences between West Germany and Bavaria stay more or less the same as they are empirically. In Bavaria, compared to West Germany, the figures equal more or less the real results, controlling for socio-demographic characteristics.

These results suggest that the differences between the party systems of the three German regions do not result from the social composition of the respective electorates, but are rooted more deeply in the political culture of the regions.

Political Centers of Gravity

What relevance do these differences in the regional party systems have in terms of political objectives? As mentioned earlier, several studies have shown that citizens in the new *Länder* possess different political attitudes and have a different vision of democracy. In particular, the demand for a strong role of the state and for more direct political participation is higher in the East (Rohrschneider and Wolf, chapter 2 in this volume). With regard to the party system(s), it is of crucial importance to clarify whether the observed differences of more formal characteristics also translate into general differences in content, that is whether the regional party systems have different centers of political gravity. "Center of gravity" is a spatial concept based on the traditional political Left–Right dimension. Left and Right refer to different generalized policy positions. Fuchs and Klingemann have shown in a comparative study of citizen's attitudes that the general understanding of Left includes equality and solidarity of values, whereas the Right is loaded with values like individualism and freedom (Fuchs and Klingemann 1990: 212–16). They argue, that the Left–Right schema is an indicator that measures generalized political positions and can be taken as a summary statement of many issue positions of the day. Thus, differences in the political center of gravity of party systems indicate differences in the generalized political demand structure. The center can

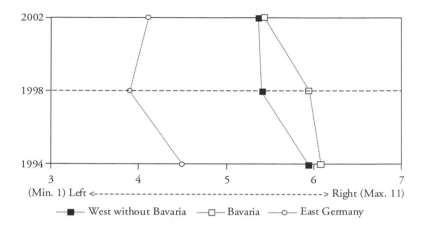

Figure 3.4 Center of Left–Right gravity in German regions (1994–1998)[a]

[a] Calculations based on Left–Right self-placement of party voters weighted by election results.

Sources: Post Election Survey 1994, WZB, ZUMA, ZA-No. 2601; Post Election Survey 1998, WZB, ZUMA, ZA, ZA-No. 3073; Post Election Survey 2002, Forsa Post Election Study 2002.

be determined by observing individual Left–Right self-placement of voters weighted by the vote share of the parties.

Figure 3.4 presents the results. The political center of gravity in East Germany is significantly to the Left of West Germany, West Germany a little to the Left of Bavaria at all three elections. The center of gravity is not fixed but volatile over time. Electorates in all three regions have moved a little to the Left between 1994 and 2002. However, differences between the regions remain very much the same. Whereas the move to the Left should be overemphasized, the differences between East and West are striking. They clearly indicate that the discrepancies between the regional party systems are not only of a formal nature, affecting the structure of political competition, but also carry differences in political content, for example, in demand. That the center of gravity is more to the Left in the East indicates an electorate showing stronger interest in and higher demand for policies and more oriented toward social equality, social justice, welfare, and so on. As Roller has shown, this higher demand is not situationally determined but deeply rooted in different regime experiences and political socialization (Roller 1997). Given the fact that these patterns of differences in the regional party systems have been persistent in formal terms as well as in terms of content over the last 12 years, the expectation that this feature will accompany Germany for some time longer is not unrealistic.

Consequences

Obviously, the German party system is in flux. After concentration and consolidation in the 1950s, the party system was "super-stable" until the 1980s, experiencing the first major change in 1983 when the Greens entered parliament. The second change came with German unification in 1990. Since then, the party system can be regarded as quite strongly regionalized. The findings, which support the hypothesis formulated here, indicate that Germany's national party system has three regional layers: the new *Länder*, Bavaria, and the rest of West Germany. Whilst this analysis concentrates on the post-unification period, it does not mean that the regional divide between Bavaria and the rest of the FRG did not exist before unification. Quite the contrary, election research lets this assumption seem quite likely. However, with unification the problem of regionalization has obviously reached a critical point.

Results indicate that party system characteristics at the district level are so homogenous within regions that the boundaries between regions are quite firm and not only of statistical significance. Furthermore, this differentiation is not due to socio-demographic composition effects. Controlling for district-level demographics, differences between the regions remain the same or would be even stronger if the social structure would be identical between regions.

What are the consequences? First, the mechanisms of party competition differ between regions. If parties would take up these differences they would increase responsiveness on the one hand, but reinforce tendencies of regionalization on the other hand. Thus, the core problem of regionalization is the trade-off between unity or governability and representation. The German electoral system is an attempt to serve both purposes. The *national* 5 percent/3 seats threshold obviously favors unity; the allocation of seats according to national list vote distribution promotes representation. This implies that parties with regional strongholds and very little votes elsewhere may fail representation. The PDS is a case in point. In 1990, it made it into the *Bundestag* only because the threshold was applied separately in the East and in the West. With the nationwide threshold up again in 1994, the PDS did not get over the 5 percent threshold though gaining 19.8 percent of the votes in the East. But it won three direct seats and therefore took part in the allocation of seats according to the share of list votes. In 1998, 21.6 percent in the East and 1.6 percent in the West added up to a vote share of 5.1 percent, thus the threshold was taken. Vote share dropped considerably to 16.7 percent in the East in 2002—probably due to the closeness of the race and an anti-Stoiber effect drawing votes from the PDS to the Social Democrats—and the PDS failed the 5 percent as well as to gain the alternatively required three direct seats, the latter partially a result of redistricting in order to reduce the number of parliamentary seats from 656 to 598.

Thus, the balance between governance and representation (Shepsle 1988), so nicely in equilibrium before unification, is disturbed. The regional division line persists but does not find its representation (or only by the two direct seats won by the PDS) in the national parliament. One possible question is whether challenge to the norms of democracy embedded in the electoral system is strong enough to start a discussion about electoral reform. Given the two goals the German electoral system wants to serve, the legal or normative discussion would have very little ground. However, the problem can also be discussed politically. One could argue that there is good reason to talk about the specific regional division line resulting from unification. But in public discourse no such discussions have been launched. Maybe, this is because of the consequences. Whereas electoral reform might be able to solve the problem of representation in a regionalized party system, it might at the same time produce stronger party system fragmentation with considerable consequences for government formation and political stability. It seems as if one has chosen the implicit alternative to keep rules as they are and to wait for the electorate to learn. Learning would imply to give up the PDS in order not to waste votes. This implies, however, that the parties to which these voters would turn would have to cope with stronger intra-party tensions. Regionalization of the party system would be resolved but may result in the regionalization of parties.

CHAPTER 4

Gerhard Schröder as "Coordination Chancellor": The Impact of Institutions and Arenas on the Chancellor's Style of Governance

Sabine Kropp

In the year 1998, for the first time in postwar German history, a German federal government was voted out of office, and a Red–Green coalition assumed power. The new government not only raised hopes for rapid and far-reaching reforms but it also stressed that the character of political leadership in Germany had to change and proclaimed that broad societal and political consensus would be one of the Red–Green coalition's outstanding priorities for enacting a "new type of innovative governing style." Decisions would be arrived at by exercising "consensus leadership" that would reflect the "general will."

Early on, however, Schröder encountered serious obstacles to his intended reforms. The chancellery's ideas evidently conflicted with reality. In order to carry out some of the aforementioned reforms and to strengthen his authority, Schröder had to resort to unusual or, as critical observers underline, even "dubious" means of bargaining. His strategies can, in part, be attributed to the German polity, which offers several veto-points, which might lead to blockades in legislation or at least force a chancellor and his government to agree to compromises and package deals. Thus, intended reforms often get incrementally reduced to small-range decisions.

Moreover, the chancellorship requires the coordination of different and interdependent arenas of action. The following analysis proceeds, therefore, from the assumption that we have to look into the institutional framework and the interdependent arenas that shape the governmental process in order to explain Chancellor Gerhard Schröder's style of governing. Other research similarly identifies both "resources" and "negative resources" of the chancellorship (Smith 1991, 1994). This is not to deny that the personal factor plays a considerable role in rationalizing the strategies of the chancellorship, but to dwell exclusively on the explanatory power of personality would mean neglecting the fact that political actors are bound to institutional settings. What follows is a more extensive interpretation of the chancellorship chiefly on the basis of institutional arrangements.

Resources of German Chancellorship

Today a growing body of literature has explored the challenges and restrictions of governing in complex institutional settings. Yet media and many branches of political science also focus on the chancellor as the most powerful actor in the governmental and the parliamentary arenas, and reinforce their argumentation with evidence from the rules and norms of the constitution, which allocate considerable leadership powers to the chancellor. Article 63 of the German constitution empowers the chancellor to set policy guidelines, which may be understood as the general authority to take the lead in government (*Richtlinienkompetenz*). The chancellor is granted the formal right to enforce his aims and notions in all questions he chooses to define as core issues. Therefore, the German government system has traditionally been labeled as a "chancellor's democracy" (*Kanzlerdemokratie*). Moreover, the chancellor is invested with the power to reorganize the executive branch (*Organisationshoheit*), and can ask the federal president to appoint and to dismiss ministers (*Personalhoheit*). The federal president is then obliged to follow the chancellor's request. Thus, the chancellor principle (*Kanzlerprinzip*) eclipses the so-called *Ressortprinzip* (departmental principle, Article 65), which stipulates that, within the guidelines determined by the chancellor and cabinet decisions (*Kabinettsprinzip*), each minister is given the right to conduct the affairs of his ministry as he deems appropriate.

Depending upon the chancellor's personal style of governing, a significant portion of the federal government's work may be conducted by the chancellery (Gros 2000; Murswieck 2003), involving planning and coordinating policy issues and defining policy guidelines. The chancellor's office consists of divisions that reflect the organizational structure of the ministries (*Spiegelreferate*). These divisions demand information from the ministries in order to coordinate politics and to prepare the official meetings and statements for the chancellor. This way, the chancellery parallels the ministries' organization to a certain degree. As a result, the chancellor's office, the sovereignty of the chancellor in personality questions, and his ability to structure the executive organization are regarded as the most important institutional preconditions for exercising strong chancellorship.

Even everyday experiences confirm the outstanding role of the chancellor in the governmental process. Niclauß (1988, 1999) has identified the following characteristics within the German chancellorship: first, the chancellor enjoys a huge personal prestige and authority and thus becomes personally identified with governmental successes and failures. Consequently, it is primarily the chancellor who is tasked to present a media-effective version of governmental politics to the public. This has led political scientists to speak of a growing presidential scope of government even within the parliamentary system (Korte 2000a: 14), many employing the term "presidentialization" as a synonym for "personalization" (Poguntke 2000). Second, it is up to the chancellor to push through important decisions in his own party and in the parliamentary groups supporting the government. Additionally, the majority of the German chancellors have also served previously as party leaders and have thus had the opportunity to orientate the party apparatus to the needs of government. As a result, the governing party tends to be more centralized than the oppositional parties. Finally, the chancellor determines the parameters of foreign and European policy. In declaring foreign policy one of his domains, he exerts control over the coalition partner and the vice chancellor, who is usually also head of the Ministry for Foreign Affairs.

New Institutionalism as a Suitable Approach for Analyzing Chancellorship?

If we focus exclusively upon the characteristics that empower personal leadership, we neglect fundamental features of governance, for the chancellor is ultimately embedded within a framework of institutions and arenas that restrict the scope of his action. Not only does the coalition partner limit the *Richtlinienkompetenz* and the chancellor's ability to appoint and dismiss ministers, the German governmental system's highly fragmented structure also forces the chancellor to coordinate policies with other veto-players. According to Tsebelis's definition, veto-players are individual or collective actors whose consent is a prerequisite for enacting any changes to the status quo (Tsebelis 1999: 593). In addition to the restrictions that inhere in a coalition, a German chancellor may find his hands bound whenever he needs the support of non-majoritarian institutions. Consequently, policy outputs usually reflect the package deals or the compromises that the chancellor has to concede to other institutions and powerful actors.

This analysis is congruent with the new institutionalist approach pursued in political science. The various discursive strands of the new institutionalism concur with the proposition that individual and collective actors pursue their aims and projects in an institutional context that not only constrains actions and shapes desires, preferences, and motives (Goodin 1996: 19–21) but that can also be understood as opportunity structures. Many political theorists today are, thus, inclined to stress the complementarity of institutionalism and actor-centered theories (Ostrom 1991; Scharpf 1997). According to that perspective, institutions are the context in which actors make choices. Therefore, a chancellor's governing style can be conceptualized as being shaped (but not determined) by the institutional arrangement of a governmental system. This also raises the question of how a chancellor makes use of the institutional resources the governmental system offers to him.

The German system of government can be understood as a complex interplay of interdependent and overlapping arenas that form the chancellor's scope for action. For our following considerations, we can single out five arenas: the coalition, the federal arena, intra-party processes, how to win the support of the electorate and of organized interests, and the parliamentary arena (see figure 4.1). Leaving aside the issue of European policy-making (see Barbara Lippert, chapter 12 in this volume), what follows is an exploration of those arenas shaped by national institutions. These arenas are differentiated according to their mode of decision-making and are shaped by certain institutional arrangements (Benz 1995; Kropp 2001: 52–91). The chancellorship involves coordination of these different arenas and, therefore, of finding compromises between the conflicting aims that political elites in these arenas are striving for (*Koordinationsdemokratie*, see Jäger 1988). As noted earlier, some of the institutions and collective actors, above all the German *Bundesrat* and the coalition partner, also hold the position of "veto-players" (Tsebelis 1999), thus forming an institutional setting that shows features of a "consensus model" of democracy (Lijphart 1999).

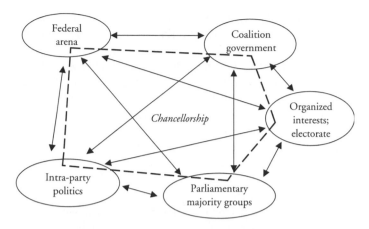

Figure 4.1 A simplified model comprising some interdependent arenas of German chancellorship

However, majoritarian institutions remain vivid in the German polity at the same time.

Given theoretical considerations, it is evident that the German chancellor presides over a broad range of formal instruments that bring into definition his outstanding role in decision-making processes. However, the particular shape of the German governmental system forces him to overcome vetoes and to seek consensus and compromises amongst a considerable number of actors and institutions. Within the two-stage approach I have been mapping out, there are two core questions that need to be raised about chancellorship: First, from the chancellor's perspective, what does the interplay of the main arenas look like? Second, how can the head of government get these interacting institutions and arenas under control, particularly if institutions as well as individual and collective actors have veto power? Can we identify typical strategies and patterns of action that, on the basis of the given institutional setting, form Chancellor Schröder's governing style?

The Impact of Interplaying Arenas and Institutions on Gerhard Schröder's Chancellorship Coalition Politics

The five aforementioned arenas indicate the maneuvering room available to the chancellor. While these arenas are a consistent presence, their shape and the way they are interconnected may change over time, offering variations of order within the governmental system. While they are empirically connected, in the ensuing sections we will analyze them sequentially. To begin with, the government coalition itself is one of the main arenas restricting the chancellor's *Richtlinienkompetenz*. As all federal governments have been party alliances since 1949, coalitions have created a permanent veto-point within the German governmental system. Spoken in the terms of game theory, coalitions are playing mixed-motive games; everyday coalition politics are shaped by both consensus *and* conflict. While these partners are willing to cooperate in order for their agenda to succeed and for a party to enter into office and implement their policy preferences, it is also true that a coalition internalizes a part of the party system's competition. As a consequence, competitive patterns of behavior exist throughout the whole legislative term. Compromises are difficult to achieve during the election campaign, as conflicts grow and the stock of trust dwindles.

A usual constellation at the level of the federal government has been for a large party to lead with the support of a smaller partner. The smaller party, for its part, can normally gain more than the proportional share of governmental offices as "payment in kind" for its support (Hogwood 1999: 29). According to de Swaans "minimal-distance" theory (de Swaan 1973), parties with the smallest ideological range on the Left–Right scale will probably form a coalition because polarization within the coalition will remain relatively small. In Germany, this has not always been the case, but the SPD and the Greens are definitely closely allied on a number of policy positions. According to hypothetical considerations and empirical findings, this would enlarge the ability of both government and parliament to produce significant laws (Tsebelis 1999). From public administration studies, however, we have observed that conflicts between ministers, as members of one and the same party but representing different policy interests, are often just as passionate as they are between coalition parties. The power relations within a coalition furthermore serve to define the options for negotiation. If one of both parties is able to play the coalition game as a "dominant player" (i.e., a party that can choose among alternative partners), it will not only have the power to "voice" against its coalition partner but also to threaten it with the "exit" option. Thus, a dominant player should also be regarded as a powerful actor in the governmental process (Van Roozendaal 1992).

In this context, it is worth noting that the position of the Green party in coalitions is usually worse than that of the FDP. The SPD is the Green party's only possible coalition partner, whereas the FDP, which holds a "pivotal" position in the party system, is able to move on the Left–Right scale from the CDU/CSU to the SPD. The SPD, in turn, can form alliances with the FDP, the CDU/CSU, and the Green party (and, to a restricted extent, with the PDS at the state level). Thus, the SPD has the potential to threaten its coalition partners with the "exit" alternative. Prior to the 1998 elections, the FDP stated that it would form a coalition with the CDU/CSU. Because the FDP wished to demonstrate credibility to their electorate, it was not able to join a party alliance with the SPD. And indeed, after 16 years of cooperation with the CDU/CSU, the Social Democrats would not have taken the Liberals into serious consideration as a coalition partner. The SPD, in contrast, was able to play the coalition game as a strong player, since a grand coalition remained at least a hypothetical alternative. Furthermore, during the legislative term the chancellor met with representatives of the FDP several times in order to demonstrate to the Greens that, if needed, he was able to play "the taming of the shrew."

Since the veto power of the Greens in the coalition continues to remain limited, the chancellor has experienced less resistance than would have been the case with other party alliances. Aware of his strong position vis-à-vis the Greens, the chancellor chose to reduce the Green minister's authority on several occasions, thereby extending his *Richtlinienkompetenz* at the expense of the departmental principle. One of the most striking incidents was the dispute between the chancellor and his Green Minister for Environment, Jürgen Trittin, about how to vote in the Council of the EU. Gerhard Schröder even threatened to dismiss Trittin if he did not oppose a new EU directive specifying that automotive industries be required to take back their products for scrapping (*Altautorichtlinie*, see Raschke 2001: 153–57). Although Germany was finally overruled in the Council by a qualified majority, it was able to get the directive slightly altered, stipulating that the industry was obliged to take back old cars beginning in 2006, rather than from 2003 onward. This and other cases offer evidence of the coalition's lack of professional management, and caused some observers to conclude that the chancellor's behavior toward the coalition partner has not been motivated by the "protection of minorities" principle (Korte 2000b: 26), but rather operates according to the "law of the strongest."

The composition of the coalition is not the only factor shaping the extent to which the chancellor can assert leadership. It is also defined by how a coalition is run, that is, by questions of coalition management. Although the conventions of coalition government have coalesced over time into rules of coalition management mutually passed on from the federal to the state level and back (Kropp 2001: 52–89), the "personal factor" also shapes the variety of informal circles and rules for coalition government in Germany to a certain degree.

Due to its lack of experience, this particular coalition encountered some difficulties while developing informal rules for managing bargaining procedures inside the government and parliament. At the beginning of the legislature, the coalition refused the high level of informal decision-making that had characterized earlier federal governments and which the coalition regarded as lacking transparency and as ultimately a nondemocratic style of governing. Although the SPD and the Greens agreed to a coalition steering committee in the coalition treaty, it had not been designed as a standing body (Helms 2001: 159), leading to many problems as the coalition was soon lacking a working pivot for mediation and planning. After encountering severe difficulties in managing even middle-range conflicts, stable management structures were set into place. In this regard, the Red–Green coalition went through similar experiences as had other federal coalitions, which also installed extra-constitutional steering bodies in order to reduce sources of friction as well as to guarantee more effective structures of decision-making (Rudzio 1991).

Like most coalition committees in Germany, the Red–Green one is composed of the party leaders, the chancellor, the vice chancellor, as well as the chairs of the parliamentary groups and the chief of the chancellery. This composition is regarded as a precondition for integrating the most important actors into decision-making. The meetings of the committee were prepared in the chancellery, which has developed into one of the central governmental agencies. In this instance, the committee was supplemented by different informal circles, the most outstanding one consisting of the chancellor, the Vice Chancellor Joschka Fischer, the Minister for Environment Jürgen Trittin, and the former SPD party leader, Oskar Lafontaine. While this elite circle had the authority to bargain conflicts and fundamental questions of government, it was supplemented by weekly meetings, routinely held by the chairpersons of both governing parliamentary groups. The Red–Green coalition herein elaborated a flexible network of informal committees and bodies just as its predecessors had done.

Intra-Party Politics

A second arena is shaped by the relationship between intra-party politics and coalition government (Maor 1998). The complexity of the intra-party structure is grounds enough to regard parties as "coalitions in themselves" (Bull 1999). As their organizational structure not only reflects different policy positions but also federal and regional interests, most of the German parties are notoriously fractious. Acknowledging that parties are scarcely unitary actors means that empirical research has to address the task of conceptualizing the important party wings and organizational units. Because these units may also veto decisions in the governmental process, the obstacles to majoritarian decisions sometimes increase multifold, and coalition governments tend to be less stable than those consisting of more unitary parties (Druckman 1996: 403).

As noted above, the logic of the parliamentary system supports centralization of the political will inside the governing parties. If the chancellor is elected head of government and party leader at the same time, he has got strong resources to gain support for governmental policies and package deals even if decisions do not correspond with or are even contrary to the party manifesto. In 1995, however, Oskar Lafontaine, who represented the left-wing (i.e., the traditional wing) of the SPD, was elected party leader. This was by no means the first time that a German chancellor did not simultaneously hold the party leadership, but no other party chairperson has assumed the governance of a ministry. Lafontaine, however, was successful in his bid for an influential office, chairing the cabinet as a powerful "super minister" for financial affairs. Thus, the resources at his command were actually broader than those available to the chancellor, although Schröder held formal control over the establishment of policy guidelines. As a result, in the first year of Gerhard Schröder's chancellorship, the policy discrepancies between the party leader and the chancellor blocked any possibility of modernizing the labor market or the social security system. Both politicians symbolized and represented different conceptions of how the SPD and governmental policies should be positioned in the ongoing process of societal modernization. Responding to these restrictions, Gerhard Schröder began to strengthen the chancellery as a powerful coordination center early on. The head of the chancellery, Bodo Hombach, soon began to challenge the authority of Lafontaine as party leader, seeking to provoke the left-wing of the party with suggestions about a possible social democratic "Third Way."

When Lafontaine unexpectedly exited the stage as minister as well as party leader in March 1999, Schröder himself was forced to take over the party leadership. Before that, the Red–Green coalition in Hesse had lost the elections, and the coalition's success appeared "to have reached rock-bottom" (Lees 2000: 176). Observers argued that Schröder was not sufficiently down-to-earth to lead his party successfully. As a strategy to overcome potential reservations within the party membership, Schröder created a new position, that of secretary general, held by Franz Müntefering. Müntefering was said to be closely attached to the party apparatus. He was quite successful in transmitting governmental policies top–down into the party membership, thereby creating a kind of subordinate status for the SPD party organization in relationship to the government. As scholarship on Schröder's governing style has underscored, the chancellor used his *Richtlinienkompetenz* in order to institute programmatic changes in the SPD's profile (Korte 2000b: 24). However, this barely constitutes a new feature of chancellorship, as this was already evident in the governing style of Konrad Adenauer and Helmut Kohl.

With their roots in the new social movements, the Greens declined any options for compatibility between party leadership positions and seats in parliament. While in opposition the Greens could well adhere to a dispersion of power between the party and the parliamentary group, things changed when the Greens became a coalition partner in the federal government. Since then there seems to be no end to discussions on this issue. The two former party leaders ("party spokesmen"), Gunda Röstel and Antje Radtcke, who were elected in order to achieve proportionality (*new Länder* versus *old Länder* and pragmatic party-wing versus fundamental-wing), were not sufficiently integrated into parliamentary and governmental procedures. Consequently, party speakers could not successfully act as mediators between governmental politics and the Green party membership. They lacked the instruments for switching routinely between the governmental arena, the parliamentary arena, and the party. Their awkward position within the coalition game, the incompatibility between seats in parliament, in governmental office, and in Green party leadership positions, has furthermore weakened the Green's ability to assert itself in the government coalition.

Recognizing that these principles were becoming increasingly inappropriate, the new "double head" (*Doppelspitze*) of the Green party, Claudia Roth and Fritz Kuhn, chose to become candidates on the party lists in 2002. This development was interpreted as a further step on the part of the Greens toward miming the normal operations of a party in government. The operative premise here was that if politicians become "multi-functional" actors, able to coordinate different arenas by holding positions within each of them, it may be easier for them to give priority to the needs of governing. Even some critical members of the Green party who harbored strong reservations against the plurality of offices, finally conceded that the founding ideas of the Green movement had become an obstacle to governmental efficiency. However, at the party conference in December 2002, a blocking minority of 33 percent of the delegates refused any revision of the Green party statutes. Claudia Roth and Fritz Kuhn consequently had to give up party leadership in order to keep their mandates. As during the first Red–Green federal coalition, the Greens again seemed to lack the ability to coordinate different levels of action.

Parliamentary Majority Groups

Within a parliamentary governmental system, the executive branch emerges out of the parliament, with the parliamentary majority groups acting as team players with the government. The resulting strategy among the members of the majority parliamentary groups in the *Bundestag* is to avoid actions that undermine the stability of government, more specifically, of "its" government. However, an expert survey revealed that the compatibility of government office and mandate was in disfavor among 36 percent among German members of parliament (MPs) at different state levels (Patzelt 1998: 741). In particular, those who support a grassroots model of democracy see fundamental problems in exercising party discipline—problems that ultimately seem to undermine the free mandate of an individual MP.

It has become common for the chairpersons of the parliamentary majority groups to take part in the weekly cabinet meetings in order to ensure a strong cohesion between the executive branch and the supportive parliamentary majority. Since this arrangement often works in favor of the executive, the chairpersons of parliamentary majority groups, Peter Struck (SPD) and Rezzo Schlauch (Greens), were concerned about being reduced to mere agents of the government and, thereby, losing the trust of their parliamentary groups. In an effort to counter this possibility, both chairpersons strictly avoided participating in cabinet meetings.

Indeed, governmental efficiency presupposes that the chairpersons of the parliamentary majority group are able to organize support for legislation. Since the chairperson is elected by the parliamentary group, he (or she) usually enjoys the trust of "his" (or "her") MPs (Patzelt 1997). This vertical dimension of trust is also reinforced horizontally, through mutual trust between chancellor and chairperson. Mistrust and conflict between the so-called backbenchers on the one hand, and parliamentary chairpersons and the government on the other, result from asymmetrical access to information and different interests, as frequently summated by means of the "principal–agent" paradigm (Lupia and McCubbins

1994). Although these problems do exist, the leading personnel, the chancellor, the chairperson, and the policy spokesmen of the parliamentary groups all depend on the support of their entire parliamentary group. This prevents the "agents" from neglecting the will of the MPs (as the principal) over the longer term.

A broad range of relationships is possible between the chairperson of the majority party and the chancellor. A chairperson may be at once confidant and veritable counterpart to the chancellor, ensuring the interests and policy positions of his or her MPs, while also organizing a majority for the government. In applying principal–agent theories it is sometimes overlooked that the chairperson's responsibility toward the parliamentary group exerts a strong influence. For instance, the chairperson of the social democratic parliamentary group, Peter Struck, successfully tried to diminish the importance of the coalition committee at the beginning of the legislature. Struck used his position to foil the committee's weekly meetings because he feared that this informal circle could jeopardize the parliamentary group's scope for action. The SPD parliamentary group was furthermore not following the Chancellor's will in all cases. For instance, in a controversy between the chancellor and the Minister of Labor, Walter Riester, regarding low-wage jobs, the MPs supported the minister but not the head of government. However, it was precisely the lack of informal coordination structures that enabled the chancellor to extend the importance of the chancellery as a central agency of policy formulation (Korte 2000b: 27).

In late 1999, after Schröder had assumed party chairmanship, the chancellery was reorganized. After Bodo Hombach had resigned from head of chancellery, it became an efficient power resource. In order to deepen the relationship between the chancellor and the parliamentary group, the minister of state in the chancellery, Martin Bury, and Frank Walter Steinmeier, successor to Bodo Hombach, gradually improved the communication between the chancellor's office, the party organization, and the parliamentary group. During the legislature, the relationship between the chancellor and Peter Struck also became more trusting and the parliamentary policy experts also found their role partners within the ministries, that is, the division heads and the heads of departments.

Federal Arena

Some political scientists consider the federal arena as the one giving the German governmental system its specific shape (Lehmbruch 2000). The upper house (*Bundesrat*), which consists of the governments of the states

(*Länder*), is one of the most powerful veto-players in the legislative process. About 50 to 60 percent of all laws have to be approved by the *Bundesrat*, which holds an absolute veto in these cases (*zustimmungspflichtige Gesetze*). It is a peculiarity of the German political system that the upper house has considerable veto powers and may not be controlled by the same majority as in the lower house (Tsebelis 1999: 593).

Since 1949, there were long periods of an oppositional majority in the *Bundesrat* that forced the federal government coalition to find agreements with the opposition (Schindler 1999: 2427–53). This made political scientists speak of the "Grand Coalition State" (Schmidt 1996). This constellation will become even more difficult, if there are coalition governments on the state level that consist of one party belonging to the federal government and another one that counts as part of the opposition in the *Bundestag*. Generally, the votes of the *Länder* are cast as a block vote. According to most coalition treaties, a state government has to abstain from voting, if its "mixed" coalition is not able to find a compromise. These abstentions, however, are counted as "no" and are therefore lost for the federal government.

Nevertheless, for most part of legislation, the *Bundesrat* does not make use of its veto. Even if the opposition had a majority in the second chamber, no more than 4 percent of all federal bills were blocked after they had been referred to the mediation committee (Schindler 1999: 2397). Although this seems to be a very small figure, it is often the controversial bills that are stopped by an "oppositional" *Bundesrat*. But experience shows that, if bills dealing with the equalization of revenue between the Länder and the Federation have to be decided, the *Länder* will not vote along party discipline. As the minister presidents of the *Länder* have got their own legitimacy independent from the federal level, they often decide questions of finance according to state interests and even vote against the politics of their "own" federal party. As a consequence, the chancellor and his coalition not only have to gain the support of the opposition in cases of conflict. They also have to find working compromises with those minister presidents and coalitions, whose composition is the same as the federal government (Kropp and Sturm 1998: 131–48). Therefore, the construction of German federalism creates the preconditions for a complex bargaining process between different policy positions as well as between regional and federal interests within parties.

In 1998, the Red–Green coalition held a stable majority of votes in the *Bundesrat*. Still, as described here, the coalition was preoccupied with the organization of the governmental apparatus at the beginning of the legislature. Moreover, the SPD had to overcome serious intra-party conflicts. The power struggle between Oskar Lafontaine and Gerhard Schröder prevented the government from formulating clear and unambiguous policy positions. Most of the promised reforms (e.g., concerning social security and an immigration law) were passed after 1999, when the majority in the *Bundesrat* had already changed. Since 1998, the SPD and the Greens have lost most elections on the state level. In Hesse, Hamburg, Saarland, and Saxony-Anhalt the SPD or Red–Green coalitions were replaced by the CDU or coalitions of CDU and FDP. In Hamburg, a coalition of CDU, FDP, and the so-called Schill-Party (a populist party standing for issues of law and order) was formed; in Brandenburg, the SPD was forced to share its power in a grand coalition with the CDU.

As a result of the Hesse elections in February 1999, the Red–Green coalition lost its majority in the *Bundesrat*. It was clear that the government would now suffer from the same institutional gridlock that had already restricted Kohl's chancellorship. Schröder therefore quickly pushed through the reform of the income tax system in March 1999, before the already elected conservative majority in Hesse came into office. Afterward, the Red–Green coalition was confronted with a majority of opposite governments and mixed coalitions in the *Bundesrat*. From that time on, the coalition has tried to bypass some parts of bills by dividing them into several pieces, some of them not requiring the consent of the *Bundesrat*. However, a huge part of the legislation still had to pass the upper house where the opposition was able to veto.

Electorate and Organized Interests

In everyday politics, polarization between coalition partners remains vivid. In order to achieve and to enlarge the support of the electorate, coalition parties try to sharpen their party profile even if their parliamentary groups and their ministers agree to compromises in the coalition. Therefore, parties not only wish to influence policies and not only strive for offices, but they must also be regarded as "vote-seekers." But again, rational strategies of vote-seeking tend to increase conflicts within the government, particularly if elections are just around the corner. If party competition becomes stronger during election campaigns, even incremental reforms may be blocked. In these times, governments do not dare to take measures that are in clear disadvantage of its electorate. In general, under the conditions of shrinking budgets, a lot of reforms inevitably aim at redistributing collective goods, thus removing vested rights of collective groups. Moreover, policy researchers regard it as a feature of modern governance to include those organizations into policy networks, which are able to give expertise and support for policy-making. According to that (Steinmeier 2001b), the Red–Green coalition adopted a markedly consensus-seeking strategy, inviting representatives of organized interests to cooperate in commissions and alliances.

Interplaying Arenas in the Governmental System: Regularities and Contingency

Up to that point of analysis, we found that there is some impact of context-dependency on Schröder's governing style. The dynamic architecture of the governmental system forms different constellations that work as a frame for a chancellor's leadership. As we have seen, the shape of that whole frame is contingent to a certain degree. In the last legislature, the chancellor had to overcome resistance within his party organization and in the SPD parliamentary group, whereas the blackmail potential of the coalition partner was relatively small. In other federal party coalitions, of course, these specific constellations alter.

However, after about one year to get going, the Red–Green coalition adopted informal rules for coalition management similar to those that are well known from the German history of chancellorship and governing. Such blueprints can be explained by the fact that, even after a change of government, the interplay of the different arenas forms typical structures and patterns, although there is of course some variation in the shape and the order of these arenas. As a government must be interested in efficient policy-making (at least for vote-seeking reasons), it develops informal rules and procedures that correspond to the institutional arrangement of the governmental system. This shows that not only formal institutions, but even informal institutions bounce back in everyday politics. Our next step is to explain the Chancellor's governing style by looking into typical strategies that characterize the "personal factor" of Gerhard Schröder's chancellorship.

Gerhard Schröder as "Coordination Chancellor": Strategies and Styles of Chancellorship

Reducing the broad variety of governmental actions, the following section will confine itself to two cases that highlight some typical strategies to overcome the outlined veto-points in the political system. First, this section will identify bargaining procedures between the federal government and the *Bundesrat*. Second, it will analyze the context of Gerhard Schröder's vote of confidence (*Vertrauensfrage*), which is considered to be the final instrument to ensure the chancellor's authority.

A third marked feature of the Schröder government (as of other European governments, see Murswieck 2003) are commissions, round tables, and corporatist alliances, which are thought to elaborate innovative policies. To deal with complex issues, nowadays most parliaments and governments rely on the opinions and the competences of experts. Thereby, Schröder tried to cultivate his image as "consensus chancellor," integrate potential opposition, and organize a broad consensus for his policies. These opinions on the role and the functions of governmental advisory commissions show that they can hardly be reduced to a common denominator (Heinze 2002). Therefore, the following case studies concentrate on the federal as well as on the parliamentary arenas.

Bargaining Procedures between the Federal Government and the Bundesrat

In 2000, the reform of the tax law for enterprises was a highly controversial issue. The *Länder* governed by the CDU and by mixed coalitions had already achieved a majority in the *Bundesrat*. They could therefore stop the bill, which inevitably required the consent of the upper house. Moreover, all *Länder* ministers of financial affairs were afraid of losing a considerable amount of taxes as a result of this reform. In order to push through the bill, the Federal Minister of Financial Affairs Hans Eichel tried to break the oppositional front in the *Bundesrat* by choosing a tempting bargaining procedure. In exchange for a positive vote, Eichel offered considerable side-payments. It is worth noting that these bargaining procedures took place outside the mediation committee, where MPs of the CDU parliamentary group can exert influence upon the bargaining process. The mediation committee consists of 32 members, 16 of them representing one state each, while the other 16 are composed of MPs appointed in proportion to the relative strengths of their parliamentary groups. In contrast to the voting procedure in the *Bundesrat*, the members of the mediation committee enjoy free mandates. This is thought of as an indispensable prerequisite for bargaining.

In the end, the federal minister was successful; the Red–Green government gained a majority in the upper house. The winners of this package deal were the grand coalitions of Berlin, Bremen and

Brandenburg, the SPD/PDS-coalition in Mecklenburg-West Pomerania, and the SPD/FDP coalition in Rhineland Palatinate as well as the Saarland, where at that time a single-party government headed by the CDU had already come to office. This group of states had agreed to the offered package deal, receiving considerable financial resources designated to improve their infrastructure. Their governments obviously considered their ailing state budgets to be more important than the party discipline inside the CDU. Their initial resistance, therefore, quickly receded.

Including a party in opposition, mixed coalitions are in charge of a considerable blackmail potential. Thus, they were able to act as veto-players vis-à-vis the federal government. The Red–Green coalitions and the SPD-headed single-party governments that voted for "their" government, however, came to nothing. For that reason, the federal government remedied their claims by supporting their budgets with some millions (DM), too. In the end, this bargaining process proved itself as a successful strategy to get the support of the *Bundesrat*. Concerning the federal budget, however, it was an extremely expensive method to organize package deals. Furthermore, law experts criticized this procedure as not conforming to the norms and the principles of the constitution.

One year later, similar bargaining patterns were applied again. In order to reform the pension scheme, the federal government aimed at privatizing a part of the retirement insurance. As a consequence of these ambitious plans, the states feared a considerable loss of income taxes. The conflict was not so much a question of policy distances between the parties, but, as it dealt with the financial relationships between the federation and the states, was regarded as mainly a federal problem. As on previous occasions, the federal minister of finance tried to tempt the "mixed coalitions" by offering financial incentives: as the federal law on financial equalization was soon to be reformed, Bremen, which suffers from a huge deficit, was promised financial advantages. Berlin and Brandenburg were assured that a new administrative agency with about 900 jobs would compensate the financial losses of the new law. Meanwhile, Rhineland Palatinate, where the SPD shared power with the FDP, was promised that aspects of housing property would be introduced into the pension reform. Furthermore, the Minister-President of Mecklenburg West Pomerania, Harald Ringstorff, who headed the only SPD/PDS-coalition at that time, broke the coalition treaty with the PDS in order to ensure the majority in the *Bundesrat*. As he was entitled to vote for the state, Ringstorff did not abstain from voting (as it was agreed upon in the coalition treaty) but supported the federal coalition in the *Bundesrat*—notwithstanding the fact that the PDS opposed this reform. Although this behavior caused serious coalition conflicts, both parties decided to continue their cooperation. As his predecessor Helmut Kohl, Schröder had to accept that the blackmail potential of minister presidents belonging to his own party as well as the bargaining power of mixed governments extraordinarily grow in constellations that confront the federal government with small or missing majorities in the *Bundesrat* (Renzsch 1989).

Further bargaining procedures also confirm the hypothesis that the German chancellor is embedded in a framework of institutions and arenas that restrict his scope for action. In March 2002, the chancellor and his coalition had to resort to controversial means again in order to avoid a standstill of legislation. Now, the question was how to organize sufficient support for the new immigration law. After the coordination between the parliamentary group of the CDU in the *Bundestag* and the self-conscious minister presidents of the CDU-headed *Länder* had failed several times, the leader of the federal party organization, Angela Merkel, and the chairperson of the CDU parliamentary group, Friedrich Merz, were eager to restore their crumpled authority. With former experiences in mind, Merkel and Merz executed a strong party discipline. Moreover, the immigration law was supposed to be a test to find out whether the challenger of the Chancellor, Edmund Stoiber, was able to assert himself. Coming from the Bavarian sister-party CSU, some state party organizations of the CDU still had mental reservations against Stoiber, who was seen as a representative of the party's right-wing. Mass media and political scientists also regarded the immigration law as the early beginning of the election campaign. From that point on, the chancellor could not count on a majority in the *Bundesrat*, nor had he any chance to make use of side payments and package deals in order to break off the oppositional front. Even after the SPD/FDP coalition in Rhineland Palatinate had signaled that it would vote for the bill, the Red–Green coalition could just rely on 31 of 69 votes in the *Bundesrat*. Therefore, it was the four votes of the grand coalition in Brandenburg that would tip the scales. Taking all possible strategies into consideration, the executive committee of the SPD refused any mediation procedure, for the Red–Green coalition feared that the CDU would try not only to alter some parts of the bill, but to achieve a completely restrictive new law. As a result of a meeting one day before the vote, the chancellor, the executive committee of the SPD, and the minister presidents of the SPD-headed state governments decided not to accept any further bargaining procedure with the opposition. As is often the case in

German politics, the party organization worked as a platform for coordinating the federal and the parliamentary arenas as well as the governmental one. Once this decision was taken, both sides closed their backdoors for further negotiations.

As noted earlier, the votes of one single government have to be cast as a block vote. Therefore, conflicts between the coalition partners of how to vote must be cleared up before the bill is brought into the *Bundesrat*. In the given case, both federal party organizations (respectively the federal government and the party leaders of the CDU/CSU) exerted an enormous pressure on the Brandenburg coalition before the formal voting procedure took place. Both partners were not able to evade these demands. As a consequence, this led to a highly dubious voting procedure. Brandenburg's Minister for Social Affairs Alwin Ziel (SPD), first voted with "yes," whereas the Minister of Internal Affairs and representative of the Minister President, Jörg Schönbohm (CDU), refused the bill. Asked once more for a consistent position, Brandenburg's Minister-President Manfred Stolpe (SPD), voted with "yes," while his representative confirmed his contrary position again. Such procedure was completely new in the history of the upper house. Klaus Wowereit (SPD), acting as president of the *Bundesrat* and at the same time as head of government in Berlin, however, counted the vote of Brandenburg as a consent. He justified his decision with the competence of the minister president to set the policy guidelines.

Obviously, both sides, the federal government and the opposition, had written their screenplay for action before the vote in the *Bundesrat* took place. Regarding this procedure as a breach of the constitution, the CDU-opposition ultimatively asked the *Bundespräsident* not to sign the bill. The *Bundespräsident*, however, decided to sign it. In December 2002, the constitutional court decided that the formal voting procedure was not in line with the constitution.

Hierarchy: The Vote of Confidence in November, 2001

If a governmental system is parliamentary, the government depends on the trust of the parliamentarian majority. Governments that are not able to gain the support of "their" MPs are therefore regarded as weak and incapable of acting. Just as in the foreign policy area, however, the Red–Green coalition was not able to count on an own majority in parliament. Having their roots in the peace movement, a considerable part of the party membership and of the Green MPs were critical of any participation of German armed forces in peacekeeping actions. They

also refused playing an active part in the international anti-terror coalition after 11 September 2001. As a consequence, 12 MPs of the Greens
and four of the SPD were not willing to vote for the stationing of troops
in Afghanistan. Even though the parliamentary opposition signaled
support to the government, the international alliances may have raised
the question whether the German government could be considered a
reliable partner. After the chancellor had already failed to gain the
Red–Green majority support for sending troops to Macedonia (the
government had gained the majority with the help of the opposition),
the vote of confidence was used as an ultimate mean to discipline the
parliamentary groups and, thereby, to strengthen the chancellor's
authority. Still, even without raising the vote of confidence, the chancellor would have gained an overwhelming majority of the *Bundestag*.

It made the situation more difficult for the coalition that the party
organizations decided upon their candidates' rankings on the party lists
at the same time. As the Green candidates felt strong resistance within
their party membership toward the anti-terror coalition, some of them
feared losing the support of their local party organizations. Some days
before the vote, eight MPs had announced that they would not support
the government in the given question; another seven were regarded as
being unreliable.

A closer look at this case reveals two dimensions of governing. The
first is a conflict between the executive branch and (at least partially) its
parliamentary majority groups. The second is an intra-party struggle of
the Green party, which was fought out between the pragmatic wing (the
Realos) and the fundamental wing (*Fundis*). This controversy not only
touched the self-consciousness of the Green party. It was also regarded
as having consequences for the future position of the Green party in the
German party system, since the PDS had remained the only party that
rejected any German participation in armed deployments.

In this situation, the chancellor decided to combine the vote on the
deployment with a vote of confidence (Article 68 of the constitution). A
vote of confidence is used as an exceptional means of exerting leadership; in German postwar history, it has been applied just four times. It
is suitable to exert pressure on MPs who are not willing to keep party
discipline, but it was also used by Chancellor Willy Brandt in 1972 as
well as by Helmut Kohl in 1982 in order to dissolve the parliament and
to bring forward elections. In its original meaning, a vote of confidence
indicates a deep governmental crisis. In the given case, however, neither
the Green party nor the SPD were eager to terminate the cooperation or
to end the legislature. After the chancellor had announced that he would

request a vote of confidence, the chairpersons of the parliamentary groups hastily tried to convince the renegades not to risk the existence of the coalition. As a result of these attempts, in the SPD parliamentary group just one MP refused to keep party discipline. In the end, the Red–Green coalition mustered an own majority. As a result of an agreement within the parliamentary group of the Green party, a split vote came out: with respect to their chances of being nominated for the party lists, four of the eight "rebels" were acknowledged to vote against the German participation in the anti-terror deployment; the other four voted for the government's line. This way, the Green party was able to demonstrate its critical support as well as maintain the coalition. The Green's party conference, discussing the behavior of the parliamentary group some days later, followed this line after a controversial debate. These findings confirm that governing may alter the political position of a party in the party system: After three years of governing in a Red–Green coalition and feeling the constraints of government, the Greens had obviously removed from their roots as fundamental peace movement.

Conclusion: Evaluating Institutional Settings and the "Personal Factor"

As our empirical findings show, Gerhard Schröder's governing style was partly an answer to the institutional arrangement of the governmental system, which, in the German case, requires the support of veto-players in order to alter the status quo. By looking into the opportunities and constraints of chancellorship, we also notice interconnected arenas, which form the scope of government for a chancellor. While formal institutions (in a narrow sense) are relatively robust to change, we must remain alert that the relations between the different arenas form more contingent constellations. In our perspective, a chancellor's governing style is *partly* an answer for the complex interplay of arenas at a certain time.

Mostly, institutions and arenas do not determine actions, but work as opportunity structures. Once more, this points out that actors are relevant in institution-centered theories. These findings remain true, although we have learned from the case of the Red–Green coalition management that the need to comprise the different levels of action within a governmental system produces similar informal rules and procedures, even if a government has changed. Indeed, a chancellor is in charge of different choices to exercise leadership. While the constitution offers tools for hierarchical leadership, governmental reality is marked by the features of a "coordination democracy." The way a chancellor makes use of bargaining strategies and the extent to which he falls back upon hierarchy or even extends or breaks the rules mold his personal governing style. The constellation of arenas that formed the scope of action for Chancellor Schröder gradually differed from those his predecessors were confronted with. However, facing growing problems with reforming the social security system and the labor market, to a greater degree than the chancellors who preceded him, Schröder was willing to extend formal procedures, rules, and bargaining strategies in order to avoid a further standstill of the legislation.

As a result, further investigation of the German chancellors' governing style has to reckon with a certain degree of contingency while looking into the constellation of arenas as well as into the "personal factor." Although the number of empirical cases is too small (Helms 2000) to work out typologies of leadership styles, a two-stage theoretical approach based on the idea of new institutionalism and interplaying arenas can offer a heuristic framework for analyzing the German chancellors' governing style.

Note

I am grateful to Alison B. Alter for her helpful comments on this chapter.

PART TWO

"Old Politics": Economic and Social Policy

CHAPTER 5

The Red–Green Government, the Third Way, and the Alliance for Jobs, Training and Competitiveness

Werner Reutter

The Alliance for Jobs, Training and Competitiveness was a cornerstone of the Red–Green's reform program. Notably the SPD pointed out during the election campaign in 1998 that it planned to reestablish the former Alliance for Jobs and Securing Competitiveness (*Bündnis für Arbeit und Standortsicherung*) that was proposed by Klaus Zwickel, the head of the powerful metalworkers union (*IG Metall*, IGM), in November 1995 and that Helmut Kohl had put into practice by so-called *Kanzlergespräche*, chancellor talks, in 1996. However, the halfhearted and more symbolic attempt of Helmut Kohl to coordinate economic and labor market policies by tripartite talks lasted only a few months and was a "total flop" (Mückenberger 1999: 181), and the trade unions left this first Alliance for Jobs after only three meetings. For Gerhard Schröder and the SPD—the Greens only played a marginal role in this field—this created a perfect opportunity. Because in this respect Gerhard Schröder could also convincingly promise to make things "better" than the Kohl government without making everything different.[1] In consequence, a restructured and revalued tripartite Alliance for Jobs was to play a prominent role to initiate overdue reforms mainly in the labor, economic, and the social policy (SPD and Bündnis '90/Die Grünen 1998: 5–6; G. Schröder 1998c: 22–23; Bundesregierung 1999: 6–8). And in fact the newly formed Alliance for Jobs, Training and Competitiveness was quickly convened after the elections and already met for the first time on 7 December 1998.

The Alliance for Jobs, Training and Competitiveness also seemed to fit perfectly well into the overall picture social scientists had drawn of Germany (Katzenstein 1987; Esser and Schroeder 1999; Streeck 1999). Generally this kind of tripartite political exchange is regarded as a necessary and striking feature of the "German model" or the "Rhenish Capitalism" (*rheinischer Kapitalismus*), and hardly anybody writing about this subject can avoid referring to the long and widespread tradition of social partnership and cooperative industrial relations in Germany (e.g., Steinmeier[2] 2001a). Many social scientists have—at least in the outset—put the Alliance for Jobs of the Red–Green government into this tradition and interpreted it as a possible reemergence of a corporatist mode of decision-making and interest mediation (Wessels 1999, 2000a; Hassel 2000; W. Schroeder 2001).

Most of the high expectations associated with this kind of macro political coordination in the beginning have nevertheless been disappointed (Hassel 2002; Lang 2002). Even if one admits that many expectations were unrealistic and the Alliance for Jobs can indeed claim some successes, for many the failure to significantly reduce unemployment was not only the result of an erroneous labor market policy, but it also symbolized that the Red–Green coalition in general and the SPD in particular had never really been able to balance out the tradition and values of the "old left" with the needs to modernize and reform the German economy and society.[3] This problem mainly has its roots in the policies of former governments, but it is also due to programmatic deficits of the Red–Green government and has manifested itself in a particularly consensus-oriented governing style with a chancellor who saw his function in moderating rather than in managing and leading the policy process (Steinmeier 2001a; see also Kropp, chapter 4 in this volume). These factors put the Red–Green coalition also in these policy fields in a defensive position when it embarked on long overdue reforms and attempts at societal modernization. It will be shown that this was also the case as far as the Alliance for Jobs was concerned.

The Concerted Action and the Alliance for Jobs of 1996: A Corporatist Tradition?

As already mentioned, at the sectoral level institutionalized cooperation between state agencies and interest groups is a well-known and widespread feature in Germany (Reutter 2001). Compared with this sectoral cooperation, the Concerted Action and the Alliance for Jobs of 1996 are exceptions which prove the rule that intersectoral, macroeconomic concertation is a rare instance in Germany. The Concerted Action (1967–1977) and the first Alliance for Jobs (1996) were due to specific political and economic circumstances rather than necessary elements of a distinguished German model.

The Concerted Action was established in 1967. It was an offspring of a Keynesian approach to global economic steering even though it goes back to proposals of the Scientific Committee at the Ministry of Economics (*Wissenschaftlicher Beirat beim Wirtschaftsministerium*), which in 1956 had recommended to publish macroeconomic data in order to enable the social partners to adapt their economic strategies accordingly (Adam 1972; Kern 1973; W. Schroeder 2001: 31–40). It took more than ten years, before the then ruling parties adopted this idea, and due to an initiative of the SPD the Grand Coalition decided to include the possibility for a Concerted Action into the Bill on Stability and Growth (*Gesetz zur Förderung der Stabilität und des Wachstums*) that was being passed in 1967. The Concerted Action was to be a means to coordinate the macroeconomic behavior and the policies of the state, trade unions, and employer organizations in order to secure economic growth, a positive trade balance, a high level of employment, and low inflation (Adam 1972: 10–41; Kern 1973: 14–28). The most important means to achieve these goals were incomes and fiscal policy as well as guidelines for collective bargaining that were to guarantee that the pay policies of the trade unions served these goals and especially secured a low level of unemployment.

The first top-level meeting of the Concerted Action with 34 persons from nine organizations took place on 17 February 1967. In later meetings up to 200 persons were present and the agenda was substantially broadened (W. Schroeder 2001: 32). At the outset the Concerted Action was able to successfully counteract the first severe postwar economic recession with a negative growth rate of −0.1 percent in 1967 and a rate of unemployment of 2.1 percent. Already in 1968 the GNP again increased by 5.8 percent and the rate of unemployment dropped to 1.5 percent (BMAS 1986: tables 1.1 and 2.11). According to many contemporary experts this was mainly due to the policies of the government that, referring to discussions in the Concerted Action, had recommended modest increases of wages and salaries of about 3.5 percent for 1967 and between 4 and 5 percent for 1968 respectively (Adam 1973: 54). The trade unions, hoping that they would be recompensed in later years, followed these recommendations very closely. In 1968, however, the profits rose by almost 15 percent and the gross income for dependent work by only 7.4 percent (BMAS 1986: tables 1.10 and 1.12). When the trade unions once more demanded only modest increases in 1969, thus again sticking to "official guidelines," this caused wildcat strikes and in their aftermath, a reorientation of the unions' pay policies. In later years the trade unions refused to follow the recommendations of the government any more, thus producing exceptionally high wage increases and devaluating the Concerted Action into a rather useless round of talks even though it took another six years before it was officially dissolved.

History, performance, and dissolution do not necessarily qualify the Concerted Action as a model for macro political cooperation. Nevertheless three lessons can be drawn from the Concerted Action. First, the myth that this kind of cooperative policy-making, if it is regarded as such, limits strikes and lockouts cannot be validated with the Concerted Action. During the ten years of its existence, some of the most important and longest labor disputes in German postwar history occurred. Furthermore wildcat strikes increased substantially in the late 1960s and early 1970s. Second, even at that time it was obvious that an economy so dependent on exports could not be governed by nationally limited institutions and merely by regulating the increases of wages and salaries. Finally, the Concerted Action showed that the capacity of trade unions to act strategically and make political exchanges was limited. Albeit in later years, the wage settlements partly corresponded with the recommendations of the government, it was impossible for trade unions to present this as part of a political exchange in order to stimulate economic growth and fight unemployment without running the risk of losing members and stirring up internal conflicts and opposition (Esser 1982: 114–16).

It is doubtful that Klaus Zwickel had these lessons in mind when he made his aforementioned proposal in November 1995. In retrospect and after 13 years of a Liberal-Conservative government, the Concerted Action may have looked differently than in 1977 when the trade unions had left the Concerted Action because the employers had filed a constitutional complaint against the Co-Determination Act (*Mitbestimmungsgesetz*). Zwickel's proposal was at least implicitly based on the assumption that wage restraint might lead to higher employment. Therefore it resembled the Concerted Action not only because of its tripartite character, but because it shared some macroeconomic premises as well. This also marks the major difference to other chancellor talks that had taken place in the 1990s at various occasions. But the actual functioning, the goals, and the performance of the first Alliance for Jobs differed that much from the Concerted Action that it is hardly imaginable that Zwickel could possibly hope to revive this institution—especially as he then flatly refused to discuss the system of collective bargaining and the wage policy of his union in the framework of the first Alliance for Jobs.

In particular Klaus Zwickel demanded that the employers avoid redundancies for operational reasons for three years, create 300,000 new jobs, take on 30,000 long-term unemployed, and increase the number of trainees each year by 5 percent. The federal government was supposed to make a "binding commitment" to abstain from further cuts or additional tightening of the Employment Promotion Act (*Arbeitsförderungsgesetz*), guarantee a sufficient number of training places, and put a levy on those companies that fail to contribute sufficiently to training. In exchange Zwickel promised to do what he could to limit pay increases to the inflation rate and accept lower rates over a limited period of time, if companies were to recruit long-term unemployed (IG Metall 1995; Bispinck 1997: 64). In order to achieve these goals and to manage the decision-making processes, Klaus Zwickel asked the government to establish an Alliance for Jobs, whose structure or task he simply did not dwell upon.

Albeit the actors involved jointly agreed at the first meeting on 22 January 1996 to reduce unemployment by 50 percent by the year 2000,[4] it very quickly turned out that there was profound disagreement between the trade unions on the one side and the government and the employers on the other. The latter mainly focused on improving the competitiveness of the German economy by reducing the share of social security contributions and by further deregulation of the labor market without giving the guarantees or the commitments Zwickel had demanded. This strategy not only met the fierce opposition of trade unions but also made clear that the policies to reduce unemployment differed fundamentally. Hence it was almost unavoidable that the unions withdrew from the Alliance for Jobs in April 1996, after the government had announced a further package of cuts in the social security system.

Regardless of the political, ideological, and structural differences between the Concerted Action and the first Alliance for Jobs, both examples reveal that a tripartite macroeconomic cooperation is a rare exception in Germany. Furthermore, these exceptions hardly constitute a tradition of effective corporatist policy-making. Even the Concerted Action was based more on the hope that shared information would lead to macro economically adapted behavior rather than on the capacity to implement decisions. In addition, the Concerted Action was short-lived and not able to comply with trade unions or employer organizations on guidelines, apart from the fact that both interest associations did not possess the organizational structures for this kind of political exchange. Altogether it might, therefore, be doubtful to qualify this institution as corporatist. The Alliance for Jobs of 1996 even lacked the minimal formal characteristics of corporatist policy-making. It was neither properly institutionalized nor did it have any clear competencies nor was incomes policy part of its agenda. For Gerhard Schröder and his government, it was thus not very difficult to make things "better" than the Kohl government. More interesting are, however, the questions: did he indeed make things different and did he do them well?

The Alliance for Jobs, Training and Competitiveness and the Third Way

Social scientists and politicians have difficulties in identifying the character of the Alliance for Jobs, Training and Competitiveness. Many put the Alliance for Jobs in the tradition of the Concerted Action or they compare it with other successful examples of corporatist policy-making (Leggewie 1999; Federal Government 2000: 4–5). For others, however, the Alliance for Jobs was the most important means for a Red–Green coalition to flank the ambiguous process of programmatic changes, bridge the gap between the "old" and the "new" Left and form a basis for the modernization of society (Esser and Schroeder 1999; Wessels 1999, 2000a). Accordingly an Alliance for Jobs was indispensable for the reform of the labor market, the improvement of the competitiveness of the German economy, and the restructuring of the social security system.

While these interpretations seem to contradict each other, they just reflect the ambiguous character of the Alliance for Jobs. This institution represents both the "old" Social Democratic tradition as well as the prospect for a renewed Social Democracy and a Third Way. Although the idea of a Third Way remained a vague concept (Merkel 2000; Jun 2000), the debate about it still conveys important messages as far as the Alliance for Jobs is concerned: Implicitly, at least, it is acknowledged that the "class politics" of the "old left" with its redistributive policies and its emphasis on equality and state intervention does not fit any more with the structures of a modern society, the development of the EU, and the further globalization of the economy (Giddens

1998; Schröder and Blair 1999b). At the same time the neoliberal approach is contradictory and neglects the social preconditions for liberty and democracy. Hence, it is necessary to find a new balance between equality and liberty, between social justice and innovation, and between state regulation and market forces. Strategically, these programmatic changes were to move the SPD into the political Center. Only if the SPD is able to win over voters from the Center and the middle classes, can it also win elections in the long run. Altogether this ends up in the squaring of the circle. It includes an attempt to combine conflicting interests and ideologies and to develop a program that is open enough to integrate the "old" and the "new" Left as well as parts of the middle classes.

Consequently it is misleading to put the Alliance for Jobs in the same category as the Concerted Action. While the Concerted Action was a single centralized institution at the federal level with redistributive tasks and based on a "strong," interventionist state, the Alliance for Jobs was to be a multifunctional institution integrated in a set of actors to be found at various levels and presupposing a "cooperative" state. The later references to the Concerted Action by Schröder and others as well as the tripartite structure of the Alliance for Jobs were, hence, a sort of symbolic tribute to "old" traditions and the promise to "restore social justice," while substantially the Alliance for Jobs had to embark on reforms.

The Alliance for Jobs, Training and Competitiveness: Structure and Performance

In its first meeting on 7 December 1998 the Alliance for Jobs defined its tasks, drafted its agenda, and established a permanent structure. In a statement the three parties declared ". . . to work jointly towards reducing unemployment and attaining lasting improvements in the competitiveness of the economy" (Federal Government 2000: 12).[5] The basic idea was to establish a macro political arena in which separate policies could be integrated and new ideas, as well as compromises, found. Accordingly the Alliance for Jobs was set up ". . . as a permanent consultation process with the aim of creating mutual trust while allowing diverging interests and opinions to be aired" (Federal Government 2000: 12). At the same time the Alliance for Jobs had to contribute to a significant reduction in unemployment and the improvement of competitiveness. Thus: "Rapid and far-reaching reforms are indispensable to achieving sustained growth in employment and improving the dynamic strength of the economy. Initially, effective action is possible now" (Federal Government 2000: 12). In consequence, the long-term process of consultation and trust-building was to be combined with short-term decision-making and reforms.

The institutionalization was to make sure that new ideas, compromises, and consensus were more likely to arise because debates could be sustained and open-ended. Clearly, this was to foster the trust-building and discursive elements that were further supported by the internal structure of the Alliance for Jobs that comprised three levels. (1) top-level meetings, at which decisions were to be made and "pacts" to be closed, should take place on a regular basis. (2) The Steering Committee, which was composed of high ranking officials from the three parties and which was led by the director of the Chancellor's Office, had to prepare the top-level meetings and coordinate the decision-making process. (3) The working groups and expert groups were managed by the ministries appropriate for the issues in question. They were to find compromises in their respective areas and, if possible, make proposals to top-level meetings. The most important working group was the Benchmarking Group consisting of scientific experts nominated by the director of the Chancellor's Office, the minister for social policy, the trade unions, and the employer organizations. In total the Benchmarking Group was to present scientific expertise based on international comparisons. Even though this structure looks sufficiently differentiated to manage the decision-making and the consensus-building processes as well as to become the focus for relevant debates, the actual performance of the Alliance for Jobs showed severe deficits in both respects. The Alliance for Jobs neither had the power to make effective decisions nor to shape the political and social discourses and thus failed to become the nucleus for change.

By far the most important events were the eight top-level meetings that took place at irregular intervals. Apart from the first meeting on 7 December 1998 there were three and two meetings respectively in 1999 and 2000, while only one meeting was convened in 2001 and 2002 each year. At the last meeting on 25 January 2002, the parties even failed to publish a joint declaration. These meetings (like all other meetings) had a tripartite basis and involved a limited number of top representatives from the state, employer organizations, and trade unions. It was assumed that these top-level meetings could agree on compromises, thus wedding the involved parties to the adopted policies. However, many of the 12 topics put on the agenda at the first meeting were never dealt with and others only sporadically, because the Alliance for

Jobs lacked the competency to make decisions in these fields (like tax reform, reform of the social security system, reform of the pension schemes or co–determination). Instead these decisions were framed by the "normal" political process. The Alliance for Jobs was just a "policy taker," even though some of their members played important roles in these decision-making processes.

In other fields, decisions depended on the willingness of the parties to commit themselves to compromises found in these meetings. However, as it turned out, there were not only conflicts between trade unions and employer organizations, but also between members of the two groups. While, for example, Dieter Hundt, the president of the Confederation of German Employers' Associations (*Bundesvereinigung der Deutschen Arbeitgeberverbände*, BDA) supported this institution and the idea of a social partnership based on consensus and compromises (Hundt 1999), Hans-Olaf Henkel from the Federation of German Industries (*Bundesverband der Deutschen Industrie*, BDI) strongly opposed this view.[6] These conflicting attitudes of Dieter Hundt and Hans-Olaf Henkel partly reflect different organizational traditions and interests. While the members of the BDA make wage agreements every year and have thus built up a tradition of bargaining and social partnership with trade unions, the BDI is basically just an interest group with limited functions and faces shrinking membership. Altogether this has led the BDI to adopt more radical views as far as collective bargaining or social partnership is concerned. Similar conflicts can be found among trade unions.

On the one side Klaus Zwickel (IGM) and Frank Bsirske (*Vereinte Dienstleistungsgewerkschaft*, Ver.di) were rather critical toward the Alliance for Jobs and refused to discuss guidelines or principles of wage policy and the system of collective bargaining in the Alliance for Jobs in other than in a most general way. On several occasions Klaus Zwickel[7] threatened to leave the Alliance for Jobs, if pay policies were discussed—in spite of the fact that it was part of his initial proposal in November of 1995 and that it was one of the cornerstones in other social pacts in Europe. On the other side Dieter Schulte (German Confederation of Trade Unions, DGB) and Hubert Schmoldt (Trade Union for Mining, Chemicals, Energy IG BCE) favored a cooperative approach more publicly. The DGB, for example, accepted in a joint declaration with the BDA that: "Productivity growth should primarily serve the promotion of employment. Performance-linked pay is part of this" (Federal Government 2000: 25). And Hubert Schmoldt, chairman of the rather cooperative IG BCE, transformed these and other recommendations (for early retirement) into an appropriate collective bargaining policy in 2000/2001.

Again these differing attitudes can be linked to specific organizational traditions and structures. Accordingly, the more conflict prone IG Metall only demanded modest wage increases in 2000 and 2001. But IG Metall was not able to "sell" this as a strategy including barter transactions with employers, because it currently faces severe organizational tensions and problems. Apart from massive losses of members—a problem that other trade unions, the BDA and BDI, also have to deal with—the IG Metall is also comparatively decentralized with districts that have the power to make collective agreements. Similarly Ver.di[8] not only has had to integrate unions (Trade Union for Trade, Banking, and Insurance, HBV and Trade Union for Media Workers, IG Medien, and partly Trade Union for Public Services, Transport, and Communication, ÖTV), which were against the Alliance for Jobs from the outset, but also the task of transforming a rather heterogeneous construct into a powerful organization has limited the room for strategic behavior for its chairmen considerably (Hassel 2002). Consequently, the chairmen of the IG Metall and of Ver.di currently do not possess the independence for political barter transactions.

These structural limits of trade unions and employer organizations affected, of course, the agenda and the performance of the Alliance for Jobs. As already mentioned and in contrast to the Concerted Action, the agenda of the Alliance for Jobs comprised a number of more or less related topics. In total 12 primary topics were already listed in the first meeting and a few others were added to this list in later meetings (like immigration, enlargement of the EU, women and labor market). Albeit the government claims that the Alliance for Jobs was important for almost every decision taken in these fields (Bundesregierung 2002i) a more realistic analysis has to reduce this list to few cases, and after a closer look many of these cases can hardly be regarded as overwhelming successes. This can be illustrated by three examples:[9]

- With the Consensus on Training from 6 June 1999, the Alliance for Jobs promised that "Every young person who is willing and able will be trained" (Federal Government 2000: 20). This included, among other things, that training profiles for new occupations should be developed, the number of training places in IT professions should be increased and the labor offices and the Employment Services assist these endeavors. Some parts of this consensus have been successfully put into practice. By the year

2001, the number of training places in IT and media professions had increased to 60,000 and new training profiles have been adopted. However, even though numerically the number of training places exceeded the number of those who looked for a training place in 1999 and in 2000, this was mainly due to efforts of public institutions and programs. In 1999 the number of training places in private enterprises even dropped by 12,400, and in the new *Länder* the situation was regarded as "insufficient," as the Working Group on Training and Further Education reported (Bundesregierung 2002c). In 2002, there was even a new overall shortage of training places. Again this shows that the Alliance for Jobs cannot force the associations involved to fulfill the compromises.

- With the Job-AQTIV-Bill[10] (*Job-AQTIV-Gesetz*) a further improvement of the Employment Services was to be achieved (Buchheit 2002). Among other things the Bill stipulated that every new unemployed individual was to make a formal "agreement" with his or her regional labor office thus guaranteeing a closer cooperation between both sides. However, this was just another of numerous attempts to improve the instruments of the Employment Services. Additionally, since January 2002, when the Bill was put into practice, only between 7 and 10 percent of those who became unemployed have signed such an agreement (Niejahr and Tenbrock 2002).

- Finally, Anke Hassel (2002) reports that when in December 1999 Gerhard Schröder asked the social partners to regulate early retirement by collective bargaining, the social partners of the chemical industry had informally reached a settlement already, which comprised modest wage increases and improved provisions for partial retirement. This not only illustrates once again that the social partners of the chemical industry possessed a relatively high degree of strategic capacity but also that the Alliance for Jobs depended on compromises found elsewhere rather than on a consensus developed in the framework of the Alliance for Jobs.

In a nutshell the Alliance for Jobs neither had the structural capacity for effective decision-making nor had the "pacts" secured necessarily lasting and positive effects. Many of the topics needed parliamentary approval. In these cases the Alliance for Jobs was more or less just informed, but as an institution it had no impact on the decisions about tax reform, immigration, the reform of co–determination, or the pension scheme. It is most telling that at the end of the term an independent commission of experts (the so-called Hartz Commission) made proposals for a reform of the Employment Services and the labor market.[11]

It fits with this overall impression that the working groups or the so-called Industrial and Special Issue Consultation also neither made any significant contributions to a public debate nor proposals that would have been seriously discussed at top-level meetings. Some working groups apparently never met (not to mention the groups for Industrial and Special Issue Consultation) or failed to submit a proper report. The only remarkable exception in this respect was the Benchmarking Group, which submitted reports on working time, on benchmarking, low-skilled jobs, further education on-the-job, and reforms of the labor market. However, the only report that stirred up some sort of public debate, met the fierce resistance of the trade unions and was discussed only once in the Alliance for Jobs. In this report Wolfgang Streeck and Rolf G. Heinze proposed the establishment of a labor market segment for low- or unskilled workers in the service industries (Streeck and Heinze 1999; Fels et al. 1999). The trade unions opposed this strategy because it would have meant paying these employees below the agreed wage tariffs even though Streeck and Heinze suggested that these new jobs be funded publicly and be integrated in the social security system. This was basically an attempt to find a new perspective and to focus on creating new employment instead of reducing the demand for jobs by a low rate of female employment, early retirement, or long education. After this conflict the Benchmarking Group was marginalized, and the Chancellor's Office declined to officially accept this report (Hassel 2002: 59). As a consequence it was no surprise that the Alliance for Jobs no longer played a recognizable role in the last two years of this government.

Federalism and the Alliance for Jobs, Training and Competitiveness

Apart from the federal Alliance for Jobs established by the Red–Green government there are similar institutions at state, regional, local, branch, or plant level (Berger 2000; Gerlach and Ziegler 2000; Nettelstroth and Hülsmann 2000). In addition, due to the European Employment Pact,[12] these Alliances were embedded in a supranational setting that has already contributed to a harmonization of national policies in Europe. However, it would go much too far to assume that the European Employment Pact and the German Alliances for Jobs at state, regional, local, and plant level form a comprehensive set of decision-making bodies even though they can influence each other. This is true already for the interplay between the Alliances for Jobs at national and state level.

After the Alliance for Jobs had been established at the federal level, several state governments (mostly led by the SPD) created Alliances for Jobs as well (table 5.1). And as Gerhard Schröder pointed out, the Alliance for Jobs at the federal level was to assume a "guiding role for state level alliances, both conceptually and organizationally" (Federal Government 2000: 7). Many of the state alliances set up similar structures with top-level meetings, steering committees, working groups, and talks on specific issues. Additionally, in spring 1999, the Steering

Table 5.1   Alliances for jobs at the state level (1998–2002)[a]

State	Alliance established or existed between 1998 and 2002	Ruling parties between 1998 and 2002
Bavaria	11 June 1996–May 2002	CSU
Berlin	22 March 1996	CDU/SPD 1995–2001; SPD/Greens since June 2001; SPD/PDS since January 2002
Hamburg	3 July 1998	SPD/Greens; since September 2001 CDU/PRO/FDP
Mecklenburg West Pomerania	15 December 1998	SPD/PDS
Lower Saxony	21 December 1998	SPD
North Rhine-Westphalia	29 January 1999	SPD/Greens
Bremen	28 June 1999	SPD/CDU
Saxony-Anhalt	28 January 1999	SPD (tolerated by PDS) since April 2002 CDU/FDP
Schleswig-Holstein	1 February 1999	SPD/Greens
Baden-Württemberg	17 February 2000 (without unions)	CDU/FDP
Saarland	8 March 2000	SPD, since May 1999 CDU
Brandenburg	—	SPD/CDU
Hesse	—	SPD, since February 1999 CDU/FDP
Rhineland Palatinate	—	SPD/FDP
Saxony	—	CDU
Thuringia	—	CDU

[a] States with no Alliance for Jobs still may have some sort of cooperation or initiatives which are not institutionalized and not based on tripartite decision-making. In addition there may be regional, local, or plant level alliances.

Source: Based on Neumann 2000: 423; my actualizations and completions.

Committee of the federal Alliance for Jobs convened a meeting with top-level officials from the states because the states were to play an important role in the implementation of decisions and measures adopted at the federal level.[13]

However it would be misleading to assume that the Alliances for Jobs in Germany at state and federal levels form a coherent and coordinated system. It is rather an interdependent set of relatively autonomous actors and bodies. Alliances for Jobs at state level developed their own agendas and took over topics from the federal Alliance for Jobs only if these fitted into their local and regional needs. Five states even abstained from any initiatives in this respect, in others the federal Alliance for Jobs had hardly any impact at all. The Bavarian Employment Pact was already adopted in 1996, and in Baden-Württemberg trade unions rejected any involvement in the Alliance for Jobs set up in February 2000. Employer organizations refused to cooperate temporarily in North Rhine-Westphalia and in Lower Saxony.[14] Despite these problems, this multi-level approach indicates that the times of centralized national attempts for macroeconomic coordination are over. As in other policy areas competencies are dispersed. The Alliance for Jobs is thus far an attempt to regain some influence at a national level. This marks a further difference to the Concerted Action, which was rather an expression of a "strong" and interventionist state.

Conclusion

Contrary to many interpretations, the Alliance for Jobs cannot be regarded as a corporatist institution. In spite of some structural similarities it was not the Concerted Action or corporatist modes of policy-making that acted as godfather for this kind of cooperation and trust-building. Different economic settings, specific institutional structures, diverging policy areas, changed conceptions about the role of the state, and, most importantly, diverging economic and social polices hardly allow the Alliance for Jobs to be placed in the tradition of the Concerted Action or of corporatist policy-making in other European countries. There was no attempt for a Keynesian economic policy, and the Alliance for Jobs never strove to redistribute income and profits in spite of allusions made by Klaus Zwickel, Gerhard Schröder, and others. The basic differences between the Concerted Action and the Alliances for Jobs lies, hence, in the fact that the first was linked to traditional Social Democratic values and traditions, while the second was a means for the "modernization" of the economy.

As a decision-making body the Alliance for Jobs not only lacked formal competencies in a number of areas but, in addition, the parties involved were organizationally only partly capable of making these kinds of political exchanges. This already excluded that the assumed macro political approach ever could become dominant in the debates of the Alliance for Jobs. In addition, important issues needed the consent of the parliamentary and the party system, and contrary to many fears the Alliance for Jobs never became a sort of side-government. Finally it turned out that some of the most essential topics were either only implicitly dealt with or were totally neglected. The Alliance for Jobs also failed to establish itself as the main arena for consultation and for trust-building as far as the labor market and the economic policies were concerned. Many important issues were decided in the parliament, by the government or by political parties. In addition, the working groups had no impact whatsoever. Additionally the Benchmarking Group became unimportant—in spite of repeated declarations that Germany would have to learn from successful models from abroad.

Altogether the Alliance for Jobs produced only some modest successes. It could not live up to the expectations expressed at the beginning of the Red–Green government. This can mainly be explained by the programmatic vagueness of the government, the ambiguous foundation of the Alliance for Jobs, fundamental conflicts between the social partners, and structural weaknesses of actors involved. At the end of the term, many even observed a new "alienation" between the trade unions and the government. Thus, the Alliance for Jobs, Training and Competitiveness is the very reflection of the programmatic vagueness of the Third Way and the attempt of a Social Democratic party, which until now has failed to bridge the gap between the "old left" and its traditional supporters on the one hand and the "new left" and the modernizers on the other.

Notes

This chapter was first presented at a conference on the Federal Elections in Germany at the University of Minnesota (27–29 September 2002). For helpful comments and critiques I am grateful to the participants of this conference as well as to Peter Rütters and Siegfried Mielke (Free University Berlin). Unluckily all errors have to remain mine.

1. During the election campaign Gerhard Schröder, attempting to move his party to the Center, expressed the intention not "to do everything different but many things better" (quoted in Merkl 1999: 9).

2. Frank-Walter Steinmeier followed Bodo Hombach, as director of the Chancellor's Office and Chair of the Steering Committee.
3. Markovits and Gorski (1993) already discussed this question in the early 1990s.
4. In a later meeting another agreement on early retirement was found (Bispinck 1997: 67).
5. All declarations, statements, or reports published by the Alliance for Jobs can be found at: www.buendnis.de (Bundesregierung 2002c). An English version of the first five statements and declarations can be found in: Federal Government 2000.
6. For example, "Das Bündnis für Arbeit soll ein langfristiges Projekt werden," *Frankfurter Allgemeine Zeitung* (26 February 1999): 1–2.
7. "Zwickel droht mit einem Scheitern des Bündnisses für Arbeit," *Frankfurter Allgemeine Zeitung* (2 January 1999): 11; "Schmoldt: Das Bündnis darf nicht scheitern", *Frankfurter Allgemeine Zeitung* (8 December 1999): 18.
8. Ver.di was formed by ÖTV (public services), IG Medien (media), HBV (trade, banks, insurances), DAG (white collar), and DPG (postal workers).
9. A closer analysis of other examples shows similar results: JUMP (the program to reduce unemployment among young people) had already been adopted before the Alliance for Jobs was set up (Neumann 2000), and the program to integrate low-skilled and long-term unemployed was cut down from a general policy to a few pilot schemes in the Saarland and in Rhineland Palatinate.
10. The term *AQTIV* is the acronym for: *Aktivieren* (activate), *Qualifizieren* (qualify), *Trainieren* (train), *Investieren* (invest), *Vermitteln* (to get people into work).
11. The so-called Hartz Commission was set up in February 2002 and submitted its final report in August 2002 (Hartz-Kommission 2002).
12. For the European Employment Pact, cf. Hassel and Hoffmann 1999: 222–27; BMAS 2002a.
13. "Länder unterstützen Bündnis-Gespräche," *Frankfurter Allgemeine Zeitung* (12 March 1999): 2.
14. "Kein Bündnis für Arbeit in Nordrhein-Westfalen," *Frankfurter Allgemeine Zeitung* (19 August 1999): 15.

CHAPTER 6

Policy Failure: The Economic Record of the Red–Green Coalition in Germany, 1998–2002

Kurt Hübner

After being elected chancellor of Germany in 1998, Gerhard Schröder made the point that he should not be reelected if the Red–Green coalition had not reduced endemic unemployment to much lower levels. In September 2002 unemployment in Germany was again on the rise, and it was obvious that the government was not ever even going to come close to breaking the strong sclerotic structures of the German political economy. In that month, the number of unemployed remained fixed at over 4 million, the same as it had four years before at the time of the government's election. It was only thanks to the impending Iraq crisis and the strong dove attitude of the Schröder government, in combination with the floods in Eastern Germany, that opened up space for the government to divert attention from economics.

The promise to reduce unemployment significantly without presenting any bold political strategy is no recommendation of the political skills of the leader of the Red–Green government. Already some years earlier Schröder shocked his fellow Social Democratic Party comrades by informing them that there is no such thing as a leftist or rightist economic policy, there is only a successful one. More than reflecting some newly found intellectual basis for his economic political strategy, this slogan strongly reflects the highly pragmatic character of economic thought of Schröder and his loyal advisors from Lower Saxony. This also meant that the three overarching political targets proclaimed by the

Social Democratic Party, namely jobs, innovation, and social justice, had no sufficient basis in economic policy-making.[1]

Since the announcements of Social Democratic Party targets in 1998 the German public has witnessed several turns in economic policy with at least two main results. First, after four years of a Red–Green government the unemployment problem is still alive and well. Second, on a broader scale, including growth of output, budgets, equality in net incomes, and more, the economic record of the government is quite negative. After presenting data on the economic outcomes of this government's policies, I will discuss some hypotheses that attempt to explain the record. Following concepts from the "varieties of capitalism" approach, this study presents an analysis that highlights the reasons for the Red–Green coalition's dissatisfactory economic record. Given the restructured economic conditions for policy-making in the late 1990s, the German government under the Red–Green coalition was not prepared to tackle the challenges arising from this environment. At the center of the unsolved economic problems of post-unification Germany lies the policy failure of the Red–Green government.

The Economic Record

The start of the Red–Green coalition was in many respects troublesome, reflecting the two parties' lack of preparation in forming a government together. Only after the demise of the party hero and finance minister, Oskar Lafontaine, did the coalition begin to find some common basis for their political program. The demise of Lafontaine was not so much the final victory of the "neoliberal camps of modernizers" against the "traditionalists" (Kreutz 2002: 463), as an indication of the halfhearted political strategy of the coalition. Lafontaine and his two ambitious secretaries of state developed a fiscal and economic policy based on fiscal prudence by reforming the biased tax system in favor of income-earners and the private business sector. At the same time, Lafontaine went on the offensive at the international level by presenting plans for changes to the global currency system and by building up a common French–German front against the rigid behavior of the European Central Bank (ECB). It was believed that this attempt to achieve an adequate policy-mix would allow the government to meet its promises of higher employment levels, a cleaner environment, and an increase in social justice. The inability of Lafontaine's troops to explain their complex political project and to organize social support for the same led to some unsurprising results. International protests led by the United States and by representatives of the ECB, as well as domestic protests undermined his case. Ironically, it was his lack of a clear understanding of economic policy that allowed Chancellor Schröder, although involuntarily, to follow his pragmatic strategy unchallenged.

Taking over the responsibility for finance by chance, as it were, Schröder and his supporters in the Social Democratic Party nonetheless saw the need to base their economic policy on their own philosophy. The result was the so-called Schröder/Blair Paper, which attempted to give the whole political undertaking of the Red–Green government a theoretical base by outlining a *supply-side politics of the Left*:

> The past two decades of neo-liberal laissez-faire are over. In its place, however, there must not be a renaissance of 1970s-style reliance on deficit spending and heavy-handed state intervention. Such an approach now points in the wrong direction. . . . In much of Europe unemployment is far too high—and a high proportion of it is structural. To address this challenge, Europe's Social Democrats must together formulate and implement a new supply-side agenda of the left. (Schröder and Blair 1999a)

Such an agenda was never fully developed. Instead, for the period in question, the Red–Green coalition's economic policy resembled more a muddling-through with a strong bias in favor of micro-policies over meso-policies. Macroeconomic policy degenerated to a byproduct of the fiscal conservatism played out by the new Minister of Finance, Hans Eichel.

Given this development, it should come as no surprise that Germany ended up as the weakest of all European economies in countries with a Social Democratic Party participation in government.[2] Following the work of Garrett (1998), and the ensuing debates on the deteriorating effects of economic globalization, it seems to be reasonable to expect, both empirically and analytically, a superior economic performance from those economies with a federal government led by Social Democratic parties. The results of the simple tabulation (see table 6.1) confirm the more elaborate testing in literature. First, for the period that is of interest to us, Social Democratic-governed societies demonstrated growth rates in GDP slightly above the average of all 15 member states of the EU. In other words, growth of output was not hampered by the economic policy strategies of the Social Democratic parties in power. Second, unemployment was significantly lower in the first group compared to the reference group. As the figures show, there is a huge dispersion in unemployment rates. Sweden and the Netherlands on the one side, and the United Kingdom on the other, follow very different employment policies. Both groupings are much more successful than the other economies of the group,[3] and did better than the EU overall. Third, in accordance with the aforementioned literature it is also predictable that the state plays a bigger role in the group of economies with a Social Democratic party-led government than in the EU group of economies overall. The state's share in economic activities, measured as state share in GDP, was two percentage points higher in Social Democratic-led Economies (SDEs) than in the group of 15 member economies of the EU. Surprising, however, is the fourth point, the finding that the economies of the SDEs achieved superior outcomes without widening their budget deficits. SDEs were more successful in reducing their budget deficits than the EU economies overall.

The exception to the rule is the German economy, which ranks at the bottom of the Social Democratic league along all categories of table 6.1, and shows inferior outcomes even when compared to the EU average. Without entering into an extended discussion of the reasons for this disappointing outcome, it is obvious that the data rejects the validity of widespread general theses such as the "globalization argument" or the "Eurosclerosis approach."[4] The causes for the comparatively unsuccessful German economic performance during the first Red–Green government are in many respects homemade, and have to do with macroeconomic lock-in effects.

This hypothesis is supported by data on cross-border transactions. For the years 1998 to the end of 1999 the German trade balance shows an increasing surplus. It is only with the onset of the global recession of 2000

Table 6.1 Economic record of Social Democratic-led governments (1998–2002)

	Average GDP growth per year	Average rate of unemployment	State expenditures as share of nominal GDP	Budget surplus (+)/ deficit (−) as share of nominal GDP
Germany	1.5	8.3	48.6	−1.8
France	2.7	9.9	53.0	−1.9
Greece	3.6	10.9	48.2	−0.9
Sweden	2.9	6.1	58.0	+2.6
UK	2.4	5.5	39.9	+0.6
Portugal	2.6	4.5	46.5	−2.4
Austria	2.1	4.0	52.2	−1.6
Denmark	2.1	4.6	53.2	+2.4
Italy	1.7	10.4	48.0	−1.8
Netherlands	2.7	3.1	45.8	+0.3
SDE	2.4	6.7	49.3	−0.5
EU-15	2.2	8.3	47.0	−0.9

Source: SVR 2001: 48–49; 2002: 42–43; own calculations.

that this surplus decreased slightly, but with exports remaining the workhorse of the German economy. Based on econometric observation of the far-above average effects of exports on GDP, there is little surprise that the cyclical downturn of international production transformed the German workhorse into more and more of a lame duck up until the year 2002 (European Commission 2002: 13). However, the negative growth effects of a shrinking, yet still positive surplus in trade balance do not indicate a loss in German producer's overall global competitiveness. It is true that exports have been strengthened by the weak euro, leading to increased international price competitiveness outside the Euro zone on the whole. Besides this price effect, Germany owes its surplus to a renewed technological competitiveness, at least in the field of matured technological products. Since the mid-1990s the German share of research and development-intensive goods in international markets has made a U-turn and contributed to the successful export performance of the late 1990s (BMBF 2002a: xxix). This improvement coincided with an overall increase in R&D expenditures in Germany. However, upon closer inspection this increase reveals itself to be not the outcome of a deliberate strategy to increase publicly funded research, but rather mainly the result of stronger research efforts in the private sector (BMBF 2002a). In international comparisons Germany still lags behind: in overall research expenditures, as a share of GDP, as well as in the absolute amounts of public-driven research support. This is particularly true compared to Sweden and Finland, who have invested much greater amounts of private and public funds to get their economies on track toward a knowledge-based economy. Compared to the efforts in those countries, federal support in favor of the *New Middle* and its economic underpinnings was too small and thus insufficient to generate feasible economic effects.

Economic policy involves much more than state actions to strengthen allocative efficiency and macroeconomic stability. Whether the parties concerned are aware of it or not, economic policy also intervenes in the distributional arena of market economies by setting tax rates, handing out subsidies and transfers, and through regulative measures. Schäfer (2001) shows that between 1998 and the end of 2000 the distributional activities of the German welfare and tax state resulted in a difference of the gross and net shares of wage incomes in GDP of 72.3 to 69.8 percent. That is, the market results of functional distribution have been corrected in favor of non-wage incomes. This decline of the wage share in net terms is reflected in the changes in personal income distribution, where the disparities of net household incomes have increased slightly until the year 2001 (SVR 2002: 350). Due to the effects of the tax reforms of 2000, this trend will continue. Such a political turnabout in income distribution clearly shows that the Red–Green coalition, against widespread prejudices and political rhetoric, did not act as stakeholder for labor and the socially excluded. This development also highlights some of the difficulties involved in using tax incentives in an open economy. The increase in net profits, it has turned out, was no guarantee for a proportional increase in domestic investments. In fact, net profits and domestic investments were increasingly being de-coupled.[5] Favoring the private business sector, obviously, didn't pay off for the Red–Green coalition. On the contrary, sluggish investment was one of the reasons for the disappointing unemployment figures.

Arena of Policy Failure I: Fiscal Policy

Given the self-defined benchmark of political success, the outcomes of the labor market should have been front and center in the first Red–Green government's political activities. In fact, the coalition followed a twofold strategy by creating a round table, labeled the "Alliance for Jobs, Training and Competitiveness" (see Reutter, chapter 5 in this volume), and by strengthening the incentives for investment and economic growth. This combination of micro- and macroeconomic measures was intended to help overcome the strong hysteris tendencies of the German labor markets, which have resulted in a strong upward trend of unemployment since the mid-1970s. In terms of macroeconomics, this strategy was rather traditional. Stronger incentives for private investments and higher net incomes were intended to help increase demand in private businesses and households, and thus lead to higher economic growth. Higher economic growth, in turn, would result in higher employment figures.

The relationship between economic growth and employment is not, however, constant in time. According to the econometric estimations of Logeay (2001), the unemployment threshold has fallen slightly since the mid-1990s: any GDP-growth above 2 percent per year leads to an increase in employment, measured as a rise in the volume of work. Table 6.1 shows that Germany did not even attain this favorable threshold in the first period of the Red–Green coalition, 1998–2002. The reasons for this failure to achieve the critical rate of economic growth can be found in the changed landscape of fiscal policy.

In contrast to the expectations of many observers, the coalition was highly successful in breaking the gridlock of reform that had characterized the long period of consecutive Kohl governments. This was particularly true in the intensely contested terrain of the tax system, where the Social Democrats under party leader Oskar Lafontaine followed a strict policy of blocking any decision in the last year of the Kohl government by using their majority in the German upper house or *Bundesrat*. Once in power, though, it was Lafontaine who immediately prepared the political preconditions for far-reaching changes in the tax system. The tax reform of 2000, achieved after Lafontaine's demise, still bore the markings of the former finance minister's signature.

This tax reform consisted of, generally speaking, three elements conceived to stimulate economic growth. As early as April 1999, the lower house or *Bundestag* ratified the law on ecology taxes, resulting in a five-step procedure of tax increases on energy.[6] The underlying rationale of this reform was the introduction of price incentives to reduce emissions caused by energy use and to make use of the new tax receipts to reduce the tax burden for indirect wage costs. It was thought that this would lead to a decrease in the price of labor and to an increase in the price for the use of the environment.[7] To avoid too high a burden being placed on energy-intensive producers, they were given exemptions in the tax rate for energy, but still enjoyed the general reduction of employer indirect wage costs. The concrete details of this reform resulted in a mixed outcome. Contrary to many objections, the effects on income and employment have been slightly positive. However, the distributional effects were negative, shifting the main burden for the ecology tax onto private households, thereby reducing their effective purchasing power (Bach et al. 2001; Kern et al., chapter 10 in this volume).[8]

The introduction of this ecology tax was followed by an ambitious reform of the income and corporate tax system. Starting on 1 January 2001, the law foresaw drastic changes in the tax rates for income-earners and corporations, including changes in the rules for taxing corporations and shareholders. With regard to income taxes, the new law increased the basic personal allowance from approximately DM 12,300 to approximately DM 14,000 in 2001. By 2005 that amount will have risen to DM 15,000.[9] The basic tax rate was reduced from 25.9 to 19.9 percent in 2001, with a target rate of 15 percent in 2005. The top rate will be cut gradually from 53 percent in 1998 to 42 percent in 2005, applicable only for taxable incomes above DM 102,000. The corporate tax rate was cut to a uniform rate of 25 percent in 2001. Capital gains from the sale of shareholdings between corporations—including shares in foreign corporations—were generally exempted from tax, while dividends received by corporations have been tax exempt since 2002. Retrospectively, the most important change introduced with this fundamental reform was the introduction of the uniform tax rate on profits. Before the tax reform was introduced, the rate for retained profits was 40 percent and the rate for distributed profits was 30 percent. With the new law it became possible for companies to shift former retained profits to the most advantageous year so as to reduce their actual tax payments. In 2001 and 2002, this loophole resulted in net outflows from the government to the private business sector.[10]

In terms of political strategy, the ratification of the "grand tax reform" was the greatest achievement of this coalition government. To win a majority in the *Bundesrat*, the Red–Green government had to overcome the strict opposition of the CDU/CSU. This was only possible by offering the CDU-dominated *Länder* significant side payments (see Kropp, chapter 4 in this volume). The political triumph, however, was soon followed by an economic disaster. The actual tax incomes of the federal state, the *Länder*, as well as the *Städte* (cities) and *Gemeinden* (municipalities) fell far below expectations. This was particularly due to the behavior of the private business sector, which made intelligent use of the extra room for maneuvering made available by the new law (DIW et al. 2002b: 735). The enormous reduction in the effective tax burden of the business sector will not last indefinitely. When the tax reform was first discussed nobody was seriously expecting an international recession. However, it would be much too facile to explain the outcome of this reform solely by pointing to bad timing. Overwhelmed by national and international complaints of the business-unfriendly German tax system, the government initiated a reform, mainly driven by ideology, that kept many of the irrational rules of the system and added a strong pro-business bias to the system.

Given today's generally lower rates and the broad range of tax exemptions that make Germany highly competitive in terms of international tax competitiveness (Hettich and Schmidt 2001), the employers were the main winners of the Red–Green coalition tax reform. Unfortunately, this "gift" on the part of the government was not reciprocated by business. The increase in profits did not lead to higher investment in the domestic economy. Due to the slowdown in international growth and the looming recession in the United States, the German economy experienced a sluggish international and national demand, generating an increase in the output gap. In pre-Maastricht times such a development would have been countered by the workings of the automatic fiscal stabilizers, probably supported by a more active state fiscal policy and a looser monetary policy on the part of the German Central Bank.[11]

Under the conditions of the Stability and Growth Pact such a political response was no longer possible. Instead, the Red–Green government rushed to introduce a procyclical fiscal policy by adjusting its own spending behavior within the limits of the Pact. This procyclical behavior was strengthened by the hawkish anti-inflationary policy of the European Central Bank, which suffered from a reputation problem and was therefore not willing to follow the policy introduced by the US Federal Reserve in order to overcome the recession by lowering its lead interest rate (Hübner 2002).

The Stability and Growth Pact was a heritage of the former Kohl government, who together with the German *Bundesbank* was very much in favor of setting an upper limit to budget deficits. As has been shown, the modalities of the Pact make it necessary, over a medium term, to run a balanced budget. The political rationale of this norm, therefore, has to be seen in the normative establishment of a pre-Keynesian budget rule based more on ideological convictions than reflecting sound economic knowledge. Although Lafontaine, in combination with the former French "super minister" Strauss-Kahn, tried to attack this straitjacket from the beginning, and tried to increase national sovereignty in fundamental economic policy issues, neither the Social Democratic Party nor the Greens shared this critique in a strong way. On the contrary, the new Minister of Finance, Hans Eichel, was crowned the most successful minister by both business and the yellow press and developed into the government's star minister.

Unlike other SDEs in the EU, the budget of the Red–Green government never reflected a change in policy toward a *Third Way*. Instead, it introduced strong redistribution mechanisms in favor of the corporate sector and high-income earners. At the same time, the government reduced state investment expenditures in a drastic way, placing in jeopardy the infrastructure base of the new knowledge economy, which was so heavily promoted in political campaigns. Given the fact that the new political environment had long been foreseeable, the Red–Green government put forward a shockingly ill-prepared performance. This new environment can be characterized as one where the national government's economic policy no longer has any control over monetary affairs, and where the government is hampered by a Stability and Growth Pact that restrains fiscal policy enormously. Instead of taking into account the increased complexity of the situation in attempting to find an adequate policy-mix, the Red–Green coalition acted as if no changes had taken place at all.

Arena of Policy Failure II: The East

Like the Kohl governments before, the first Red–Green government was a strictly Western value-based government without any serious understanding of the deep macroeconomic changes in Germany since 1990. The politically paralyzing repercussions of the defeat in the election campaign of 1990, due mainly to the skeptical attitude of the then SPD front-runner Oskar Lafontaine against reunification, still affected the party years later. The combination of the SPD's guilt-complex toward the East with the lack of economic policy skills on the part of the Greens, along with their almost nonexistent performance in the eastern election results led to a policy of "more of the same" in regard to eastern Germany. Instead of designing a "grand strategy" for the endangered catch-up process of the *new Länder*, the Red–Green coalition followed a business-as-usual attitude by promising more of the same policies and resources. Reflecting the SPD's general campaign slogan, the government used the terms "innovation-investment-infrastructure" to mark its political priorities for the eastern part of Germany. The new program *Futour 2000* targeted start-ups by offering venture capital to overcome the difficulties in the first lifespan of newly founded companies. Companies with less than 250 employees received the offer of a much-improved tax-free investment subsidy. Start-ups as well as modernization and restructuring projects were granted a non-repayable investment subsidy. Cooperative efforts between the private business sector and universities in the East were supported by the program *InnoRegion*, which tried to establish high-tech sectors, such as medicine or biotechnology. The *Job-Aqtiv Law* introduced training and education programs to upgrade the skills of workers according to regional demand structures. The *Jump Program* tried to help those young people without a finishing degree who were out of work. More than 50 percent of the 37 billion euro for infrastructure improvements in the transportation routes (*Verkehrswege*) was reserved for the East.[12]

The most far-reaching economic policy decision of the Red–Green coalition was the new ordering of the so-called *Länderfinanzausgleich* and the passing of the *Solidarity Pact II*. The former had to be upheld by the German Supreme Court after complaints by Bavaria, Baden-Württemberg, and Hesse, all of whom feared that they would lose more and more of their financial resources thanks to the vertical transfer of resources to the less well-developed *Länder*, in particular the *new Länder* in the East. The new rule foresees a continuation of flows in favor of the weaker *Länder*. While the net payers will reduce their transfers over time, the federal government will compensate for those reductions by increasing its share of the payments. *Solidarity Pact II* prolongs the transfer payments for the East until 2020. Starting in 2005, when Solidarity Pact I runs out, the *new Länder* will have received, in total, 150 billion euro over a period of 15 years.[13]

In economic terms the outcome of the diverse programs and supports was at the very least disappointing (see table 6.2 and figure 6.1). Up until 1996, GDP growth in East Germany was higher than in West Germany. Since 1998 growth rates in the East have sunk below those of the West. This resulted in an at least momentary end of the catch-up process, hence violating the main reunification target of creating comparable economic conditions between the East and the West. The figures for the officially registered unemployed in 2001 were even slightly higher than in 1998, amounting to 1.259 million in eastern Germany. This increase has not been halted by all of the efforts to decrease the numbers of the active working population by driving them out of the labor markets. The result of all of these combined factors is a further decrease of the population living in eastern Germany, either due to movement to the West or to the decrease in birth rates. The increase in labor productivity appears to be, at first glance, one of the few bright spots. A closer examination, however, shows that even after 12 years of unification policies, and hundreds of billions of West–East transfers, the gap between the West and the East is still enormous, with the East reaching only slightly more than two-thirds of the labor productivity levels in the West. The situation is even worse if we take output per inhabitant as the indicator. In this case GDP per inhabitant has, since 1996, remained constant at the level of 61.5 percent of the rate in the West (SVR 2002: 178–79). Finally, the data also indicate that although the wage share in the East shows a steady decline, it is still far above the level in the West, contributing to the very disturbing low degree of international competitiveness in terms of costs of production in the East.

The main cause for this disappointing performance lies in the investment activities of the private business sector. Though the share of investment in GDP is about twice as high in the East compared to the West, equipment investments are still smaller in the East (Priewe et al. 2002: 36). This weak dynamic in equipment investments slowed the pace of technological modernization and thus prevented a faster increase in labor productivity. In a pure market economy such a process of unequal growth between two regions would have led to a strong polarization, where one region would continuously win and the other would lose. The politics of German unification tried to avoid such a polarization by

Table 6.2 Basic data about East German economy (1995–2001)

	1995	1996	1997	1998	1999	2000	2001
Population (in 1,000)	14,204	14,152	14,112	14,051	13,981	13,924	13,794
Change to previous year (%)	*−0.4*	*−0.4*	*−0.3*	*−0.4*	*−0.5*	*−0.4*	*−0.9*
GDP[a] (in billion euro)	200.82	207.30	210.70	212.68	217.02	219.23	219.01
Change to previous year (%)	*4.5*	*3.2*	*1.6*	*0.9*	*2.0*	*1.0*	*−0.1*
Employed persons (in 1,000)	6,048	6,007	5,936	5,950	5,983	5,917	5,799
Change to previous year (%)	*1.9*	*−0.7*	*−1.2*	*0.2*	*0.6*	*−1.1*	*−2.0*
Per 1,000 inhabitants	*426*	*471*	*485*	*503*	*516*	*523*	*522*
Employees (in 1,000)	5,579	5,536	5,450	5,446	5,467	5,394	5,277
Change to previous year (%)	*1.8*	*−0.8*	*−1.6*	*−0.1*	*0.4*	*−1.3*	*−2.2*
Self-employed (in 1,000)	469	471	485	503	516	523	522
Change to previous year (%)	*2.5*	*0.4*	*3.0*	*3.6*	*2.4*	*1.5*	*−0.2*
Underemployment[b] (in 1,000)	1,916	1,843	1,837	1,839	1,829	1,740	1,697
Registered unemployed (in 1,000)	*971*	*1,083*	*1,249*	*1,256*	*1,227*	*1,244*	*1,259*
Participants in public job creation schemes (in 1,000)	*291*	*261*	*221*	*298*	*332*	*232*	*173*
Productivity[c] (in 1,000 euro)	33.2	34.5	35.5	35.7	36.3	37.0	37.8
Change to previous year (%)	*4.4*	*3.9*	*2.9*	*0.7*	*1.5*	*2.1*	*1.9*
Wage quota[d]	64.7	62.9	61.2	60.8	61.0	60.7	59.4
West Germany = 100							
Productivity[e]	*64.8*	*66.8*	*67.7*	*67.3*	*67.9*	*68.4*	*70.1*
Wage quota[d]	*119.7*	*117.1*	*115.7*	*116.3*	*116.3*	*115.2*	*112.3*
Income per domestic employee	*75.0*	*75.7*	*75.9*	*76.2*	*77.2*	*77.4*	*77.5*

[a] In prices of 1995.
[b] Includes: registered unemployed, unemployed according to §§ 125, 126 SGB III, participants in public job creation schemes, in further education, in language courses, short-time work, partial retirement, and early retirement.
[c] GDP in prices of 1995 per employed persons in Germany.
[d] Income per domestic employee in relation to GDP per employed persons.
[e] GDP in current prices per employed persons in Germany.

Source: Statistisches Bundesamt; Arbeitskreis "VGR der Länder," Bundesanstalt für Arbeit, Calculations of the DIW and the IWH quoted in DIW et al. 2002a: 13.

introducing far-reaching and highly ambitious transfer and subsidy systems. However, the results of those efforts are mixed. In regard to household incomes and consumption patterns the East has caught up. The effective household income of the East has reached more than 90 percent of the average in the West. Those incomes were used for financing the demand for goods and services.

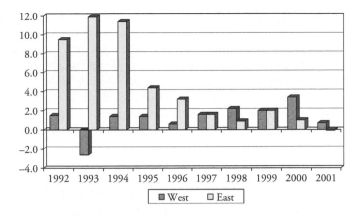

Figure 6.1   The halting catch up-process of the East: changes to previous year in GDP[a] in East and West Germany[b] (percent, 1992–2001)

[a] In prices of 1995, date of calculation: spring 2002.
[b] Former FRG without Berlin; New *Länder* without Berlin.

Source: Arbeitskreis "Volkswirtschaftliche Gesamtrechnung der Länder" quoted in BMWA 2002: 4.

Unfortunately, the overall amount of effective demand in the East is much higher than the GDP produced in the *new Länder*. In 2001 overall demand exceeded GDP by about 40 percent (SVR 2002: 177–82). Although this is a much smaller value than in 1991, when the gap was around 66 percent, it still shows that the East has an enormous regional trade deficit. As in international trade, the deficit in a regional trade balance is reflected in the capital balance. The capital balance shows that the prevailing consumption and investment patterns of the East are mainly financed by transfers from outside actors: from the second half of the 1990s until 2002 net transfers from the West to the East have been in the range of 70–75 billion euro per year, that is, about 4 percent of the West's GDP.

German reunification has brought about a dramatic change in the German political economy. The most important element of this change has been the establishment of a *regional transfer economy* within the overall German economy. This *transfer economy* is sustainable only due to the steady inflow of positive net financial resources from outside. Unlike a deficit economy on the international scale, such a *regional transfer economy* cannot default. This would not generate an economic problem if the rate of return on these transfers was positive. The private investment activities show that the Eastern Transfer Economy does not seem to fulfill the profit expectations of private actors. Based on the experiences of the recent past, it seems that the East is in an unfortunate lock-in situation that will prevail if economic policy actors do not attempt to create strategies to escape from this situation. The economic policy strategy of the Red–Green coalition has not contributed to such efforts. On the contrary, following a strict pragmatic perspective in order to avoid violating the interests of voters in the East, they perpetuated a policy that has generated the *Mezzogiorno* structure of the German political economy.

Macroeconomic Blind Spots

The Red–Green coalition came into government without having a clear-cut macroeconomic strategy in its political repertoire. Believing its own propaganda that the new government will not "do everything different but many things better" (Schröder quoted in Merkl 1999: 9), it undervalued the importance of at least two fundamental changes in the German political economy. Namely the restrictions on fiscal policy caused by the Stability and Growth Pact, and the effects of the long-established transfer economy in the East for the overall economic dynamics of the country. The restraining effects of the Stability and Growth Pact, though discussed at length in academic circles, only dawned on the ruling government when the economy started to slow down at the end of 2000. Given the negative effects on state receipts due to the tax reform, the lower than expected rates of GDP aggravated the drastic shrinkage in state revenues. After the elections of September 2002, the newly formed government was forced to admit that in 2002 the budget deficit would be between 3.7 and 3.8 percent of GDP, and thus far beyond the magic margin of 3 percent set by the Stability and Growth Pact. Immediately, the EU took formal action by initiating the disciplinary procedure for those member states who exceed the deficit ceiling. Following article 104 of the EU Charter, this could result in Brussels demanding that between 0.2 and 0.5 percent of GDP be lodged with them in the form of an interest-free deposit.

Although it is obvious that such a procyclical procedure would not contribute to overcoming the cyclical slowdown of economic growth, the second Red–Green coalition that assumed office in 2002 is making no serious attempts to effectuate political change. On the contrary, the first budget of the new government followed exactly the logic of the Stability and Growth Pact, that is, it sought to balance the budget in order to fulfill the criteria of the Pact. This response to a macroeconomic problem shows that the Red–Green coalition is still missing the opportunities it has to prepare an adequate political strategy suitable to the new institutional and political circumstances of the euro. The same holds true for the Red–Green coalition's political support for the catch-up process in the East. Instead of designing an ambitious strategy for the East based on the government's initial formula of "modernization-innovation-justice," the Red–Green coalition is following the established path of the former conservative governments without even recognizing that this path had long ago ended in a dead end street.

Sixteen years of various Kohl governments have produced the urgent need to remodel many of the institutional features of the German political economy in order to strengthen the comparative institutional advantages of the German variant of market capitalism. Unlike some other Third Way governments in Western Europe, the Red–Green government of 1998–2002 never believed in the necessity of an integrated policy design, where macroeconomic policies would play a decisive role. Instead, it followed a patchwork-like policy by introducing isolated reforms without taking into account the interplay between different political arenas. The balance of the first four years of a Red–Green government in Germany shows the devastating effects of such neglect.

Notes

I would like to thank my colleague, Claude P. Desmarais, who generously helped me improve both my English style and my thought in editing this paper. Thanks go also to my research assistant Ahmed Allahwala for his fasthands in delivering sources.

1. Harlen (2002) delivers a description of the political obstacles to the development of an adequate economic policy.
2. SDE is the abbreviation used in the text for Social Democratic-led Economies. Table 6.1 has been constructed using the period of at least two years as the minimum criteria for assessing a nation-state as belonging to the SDEs.
3. These differences are readily apparent in Moene and Wallerstein's (1999) and Scharpf's (2000) analyses.
4. A more thorough critique of the "globalization approach" is presented in Hübner (1998), while a devastating critique of the "Eurosclerosis thesis" is found in Schettkat (2002).
5. See the figures in Schäfer (2001). A theoretical explanation can be found in Hübner and Petschow (2001).
6. The first step included a new tax on electricity of two *Pfennige*, as well as an increase in the value-added tax on oil and natural gas. Those rates will increase following a pre-announced plan before reaching the final step in 2003 (see Kern et al., chapter 10 in this volume).
7. Koskela et al. (2001) demonstrate how a well-designed green tax can increase competitiveness.

8. Any effective ecology tax should lead to a rise in prices, because only then will changes in the structure of consumption result. The concrete problem with this project is that the exemptions favor precisely those sectors that make above-average use of scarce resources.

9. Due to the political-economical responses to floods in parts of eastern Germany the time schedule for achieving that level has been pushed back by one year.

10. A more detailed description and analysis of the anticipated effects of this reform can be found in Zitzelsberger 2002; Dautel 2001; Ehlerman et al. 2001, and Sorensen 2002.

11. These last assumptions may be too optimistic given the severe conflicts between the *Bundesbank* and the fiscal policy directives of former governments.

12. A detailed listing of the different programs that the Red–Green coalition designed for the East can be found in Bundesregierung (2002g). Additional support for the East comes from diverse EU programs as the *new Länder* enjoy most-favored region EU support. For details see European Commission 2002: Box 3.

13. A critical analysis can be found in Priewe et al. 2002: 118–19.

CHAPTER 7

Continuity or Change: Red–Green Social Policy After Sixteen Years of Christian Democratic Rule

Martin Seeleib-Kaiser

The key argument of the classical "parties matter theory" in comparative welfare state analysis has been that conservative parties tend to fight inflation, whereas Left or progressive parties tend to focus on reducing unemployment (Hibbs 1977). Although there are some differences in terms of the variables operationalized, it has been argued further that historically the strength of social democratic incumbency has led to the construction of large welfare states (Shalev 1983). More recent research has shown that not only Social Democratic, but also Christian Democratic parties can be characterized as welfare state parties. Nevertheless, there are said to be clear differences: Social Democratic parties promote full employment and the provision of universal social services, while Christian Democratic parties rely more heavily on the market in terms of employment policies and the principle of subsidiarity with regard to providing social services (Kersbergen 1995; Huber and Stephens 2001).

Accordingly, we should expect that the Red–Green government pursued a different approach in social policy after it came to power in 1998 than the Christian–Liberal coalition government during its rule. Consequently, the following questions guide this essay: What are the programmatic aims of the Social Democrats and the Greens? Did we witness continuity or change in social policy after their 1998 election victory, compared to the long rule of Christian Democrats? Did the Red–Green coalition follow through with the promises the two parties made during the election campaign? How are the recent social policy[1] reforms related to the normative and institutional design of the German welfare state in the golden post–World War II era?

Normative and Institutional Foundations of the German Welfare State in the Golden Post–World War II Era

In comparative research, Germany is characterized as a welfare state that resembles most closely the ideal category of a conservative welfare state regime (Esping-Andersen 1990). One core element of such a welfare state regime is its strong emphasis on social insurance; consequently, Germany has also been characterized as a "social insurance state" (Riedmüller and Olk 1994). The other core element of a conservative welfare state regime is its reliance on the family and other communal groups in delivering social services. According to the social insurance philosophy the German welfare state was primarily providing wage-centered social policies. The normative precondition for receiving benefits was a prior standard employment relationship (Vobruba 1990). Based on this institutional setting, social benefits were to be financed through equal contributions by workers and employers and *not* through general taxation. Consequently, the *main* aim was inter-temporal redistribution within the life course and not interpersonal redistribution. Furthermore, securing the "achieved living standard" (*Lebensstandardsicherung*) through the different social insurance schemes became the *leitmotiv* of postwar social policy expansion.

The second core element of a conservative welfare state regime is its heavy reliance on the family, that is, the housewife, as a provider of social services (Neidhardt 1978). Based on the principle of subsidiarity, the state would only support the family, in addition to a child allowance or the child tax credit, if traditional self-help mechanisms would fail. Hence, in contrast to Scandinavian welfare states, the German welfare state would provide public social services only in a very restricted way. Through the institution of the family the housewife and dependent children were entitled to derived social insurance benefits based on the employment relationship of the male breadwinner.[2] The strong economic growth of the 1950s and 1960s with its very low unemployment rate and the predominant acceptance by women of their role as caregivers for children and the elderly (Fröhner et al. 1956) contributed to a seemingly well-functioning welfare state.

To summarize one can argue that during the golden era, the German welfare state was mainly characterized by statutory insurance schemes, which were to guarantee the formerly achieved living standard in case of old age, unemployment, and sickness as well as grant derived benefits to family members. The family itself had the important role as the primary provider of social services. From a normative perspective the German welfare state was primarily based on the principles of social integration and cohesion, not on redistribution between the classes, or fighting a war on poverty (Goodin et al. 1999).

Social Policy During the Long Christian Democratic Rule

The expansion of the welfare state had come to a halt in 1975, with the first cutbacks in social policy legislated by the Social Democratic–Liberal coalition government.[3] After the CDU came to power in a coalition with the FDP in 1982, it not only promised to continue and strengthen the overall consolidation process within the wage-earner centered social policy, but also to shift the focus more strongly toward supporting the family. The institution of the family had allegedly been neglected by the Social Democrats (Bleses and Rose 1998; Bleses and Seeleib-Kaiser 1999).

The social policy development under Christian Democratic rule can be divided into four phases. The first two years were characterized by cutbacks, especially in the unemployment insurance program, active labor market policies, and social assistance. The old-age insurance scheme was largely left unchanged and within the health care system we witnessed measures to control cost, which were largely technocratic in nature. Starting in the mid-1980s, the government initiated some policy expansions, although the overall goal of budget consolidation and a reduction of social insurance contributions was kept in place. Most note-worthy were the expansions in family policy. The government increased the child allowance and child tax credits, which initially had been cut, recognized a limited time devoted to child-rearing as equivalent to mone-tary contributions toward the old-age insurance, and introduced parental leave as well as the parental leave benefit (Bleses and Rose 1998: 144–54). Finally in 1992, the conservatives passed legislation to expand the public provision of childcare facilities, giving every child between the ages three and six an entitlement to a place in a kindergarten. The law went into effect fully in 1999 after a transition period, during which more than 600,000 places for children in public childcare facilities were created (Bäcker et al. 2000b: 212).

The third phase came with the unification of the two German states. As a matter of principle and in order to avoid chaos in the former GDR the structure of the West German welfare state was extended toward the East. Since the conservative government refused to adequately increase the subsidies out of general revenues for the insurance funds and due to the huge social problems associated with the unification process, we witnessed a rapid increase in social spending and in social insurance contributions (see figures 7.1 and 7.2). Hence, it has to be stressed that these increases were not the result of programmatic social policy expansions, but due to the financing arrangements of the unification process within the realm of social policy and the enormous social problems, especially the rapidly increasing unemployment, in the territory of the former GDR.

After the process of unification was formally accomplished, the Kohl government in late 1992 once again started to pursue a policy of retrenchment in order to control and eventually reduce the sharply increased social spending as well as social insurance contributions. The various policy initiatives included some major changes in the unemployment insurance program, a reduction of the statutory sick-leave benefit from 100 to 80 percent, a loosening of the dismissal protection, and—for the first time in German history—a significant benefit cut for future pensioners through the introduction of a "demographic factor" into the pension formula. The changes within the unemployment insurance were basically a continuation of the policy changes initiated since the mid-1970s, that is, an incremental withdrawal from the principle of securing the achieved living standard and a promotion of a greater reliance on the market. Through the implementation of the Labor Promotion Reform Law of 1997, an unemployed worker can no longer reject a work offer outside his or her occupation or level of qualification as unsuitable. In addition, he or she must accept any job offer that pays up to 20 percent less than the previous job during the first three months of unemployment, and up to 30 percent less during the following three months. After six months the unemployed will have to take basically any job offer that pays at least the amount of the unemployment compensation payment. Based on these changes, one can conclude that the state is increasingly relying on a means-tested approach and the market with regard to unemployment policy. Furthermore, various policy reforms at the local level since the mid-1980s and reforms at the federal level in 1993 and 1996 have put an increased emphasis on workfare requirements within the social assistance program. In 1998, approximately 300,000 (former) welfare recipients participated in welfare-to-work programs, whereas the numbers for 1982 and 1993 were 20,000 and 110,000 respectively (Alber 2001: table 14). (Re-)integration into the labor market has become a primary concern, even if this means a state-subsidized increase in atypical employment paying wages below the respective collective bargaining agreements—a process that can be characterized as re-commodification (Seeleib-Kaiser 1997).

Through the implementation of the Pension Reform Law of 1999 (*Rentenreformgesetz 1999*), which was legislated in 1997, the replacement rate for the standard pensioner would have been reduced from 70 to 64 percent. Based on this measure a substantial percentage of the elderly would have had to depend on the means-tested social assistance in the future once again (Schmähl 1999: 417 f.; cf. BMAS 1998: 57 f.). Via the legislation of this law the former coalition government of Christian and Free Democrats implicitly retracted from the principle of *Lebensstandardsicherung*, which was the major achievement and *leitmotiv* of postwar policy, ever since the historic "1957 Pension Reform."

To summarize, the conservative coalition government pursued a social policy approach that scaled back on the principle of publicly guaranteeing the formerly achieved living standard, while at the same time expanding the programs for families. With the exception of the policy pursued during the unification process, the overarching goal was to limit and eventually reduce social expenditures and social insurance contributions, while at the same time to acknowledge the overall need for the government to play an active role in social policy.

Social Policy Goals of the Red–Green Government

Analyzing the 1998 party platforms of the SPD and *Bündnis '90/Die Grünen* as well as the coalition agreement, it becomes evident that they did not intend to expand the welfare state in the midterm, despite promises to revoke some policy changes of the prior Christian–Liberal coalition government in the short run. In the short term, they promised among other things to reinstate the "old" policies regarding the regulations of dismissals and the sick-leave benefit and to suspend the implementation of the Pension Reform Law. Their overarching policy approach was characterized by the following four elements:

(1) no new deficit financed economic stimulus programs;
(2) a reduction of social insurance contributions and enterprise taxes;
(3) a modernization of the welfare state, which emphasizes activation instead of compensation, a promotion of greater self-reliance, and a reduction of government tutelage;
(4) an expansion of family policies (SPD 1998: 21, 26–31; Bündnis '90/Die Grünen 1998: 23–8, 32; SPD and Bündnis '90/Die Grünen 1998: 7, 12, 32–45, 40–42).

In his first address to parliament, Chancellor Gerhard Schröder forcefully reiterated the need to reduce the budget deficit and to focus subsidies as well as social policies on the "truly needy."[4] Although some statements by the SPD chairman and finance minister, Oskar Lafontaine, were interpreted as calls for an expansionary deficit-financed approach, it was largely the press, interested in finding policy differences within the new government, which exaggerated his preference for such a policy approach. A deficit-financed stimulation of the economy at no time during the tenure of Lafontaine became an official policy goal.[5] After Lafontaine had resigned in the spring of 1999, the new finance minister, Hans Eichel, made it unmistakably clear that there was no room for any deficit-financed programs and that his primary goal was the reduction of the government deficit.[6] In order to achieve the second policy goal of reducing the level of social insurance contributions, the new coalition government called for the introduction of a new ecological tax. The revenue of this tax was to be used to contribute to the pension fund and thereby allow a reduction in the level of social insurance contributions (SPD and Bündnis '90/Die Grünen 1998: 15–16). The Social Democrats and the Greens had made it explicit in their election platforms and later restated in their coalition agreement that they would reform the old-age insurance system with the goal of an expansion of private and company-based pension plans as key elements. This approach was part of their broader strategy toward self-reliance and activation, which also included a call for "work instead of assistance" (SPD and Bündnis '90/Die Grünen 1998: 36), that is, a reform of the social assistance program. Finally, in terms of family policy the party programs and the coalition agreement called for an improvement of the parental leave provisions, expansions of the child allowance and tax credits, as well as an expansion of childcare facilities.

Summarizing the overall programmatic approach of the Social Democrats and the Greens, it seems fair to argue that the new coalition government did not publicly call for a comprehensive new approach in social policy after 16 years of conservative rule. Moreover, based on the party programs and the coalition agreement, the Red–Green coalition government would continue the general policy path pursued by the former conservative coalition government, albeit with some small alterations in emphasis. In this sense, the statement made by Schröder during the election campaign, whereby the Social Democrats in government would not change everything, but improve a lot of things, seemed to describe the programmatic approach within the realm of social policy very accurately. Compared with the social policy approaches and reform initiatives put forward by the Greens and Social Democrats, during the long dominance of Christian Democratic rule in the 1980s (Gohr 2001), this "new" approach constituted the preliminary endpoint of a substantial programmatic change during the 1990s. This change can be characterized as a social-democratic convergence toward the programmatic aims of the Christian Democrats (Seeleib-Kaiser 2002b).

Red–Green Social Policies in Government

A Quantitative View

In the view of many political observers the issue that really counts is not the publicly stated policy proposal, but the "real" policy output (Edelman 1976). One way to measure policy output is to analyze budgetary expenditures. Despite a small increase in federal spending in 1999, the Red–Green coalition pursued a policy of reduced federal government intervention. In 2001, the spending of the *federal* government amounted to 11.8 percent of GDP, which is the lowest level in the last four decades. The success of this policy combined with additional revenue from the auction of telecommunication licenses reduced the *federal* budget deficit from 1.5 percent of GDP in 1998 to 1.1 percent in 2001 (Hinrichs 2002: 23–24). This policy approach can be characterized as a paradigm shift with regard to Social Democratic fiscal policies (Meng 2002: 191). At times, the governor of Bavaria and the subsequent chancellor candidate of the CDU/CSU, Edmund Stoiber, has even criticized it as inappropriate and too rigid. During the election campaign in 2002, a prominent social-democratic critic of Schröder's economic and social policies summarized the strategy of the conservatives as "social democratism," while the SPD itself was not offering anything (Ottmar Schreiner cit. by Meng 2002: 228). Hence the rise of the overall state budget deficit, as defined and used by the EU for the determination of compliance with the deficit criterion of the Stability Pact, to 2.8 percent of GDP in 2001 cannot be attributed to an increase in federal spending. Moreover, it was largely the result of reduced government revenues, due to the effects of the tax reform of 2000 as well as sluggish economic growth. Furthermore, the federal government renewed its commitment toward the EU to reduce the budget deficit further and provide a balanced budget by 2004. However, a comprehensive strategy of deficit reduction by all territorial entities is essential in order to comply with this commitment (SVR 2001: 118–37; Deutsche Bundesbank 2002a: 50–63). Based on the "parties matter theory" one would have expected a very different approach by the new government, namely an expansionary fiscal policy.

Yet, the financial situation of the federal government deteriorated rapidly in 2002, due to the continued economic slump and rising unemployment. The biggest increase in the federal budget was caused by the rising transfers from the federal government to the pension system, the employment service, and the *new Länder* (SVR 2002: 142–46). According to the definition used by the EU to determine the state deficit, the deficit of the federal government rose from 1.4 in 2001 to an estimated 1.8 percent of GDP in 2002. Therefore, the federal government is responsible for a 0.4 percentage point increase in the overall state deficit, which rose from 2.8 (2001) to an estimated 3.7 percent of GDP (2002) (SVR 2002: 138).

As already indicated, Germany has a highly complex public financing structure through its federal system and the existence of para-fiscal institutions, such as the social insurance funds. Hence in order to grasp the overall development of social policy expenditures, we have to take a closer look at the "social budget" or social policy expenditures.[7] Figure 7.1 shows the overall social spending in relationship to GDP from 1975 to 2001. After a reduction in spending during the 1980s, we saw a reversal of the trend in the first half of the 1990s, before social policy outlays were once again consolidated during the late 1990s. Based on the overall spending data, the change in government in 1998 did not seem to substantially alter the spending pattern.

If we control spending by region for the time period 1991–2001, we by and large witness continuity in the West and a gradual, but persistent

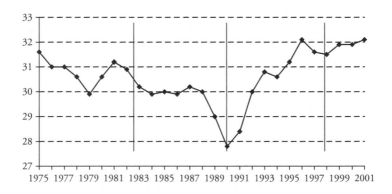

Figure 7.1 Social spending in Germany as a percentage of GDP (1975–2001)[a]

[a] Starting 1991 data for unified Germany. Data for 1999 and 2000 are preliminary, and projections have been given for 2001.

Source: BMAS 2002c: table I-1.

Figure 7.2 Employers' contributions[a] to social insurance schemes in Germany as a percentage of gross wage (1975–2002)

[a] Not included are the premiums for the accident insurance. Due to small differences between East and West, the data presented here is based on the premiums in the West.

Source: BMAS 2002d: table 7.7; BMG 2002.

increase in the East since 1997 (BMAS 2002c: table I-1). The high level of social spending in the East is financed through continuously rising West–East transfers, which in 2001 approximately reached the amount of 27.9 billion euro. These West–East transfers are largely channeled to the East through transfers from the "Western" unemployment and old-age insurance funds, which in sum totaled 25.8 billion euro in 2001 (BMAS 2002c: table III; table III, 112; table III, 16).

Accordingly, without these West–East transfers either the social insurance contributions or the tax-financed subsidies for these systems in the West could have been reduced. In order to reduce social insurance contributions despite the financial "burdens" of the unification process the Red–Green government introduced an ecological tax. The revenues from this tax are estimated to amount to 57 billion euro in the years 1999–2003 and are earmarked by statute for the old-age insurance fund. Without the revenues from the ecological tax the employers' contributions (figure 7.2) to the old-age insurance fund would have been 0.75 percentage points higher in 2002 (Truger 2001b; BMF 2002: 10; Kern et al., chapter 10 in this volume).

If we disaggregate the spending data along functions, a picture of overall continuity emerges for the categories of old age as well as health, while the outlays for the category "Marriage and Family" continued to increase and the spending for employment-related policies decreased not only relative to GDP, but even in absolute terms during the years 2000 and 2001 (see figure 7.3). The economic and demographic development would have suggested the opposite development, since unemployment

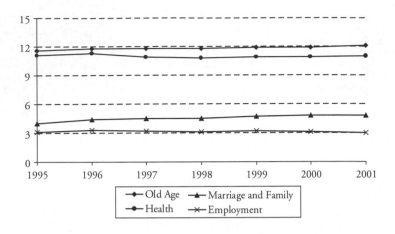

Figure 7.3 Expenditure for selected social policies by function as a percentage of GDP (1995–2001)[a]

[a] Data for 1999 and 2000 are preliminary, while projections are given for 2001.

Source: BMAS 2002c: table I-3.

in absolute numbers was higher in 2001 than in 1995 and the number of children declined over the same period.

Based on the quantitative data presented here it becomes evident that the new government did not follow a path of expansionary policies. Moreover, as was proposed in the party programs and the coalition agreement of 1998, it consolidated the public finances and gradually reduced the social insurance contributions. Within the overall social expenditure the amounts spent for the category of employment were reduced, while social spending for families continued to increase substantially.[8]

Despite the efforts to consolidate expenditures, the federal budget and the social insurance funds, especially the health care as well as the pension funds, have come under severe financial pressure during the fourth year of the Red–Green coalition government, which has made further cutbacks and/or an increase in social insurance contributions once again a short-term "necessity." Without continued reform (especially in the health insurance system)[9] and a speedy economic recovery in 2003, social insurance contributions are likely to rise and perhaps eventually even surpass the level reached during the tenure of the Christian–Liberal coalition government in the late 1990s.

Finally, quantitative data on spending cannot fully and accurately reflect policy developments. First, spending data might be influenced significantly by economic and demographic developments. Second, the data can only reflect those policy changes that have been implemented and not those that were legislated, but are phased-in over a longer time period. Therefore, I will analyze the qualitative social policy changes of the Red–Green coalition in greater detail with a special emphasis on pension reform and family policy in the following section.

Qualitative Policy Changes

The first steps of the new government in late 1998 and early 1999 were to suspend the implementation of the *Rentenreformgesetz 1999*, reinstate the 100 percent replacement ratio of the sickness benefit as well as the "old" dismissal protection regulations, and reduce some co-payments in the statutory health insurance schemes. However, these measures cannot be characterized as a sea change in policy development. The *Rentenreformgesetz* was not revoked, but its implementation was *suspended* until a comprehensive pension reform could be legislated. The reintroduction of the 100 percent replacement ratio with regard to sick pay largely benefited "only" those workers who were not covered through collective bargaining agreements.[10] Finally, the reinstatement of the "old" dismissal protection affected only approximately 5 percent of the workforce, since about 70 percent of the workers were still protected by the more stringent provisions even after the changes of 1996, and workers in very small enterprises were never covered by these rules.[11]

During the first four years of the Red–Green coalition government no major reforms were legislated in the areas of health care, active labor market policy, unemployment insurance, and social assistance. In the field of health care all reforms in addition to the seemingly regular efforts to control costs failed (BMAS 2002b: 132–41; SVR 2002: 163–73). Although some progress was made in improving efficiency, each of the two health ministers during the four years in power, Andrea Fischer (Greens) as well as Ulla Schmidt (SPD), was unable to successfully build a consensus between the various political actors in the field necessary for a comprehensive reform. Finally, the minister postponed a possible comprehensive reform until after the 2002 elections.[12]

With regard to (re)integrating or activating unemployed workers, the Red–Green coalition supported the establishment of a limited number of pilot projects, initiated a program against youth unemployment, and in early 2002 commissioned a report by a blue-ribbon commission (Hartz-Kommission 2002), which presented its findings shortly before the elections. Instead of the implemented minor policy reforms one would have expected a significant expansion of active labor market policies (ALMP), since ALMP and a commitment to full employment are said to be the hallmarks of Social Democratic welfare policy. Yet, there is no clear evidence toward an increased emphasis on ALMP by the Red–Green coalition government. Depending on the source, the number of persons participating in measures of ALMP varies slightly. According to estimates by the Council of Economic Advisers (*Sachverständigenrat*, SVR), the absolute number of unemployed in active measures declined slightly from 1.09 million in 1998 to 0.97 million in 2001 (SVR 2001: 99). Data by the Ministry of Labor show a slight increase of people in active labor market measures from 1.4 million (1998) to 1.5 million (2001) (BMAS 2002b: 37). Undisputed, however, is a clear decline of participants in traditional public works projects from an annual average of about 384,000 participants (1998) to 220,000 (2001), that is, the lowest number since unification (see figure 7.4). Despite the continuously high unemployment of about 20 percent in the East, this region witnessed considerable reductions in ALMP (BMAS 2002b: 37).

In the summer of 2002, the federal government promised to speedily implement the Hartz Commission's recommendations and thereby shift greater attention toward reducing unemployment. However, neither implementing a policy aiming at reducing unemployment via deficit-financed public employment programs nor a "left-wing" supply-side policy (Boix 1998) with a focus on increasing human capital through education and training measures are part of the recommendations.

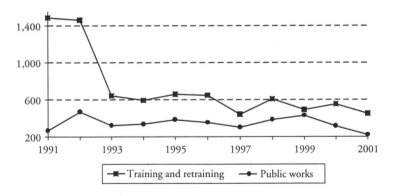

Figure 7.4 Participants in measures of active labor market policy (training and retraining, public works; 1991–2001)

Souce: BMAS 2002d: table 8.14A.

Moreover, the recommendations primarily focus on the improvement of the effectiveness and efficiency of the labor exchange offices. In addition, the commission proposes to establish more private and public agencies for temporary workers, grant low-interest loans to small- and medium-sized companies that employ previously unemployed workers, and grant financial aid to unemployed workers to become self-employed (Hartz-Kommission 2002).

During the tenure of the Red–Green coalition at the federal level, employment in workfare measures at the local level continued to increase. According to a survey by the German Association of Cities (*Deutscher Städtetag*) about 400,000 (former) welfare recipients participated in welfare-to-work programs during the year 2000, an increase of about 100,000 since 1998. About 50 percent of the participants are employed in "regular" employment relationships (Deutscher Städtetag 2001). Such employment relationships entitle the participants to receive unemployment compensation after the publicly funded or subsidized activation measure expires and he or she should still not find work in the regular labor market. Thereby, the costs of unemployment are shifted back from the local to the federal level. Hence, the main reason behind the increased emphasis on activation at the local level is to reduce social assistance expenditure. In other words, localities have a financial incentive to activate unemployed social assistance recipients, due to the existing financing structures of the German welfare state.

Pension reform

The work on a comprehensive pension reform proposal started very early in the tenure of the Red–Green coalition government. First talks between the coalition parties and the Christian Democrats were held in the spring of 1999. In the summer of 1999, Walter Riester, minister for labor and social affairs, publicly announced the cornerstones of his proposal. Finally, in the fall of 2000, the SPD and Greens formally introduced a bill in parliament to reform the pension system (BT-Drs. 14/4595). After further deliberations within the Committee for Labor and Social Affairs of the *Bundestag*, during which no consensus with the Christian Democrats could be reached, the coalition parties split the pension reform bill into two parts. The first part encompassed the provisions with regard to contributions and benefits within the public scheme, which did not require the consent of the CDU-controlled Federal Council. Although the members of the opposition parties in the *Bundestag* had voted against the second part of the reform initiative, it finally passed the Federal Council with votes of the opposition parties after further modifications. This process made obvious that the dispute between the governing coalition and the CDU was not about the principle direction of reform. Moreover, it focused on the details of the public subsidies for future private- and company-based provisions, as well as old-age provisions included in collective bargaining agreements (Unterhinninghofen 2002: 216–17; Dünn and Faßhauer 2001).

What now is the substantive content of this reform, which has been characterized by Chancellor Schröder as "epochal"? (cited in Unterhinninghofen 2002: 213). At the center of the reform is the limitation of future increases in social insurance contributions. As a result of this legislative measure the contributions to old-age insurance funds are estimated not to rise above 20 percent of the gross wage in 2020 and 22 percent in 2030, the time the baby boomers will retire. This limitation was accomplished by a significant reduction in the replacement ratio of the benefits to a level of about 64 percent for the standard pensioner in 2030.[13] In order to achieve the prior level of support during retirement, workers are encouraged through public subsidies to voluntarily enroll in certified private old-age schemes. The level of subsidies for workers who enroll in private- or company-based programs, depends on the level of income and the number of children in their household. Furthermore, the social partners are encouraged via the tax system to include old-age schemes into collective bargaining agreements. This will give unions a greater stake in shaping "company" pensions with the theoretical possibility of including redistributive elements. In the past, company pensions were almost exclusively at the discretion of employers (BMAS 2002b: 114).

However, even if workers enroll in the various certified programs,[14] there is no guarantee for a defined benefit at the previous level, because the companies offering the various financial products are legally "only" required to guarantee the nominal amount paid into the system. Hence, the overall pension system in Germany is being transformed from a pay-as-you-go system based on the principle of defined benefits to a partially funded system based in part on the principle of defined contributions. According to estimates by the *Bundesbank* a 50-year-old worker will have to save an extra 4 percent of his or her gross pay in order not to witness any income loss in retirement; the additional saving ratio for a 20-year-old worker would have to be 1.5 percent (Deutsche Bundesbank 2002c: 30). Through the progressive nature of the subsidies for those who enroll in the new programs the state intends to reduce the negative effects for lower-income workers. Still, contributions for employees who participate in the voluntary programs will be substantially higher in the future, than they would have been without the reform. They basically have to shoulder the financial burden of "privatization," while the public scheme is financed equally by employers and employees. Hence, if we combine the contributions for the new pillar and the public scheme, the reform only limits the costs for employers.

In addition, the occupational disability pension was reformed. In the future, workers can no longer draw disability pensions if they are unable to continue to work in their profession or occupation; they will have to rely on the labor market for an alternative occupation and/or on the regular disability program. Although the reformed disability insurance program now treats unskilled and skilled workers in the same way, it means a real change for skilled workers by ending the protection of their occupational or professional achievements in case of specific disabilities (Wollschläger 2001: 283–84). Finally, the coalition government de facto introduced a minimum pension effective 1 January 2003, by revoking the income and wealth test of the relatives of low-income senior citizens, when they apply for social assistance. The law requires the administrators of the old-insurance fund to inform senior citizens with very low pensions about their entitlement to social assistance in addition to their insurance benefits (BMAS 2002b: 118–19).

Overall this pension reform leads to a re-commodification and marketization of the old-age and disability insurance systems and to a withdrawal from the principle of publicly guaranteeing the achieved living standard, while at the same time improve the conditions for very low-income pensioners.[15]

Expansions in family policies
The Red–Green coalition continued to expand, albeit in a somewhat accelerated fashion compared to the previous government, the various family policies, as the spending data already suggested.[16] The expansion of family policy developed along three dimensions: (1) increasing the child allowance and child tax credits; (2) strengthening the recognition of a limited time devoted to child rearing as equivalent to monetary contributions toward the old-age insurance; and (3) improving parental leave, the parental leave benefit, as well as introducing an entitlement toward part-time employment.

In a number of steps, the Red–Green coalition government increased the monthly child allowance payment to 154 euro per child (an increase of 41.50 euro per month since 1998) and the annual child tax credit to 3,648 euro. Furthermore, parents can receive additional tax credits to defer some of the costs of childcare, if the childcare is deemed necessary due to the employment of the parents (BMFSFJ 2002; for a more elaborated analysis of the tax policies with regard to families cf. Dingeldey 2001).

Through the implementation of the Survivors' Pensions and Child Rearing Law (*Hinterbliebenenrenten- und Kindererziehungszeiten-Gesetz*) of 1986, the state, for the first time in the long history of the German social insurance system, recognized the contributions of caregivers as equivalent to monetary contributions within the old-age insurance system. Currently, the time devoted to child-caring will be recognized as a fictive contribution—equivalent to 100 percent of the average contribution—to the old-age insurance system for the duration of three years per child.[17] New is the provision that, if a parent should choose a part-time position, in order to reconcile outside work with the desire to at least partially care for the child personally, the state will contribute to the pension fund to make up for the "lost" contribution up to a limit of 100 percent of the average contribution until the child is ten years old. Through the recognition of (a limited) time spent as a caregiver and thereby creating individual entitlement rights, the state reduced the dependence of the predominantly female caregivers on derived benefits of male breadwinners (Meyer 1998).

In addition, legislation was introduced and consequently expanded to increase the compatibility of work and the responsibility or desire of parents to personally care for their children during the first years of their life. In 1986, parliament passed a parental leave scheme, whereby an employee could take up to ten months of unpaid leave from employment after the birth of a child, during which (s)he receives a tax-financed parental leave benefit. The employer has to guarantee reemployment after the leave in a similar position and with equivalent remuneration. The duration of the parental leave has been extended in a number of steps during the late 1980s and early 1990s. Since 1993, parents are entitled to three years of leave; during the first two years, the government pays a flat monthly means-tested benefit of 307 euro (DM 600) (Bleses and Rose 1998: 152).[18] The Red–Green government made it easier for both parents to share the parental leave and substantially increased the earnings limit up to which parents are eligible for the full benefit. The stated goal of the Red–Green government is that all parents with an average income shall once again receive the benefit (BMAS 2002b: 228), whereas the percentage of recipients declined substantially during the tenure of the previous government, since the earnings limit had not been adjusted since 1986 (Fuhrmann 2002: 192). Furthermore, a new provision entitles parents with children born after 1 January 2001 to work part-time up to 30 hours per week during their parental leave.

During its first four years in power, the Red–Green coalition government has not legislated any measures concerning the improvement and/or expansion of childcare facilities. However, first, it has to be acknowledged that education and childcare in principle are within the responsibility of the *Länder* and the federal government can only through regulatory policies or financial incentives promote certain institutional changes. Second, increasing the spending for the establishment of new childcare facilities and schools with an all-day schedule is a top priority of the federal government during its second term, according to the new coalition agreement. The Red–Green coalition has pledged to spend the amount of 1.5 billion euro annually for the expansion of day care for children under three years of age, starting in 2004. This program is explicitly excluded from the continued efforts to consolidate the federal budget and reduce the budget deficit (SPD and Bündnis '90/Die Grünen 2002: 10, 29). If the federal government follows through with its plans and the state as well as the local governments fully implement them, this would lead to a substantial increase in the provision of childcare facilities. The federal government estimates that after the full implementation of its program, childcare facilities will be available for 20 percent of the children under the age of three (the latest available figure for this category of childcare facilities is a provision rate of 7 percent [1998]). Additionally, at the local and regional levels we have witnessed tendencies to increase the provision of "reliable elementary school"[19] education and after-school programs, during the past couple of years. The Red–Green coalition government has promised to support the endeavor of establishing all-day schools with 4 billion euro between 2003 and 2007 (SPD and Bündnis '90/Die Grünen 2002: 31).

To summarize: the Red–Green coalition has continued the path pursued by the previous government to expand family policy. For its second term it has pledged to improve the provision of childcare. To some extent the two large parties differ on this issue, since the Christian Democrats emphasize a reformed and increased family allowance, which would give parents also the choice to buy childcare on the market,[20] whereas the SPD has put its priority on the establishment of more public institutions.

Red–Green Social Policy: A First Assessment

Using the election platforms and the coalition agreement as a reference point, the first four years of the Red–Green government can be characterized as an overall success within the social policy domain. The major accomplishments were the reduction of social insurance contributions, pension reform, and an expansion in family policy, while at the same time limiting overall spending. All these measures are in line with the four key elements of the election platforms and the coalition agreement guiding social policy.

The programmatic aims as well as the policies did not differ substantially from the goals and policy direction of the previous government. The overall social policy path pursued by the Red–Green coalition government can therefore be characterized as a continuation and partly as an acceleration of the approach followed by the previous Christian Democratic government. It should, however, be acknowledged that the finding of continuation is based on a somewhat asymmetrical comparison of the past four years of Red–Green government with sixteen years of Christian–Liberal rule. Hence, at least theoretically it is possible that the argument of policy continuation will be falsified through measures taken in the second term of the Red–Green coalition government. However, the analysis of the coalition agreement of 2002 as well as the policy statement (*Regierungserklärung*) given by Chancellor Schröder at the beginning of his second term do not give any indication that this will be the case (SPD and Bündnis '90/Die Grünen 2002; Schröder 2002b). Finally, policy continuation should not be confused with policy stalemate.

The sum of the many steps taken by the two governments in the past 20 years add up to a substantial change in the normative and institutional design of the German welfare state, which I have characterized elsewhere as a "dual transformation" (Seeleib-Kaiser 2002a). What we have witnessed is a process of an implicit withdrawal from the principle of guaranteeing the achieved living standard for wage earners in the various traditional social risk categories, while at the same time child-caring and the social service functions of the family were increasingly "socialized." This outcome was not accomplished in one big comprehensive reform or big bang, but through seemingly countless incremental reform steps.

What are the causes for the identified dual transformation of the German welfare state?[21] Institutional as well as structural explanations, very often used in welfare state analysis, do not seem to adequately explain the policy output. Especially, the change of power at the federal level in 1998 has not led to the expected change in policy based on the "parties matter theory." Moreover, we have witnessed a change in the interpretive patterns used to justify social policies. Two interpretive patterns have emerged as dominant during the past 20 years. According to one interpretive pattern the increase of social insurance contributions needs to be stopped and eventually reversed in order to stay competitive in the world economy. Furthermore, the government has to consolidate its budget and reduce the budget deficit. Consequently changes in social policy become a necessity. According to the second interpretive pattern the public support for families needs to be expanded, while at the same time the overall expenditures for social policy should not increase. These interpretive patterns became dominant during the long tenure of the Christian Democrats in power and also guided the programmatic approach of the Red–Green government toward social policies (Seeleib-Kaiser 2002a). Eventually, they have become "cognitive locks" (Blyth 2001) that will also be directing the future development of the German welfare state within the next four years (SPD and Bündnis '90/Die Grünen 2002; Schröder 2002b). The changed interpretive patterns transformed the normative and cognitive foundations of social policy in Germany and concomitantly led to an institutional policy change. With the exception of the PDS, all parties support this approach in general. With no fundamental changes in the programmatic aims of the parties and the absence of unforeseen historical junctures, only the speed of the transformation, but not its general direction, seems probable to vary in the future, depending on the parties in power (see the election platforms for the 2002 election; Bündnis '90/Die Grünen 2002; CDU 2002; FDP 2002; PDS 2002; SPD 2002). The findings presented in this chapter have two implications: first, the "parties matter theory" seems to lose some of its explanatory power at least in the case of Germany, and second, the dual transformation of the German welfare state will most likely continue in the years to come.

Notes

Revised paper of the presentation at the conference "Federal Elections in Germany 2002. The Government of the Red-Green Coalition after Four Years in Office" held at the University of Minnesota, 26–28 September 2002. I thank Peter Bleses, Antonia Gohr, Bob Holt, Werner Reutter, Martin Roggenkamp, Heinz Rothgang, and the participants of the conference for helpful suggestions and comments.

1. The analysis in this paper is based on a narrow definition of social policy with the public programs to secure against the primary social risks of old age, sickness, and unemployment at its center. Although I acknowledge that the meaning of the term social policy can and a comprehensive analysis should encompass more dimensions, space limitations do not allow a more elaborate analysis.
2. For a more elaborated analysis of the interdependence of the male breadwinner and the female caregiver see Bleses and Seeleib-Kaiser (1999).
3. This section is largely based on Seeleib-Kaiser (2002a).

4. Cf. "Schröder verspricht Konsolidierungskurs, Abbau der Arbeitslosigkeit, außenpolitische Kontinuität," *Frankfurter Allgemeine Zeitung* (11 November 1998): 1.

5. See e.g. "Lafontaines neue Kleider," *Frankfurter Allgemeine Zeitung* (14 February 1999): 34; for a perspective from the former finance minister himself see Lafontaine (1999: 222–39).

6. "Der Bundesfinanzminister verteidigt die 'bittere Medizin der Gesundung,'" *Frankfurter Allgemeine Zeitung* (25 June 1999): 1.

7. The "social budget" is the most comprehensive statistical data set of social policy expenditures in Germany and includes in addition to social spending by the various public entities at the different political levels also the social policy provisions provided by employers (BMAS 2002b: 371–72).

8. According to data published recently by the *Bundesbank*, spending for families with children is even higher. In 1999, the state spent almost 150 billion euro, or 7.6 percent of GDP, for families, which amounts to an annual average increase of almost 4 percent in the years from 1992 to 1999 (Deutsche Bundesbank 2002b: 21–22).

9. The health and social minister, Ulla Schmidt, has appointed a commission under the leadership of Bert Rürup (chairman of the Social Security Council) on 21 November 2002 to develop a comprehensive reform with the stated goal to reduce the social insurance contributions.

10. Most workers covered by collective bargaining agreements continued to receive 100 percent sick pay even after the statutory changes of 1996, since sick pay was often part of the agreements (cf. Bäcker et al. 2000a: 455).

11. The conservative government had changed the dismissal protection "only" for those workers in companies with 5 to 10 employees (Seeleib-Kaiser 2001: 144).

12. "Gesundheitsreform wird verschoben," *Frankfurter Allgemeine Zeitung* (2 December 2001): 1; "Runder Tisch zur Gesundheit ohne Ergebnis," *Frankfurter Allgemeine Zeitung* (23 April 2002): 16.

13. Although officially the government maintains that the replacement ratio of the benefits will only decline to 67 percent (BMAS 2002b: 103), this level is accomplished by creative accounting, since the pension formula was changed. Based on the old formula the replacement ratio would drop to exactly the same level that would have been achieved by the implementation of pension reform legislated by the prior government in 1997, according to the new chairman of the Social Security Council (*Sozialbeirat*), Bert Rürup, cited in "Herbe Kritik an Wahlprogrammen," *Frankfurter Allgemeine Zeitung* (7 May 2002): 16.

14. First signs indicate that a substantial number of workers do not intend to participate in the new programs. Various surveys show that 20 to 48 percent of eligible workers do not intend to sign a contract (cf. Deutsche Bundesbank 2002c: 32). Within the first four months after the law became effective only about two million employees had signed contracts for the new

financial products (cf. "Herbe Kritik an Wahlprogrammen," *Frankfurter Allgemeine Zeitung* (7 May 2002): 16. However, in order to evaluate the take-up rate systematically a longer time span is necessary.

15. For an elaborate and critical evaluation of the pension reform see Nullmeier (2001) and Lamping and Rüb (2001). For a more optimistic view see Kohl (2001).

16. For a broader analysis of gender policies during the Red–Green coalition see Fuhrmann (2002). Due to the complexity of the issue, I will also refer to specific family policy measures already legislated during the tenure of the Christian–Liberal coalition government in this section, before addressing the more recent legislative changes.

17. Initially the state limited the recognition of child-rearing time to one year on the basis of 75 percent of the average income. However, in 1989 the government began to expand these provisions.

18. During the first six months of the parental leave, parents with a joint annual income of up to 51,130 euro can receive the full benefit. Starting from the seventh month the earning limit to receive the full benefit for a two-parent household is 16,470 euro. Furthermore, since 2001 parents that choose a benefit duration of only 12 months instead of 24 months are eligible for a monthly benefit of 460 euro (cf. BMFSFJ 2002; for a legislative overview see Frerich and Frey 1996: 330–33).

19. The "reliable elementary school" (*verlässliche Grundschule*) guarantees a fixed schedule from morning to early afternoon on each school day. Traditionally, elementary school education in Germany has had rather erratic daily timetables making it very difficult if not impossible for both parents to work, even if it was only part time. For example, for recent changes in the state of Baden-Württemberg see Kultusministerium des Landes Baden-Württemberg (2000).

20. It has to be stressed, however, that the CDU/CSU in principle also supports the expansion of childcare facilities for small children (CDU/CSU 2002: 36–37).

21. Due to space limitations, I cannot fully elaborate on this point here. For a comprehensive analysis see Seeleib-Kaiser (2002a).

PART THREE

Current Issues and "New" Politics: Internal Security, Environmental Policy, and Immigration

CHAPTER 8

Internal Security and the Politics of Law and Order

Gert-Joachim Glaessner

In public debates, political controversies, and especially in election campaigns, security is always a hot issue. Successful election campaigns have quite often been based on the promise to be "tough on crime," that is, curbing crime or unlawful behavior, and improving security in public spaces. Many believe Michael Dukakis's presidential campaign in 1988 failed because he was regarded as "soft on crime" (Anderson 1995). Margaret Thatcher, on the other hand, won the elections in 1979 by promising to increase public expenditures for the police and to end social unrest by disciplining the trade unions and starting a "fight against crime." Labour in 1997 made crime and crime prevention a major topic in its successful campaign as well and promised to be tough on crime and on the causes of crime. In Germany also, security was at the forefront of the political debate in 1998, with Social Democrats running their election campaign under the slogan of "Social Security" and "Social Justice." Both issues figured prominently on the agenda and voters were given the impression that a change of government would mean a change for the better: more social security and justice without sacrifices. In its coalition agreement, the Red–Green government furthermore regarded the continuous improvement of internal security as one of its most important tasks. This governmental guideline, agreed upon by Social Democrats and the Greens in November 1998, called for a "firm stand against crime and its causes," a formula adopted by the Social Democrats from New Labour's successful 1997 campaign. Similar formulations surfaced in the agreement of 2002 forged after the coalition managed to regain a small majority in parliament (SPD and Bündnis '90/Die Grünen 2002: 54). While many of these promises did not actually materialize, there were indeed some changes in the domain of domestic security.

Following the events of 11 September 2001, these changes led to only few controversies, which was surprising given that federal elections were due. Instead nearly all parties rallied around the government, and new security measures passed by the parliament were also supported by members of the opposition. This marks a decisive difference from other European countries such as France and the Netherlands in particular. In Denmark, too, elections were heavily influenced by right-wing populists claiming they could solve the problem of growing crime and insecurity, even as general crime rates (with the exception of youth crime) have been declining.

Even the Greens, who had seemingly rejected the terms of law and order since their foundation in 1980, now acknowledged internal security as a legitimate aim of state authority. But they emphatically stressed that the threat of international terrorism was challenging civil liberties and that all precautionary measures should be taken to respond with a minimum of restriction on individual and civil rights. The Greens succeeded in a more liberal approach to the new anti-terror legislation and insisted on conducting a permanent evaluation of those laws that inflict civil liberties (Bündnis '90/Die Grünen 2002). Interestingly enough, the Liberals, guardians of civil liberties for more than 50 years, hardly mentioned the topic and made no strong argument in favor of civil liberties (FDP 2002).

Predictions and fears that the populist sentiment waging in other European campaigns would also afflict Germany and lead to a shift in the political debate, have thus not materialized. Quite the contrary: the traditional parties of the Christian Democrats, Social Democrats, and the Liberals, which have dominated political life in Germany since 1949, are fairly congruent in their positions on security and law-and-order politics. Today, the Greens seem to agree that restrictive and even coercive measures must be considered in fighting crime and other threats to security.

Security is, hence, a multifaceted concept and has been an important political issue in Germany. No political party can take the risk and fail to address this problem and promise to improve the safety and the security of the people (or to be more precise, of the electorate). If parties fail to do so, as was the case in Hamburg in 2001, the electorate punishes them right away.[1] Security is ultimately an issue with a complex and shifting meaning that demands clarification.

What is Security?

Given the relevance and the prominent role of the issue of security in public debates and political controversies, it is an astonishing fact that in social and political science there is hardly a debate about the dimensions and implications of the quest for security in modern societies. Surely Ulrich Beck's *Risikogesellschaft* (Beck 1986) provoked much talk about risk and insecurity (Bonß 1995; Earle and Cvetkovich 1995; Luhmann 1991), but security as a topic of reflection was left to writers on international relations and to criminologists. The path-breaking study of Franz Xaver Kaufmann (1970) on social security and the book of the French sociologist François Ewald *L'Etat providence* (1986) are the only ones of their kind in contemporary social science.[2]

Security, as an issue elaborated by these authors and within a wide range of books in the field of criminology, is a much broader and much more complicated phenomenon than simply crime, internal security of a given state, or national security. Even as crime and crime prevention are at the core of public awareness and unease, there is far more to the "security question": technological risks, economic uncertainties, social welfare and social security, threats to internal security by external enemies or extremists, "the enemy within," and, of course, terrorist threats or attacks.

In this regard, security is a societal concept based on the understanding that a situation is safe, and appears to be lasting, stable, and without danger or risk. Security also refers to the maintenance of a certain societal status, standard of living, and living conditions for individuals and social groups. Security is furthermore associated with certain institutional arrangements established in order to defend a society or body politic against internal and external threats. And last but not least, security could be understood as the assurance of citizen rights and provisions for procedures that will uphold these rights vis-à-vis any attempt on the part of individuals, societal forces, or state institutions to neglect or violate them. This is most fully embodied in the principle of the rule of law (*Rechtsstaat*).

Security in a narrower sense would encompass the rules, regulations, and institutions that protect citizens' human dignity, that is, their "life and physical integrity," to quote the German constitution (Article 2,2). In the preamble of the American constitution, the Union is tasked to ". . . establish Justice, insure domestic Tranquility, provide for the common defence, promote the general Welfare, and secure the Blessings of Liberty to ourselves and our Posterity . . . ." This understanding of security as life, liberty, and welfare reaches far beyond the political sphere.

It incorporates the economic and social sphere, as well as the sphere of basic norms and values of a society. This makes security an overarching concept, one that cannot be limited or restricted to one segment of a society and political order and which constitutes basic duties and goals of the state as the institutional form of a political community.

However, neither modern democracies nor authoritarian regimes are equipped to cope with all these problems at once. A modern state's ability to provide security in all these spheres is becoming increasingly restricted, and authoritarian regimes and dictatorships have often resorted to repression as a means to deal with security. In this respect the Red–Green policy on internal security exemplifies the challenges involved, incurred when democracies are tempted to trade security for liberty.

Internal Security in Germany

Within the German federal system, internal security is primarily the responsibility of the *Länder*. Germany's federal system is characterized by a vertical division of powers between the federal state and the 16 *Länder* of the federation. Legislative powers are allocated to both the federal parliament and state parliaments. Administrative tasks are divided between the federal government, which carries only a limited range of administrative functions, and the administrations of the *Länder*. While in principle, the constitution (Basic Law) is based on the assumption of responsibility by the states, in practice, most of the legislative activities have shifted from the *Länder* to the federal level.

The federal system not only allocates concrete and clearly differentiated legislative jurisdiction to the federal and state levels, but also allows administrative tasks to be distributed on the basis of subsidiarity to the individual public body—the federal government, the *Länder* administrations, and local communities and their associations. The essential characteristic of the German administrative system is that, while the federal government maintains an administration of its own in a few important areas, the majority of administrative tasks are conducted at the level of the *Länder* or the local governments. Exclusively federal administration tasks exist in only a few areas, such as the Foreign Office, the financial and tax-collecting administration, the army, the Federal Border Police, and other security bodies. Where needed, these institutions have offices of their own at the state or local level (e.g., the army has offices in the *Länder* with local administrations to organize conscription and other duties). Apart from these few exceptions, the *Länder* administrations are responsible for applying federal law.

However, there are certain distinctions in the division of tasks and authority for internal security at the state and federal levels, distinctions that are all the more important as they emanate from constitutional provisions regarded as essential democratic safeguards. While responsibility for internal security and policing rests mainly with the *Länder* and local administrations, the Federation has gained some decisive jurisdiction with regard to border control and security measures at airports, railway stations, combating international crime, drug trafficking or terrorism, and protection of the constitution (*Verfassungsschutz*). The federal government also administrates issues pertaining to espionage and counterespionage, the protection of the armed forces against sabotage and infiltration by foreign agents, and defense of the constitutional order against all sorts of threats. The police are primarily assigned to the *Länder*, with the exception of the Federal Border Police (*Bundesgrenzschutz*, BGS) and its special anti-terror brigade GSG 9.

The Basic Law provides for close cooperation between the Federation and the *Länder* in criminal police work, protection of the constitutional order (i.e., German legal norms known as the *free democratic basic order*) against enemies from within or outside the country. Article 87,1 of the constitution allows for the establishment of ". . . Federal Border Guard authorities and central offices for police information and communications, the criminal police and compilation of data for the purpose of protecting the constitution and countering activities on federal territory which, through the use of force or preparations for it, jeopardize the external interests of the Federal Republic of Germany."

The Federal Security Institutions

The Federal Border Police (*Bundesgrenzschutz*, BGS) was founded in 1951 as a paramilitary police force to secure and, in the event of armed conflict, to defend the borders of the FRG (with a special branch in Bavaria, the *Bayerische Grenzpolizei*). The Border Police has gradually developed into a sort of Federal Police with multiple duties and responsibilities. After a terrorist attack at the Munich Olympics in 1972 a special anti-terror branch, the GSG 9, was built up and served successfully in many cases, most notably in liberating a Lufthansa jet in 1977 that had been hijacked by a Palestinian commando trying to free a group of German terrorists of the "Red Army Faction." After unification, the BGS assumed responsibility in 1992 for air-traffic security and the function of Railway police. With the implementation of the Schengen agreement, border controls between the countries that had signed the agreement were abandoned and securing the outside borders of the Schengen area became a major task of the nearly 3,000 officers of the BGS.

After 11 September, the BGS was granted extended authority for stopping, interrogating, and identifying members of the public. Due to the paramount importance of aviation security at the national and international level, the German government introduced considerable improvements in security clearance checks at airports. Here, again, the BGS has served as the supervising institution, with airport security becoming one of its central duties. Officers of the BGS can also be employed as so-called sky marshals (*Flugsicherheitsbegleiter*).

A fierce political controversy surfaced over the plan of the Ministry of the Interior to grant the Federal Criminal Police Office (*Bundeskriminalamt*, BKA) far-reaching new jurisdiction. The first draft of the law aimed at establishing the BKA as just another investigating institution with responsibilities similar to those of the public prosecutor's offices. While this idea did not survive discussion in parliament, the agency has gained additional powers that further strengthen its standing in the "security community." Founded in 1951 for centralized collection, analysis, and transmission of significant information and for maintaining forensic facilities for both the federal state authorities and the *Länder* administrations, the BKA developed in the late 1990s from a relatively small unit of about 500 staff in the mid-1950s into an influential administration with over 4,500 staff members, including more than 2,000 police officers and an annual budget of almost DM 583 million in the year 2000 (BKA 2002). The office is only authorized to act in response to a request from a German state or by order of the Federal Ministry of the Interior.

Over the years, there was widespread suspicion about the BKA due both to its history and to the misgivings harbored by state governments and state police about the shift in responsibilities and the creation of parallel authority at the federal and state level. Nevertheless, following German unification in 1990, the tasks of the BKA were extended to include the five new states. The BKA thereupon became a central police agency for the whole of Germany (cf. Article 87,1 of the German Constitution). Its tasks and powers are governed by the "Law on the Bundeskriminalamt" of 7 July 1997, which established the office as the central agency for police information and communications. The new law assigned the following tasks to the BKA:

- it monitors developments in the field of crime,
- develops crime-fighting methods and approaches for the police,
- provides the Police Crime Statistics (*Polizeiliche Kriminalstatistik*) for the FRG,

- gives professional advice and support to police agencies at the federal and state levels, regarding specific cases considered significant and regarding issues of crime-fighting strategy,
- supports police offices for the purpose of solving serious crimes,
- monitors developments in the field of crime prevention in Germany and other countries,
- and maintains a special research unit on crime and crime prevention (BKA 2002).

In 2001 the authority of the BKA was strengthened by enhancing the means for data collecting: in cases where there are grounds to suspect criminal activity, the Office will be able to gather additional information without having to clarify in each and every case whether this information has already been acquired by the police force of the federal government, the *Bundesgrenzschutz* (BGS), or of the *Länder*. While the intention is to make it much easier to obtain and analyze necessary information, it is highly possible that, with the challenges that already exist in cooperation between intelligence and police institutions, these regulations may simply lead to further competition between various institutions for jurisdiction, influence, and power.

The tasks of the Federal Office for the Protection of the Constitution (*Bundesamt für Verfassungsschutz*, BFV) and the respective offices on the *Länder* level are to safeguard the democratic system and to protect the institutional order of the FRG against extremist political groups or individuals and against other activities that constitute a threat to national security. As is always the case with such institutions, the BFV has often been massively criticized for its activities, especially during the student protests, left-wing political extremism, and terrorist activities associated with the 1960s and 1970s (Braunthal 1990).

The primary function of the Federal and *Länder* Offices is to track foreign spies operating within Germany, and to collect information and provide intelligence on extremist organizations and their members to the federal and *Länder* governments, to other executive authorities, and to the courts. The offices report to the Federal Ministry of the Interior and the respective ministries in the *Länder* and cooperate with corresponding state agencies like the Federal Intelligence Service (*Bundesnachrichtendienst*, BND) or the Military Counterintelligence Service (*Militärischer Abschirmdienst*, MAD).

The federal and state offices have no executive police powers; that is to say they may neither arrest nor prosecute anyone, nor use any other means of force. The idea of a strict division of power and jurisdiction within security agencies in Germany is the product of historical experiences drawn primarily from the Nazi era; institutions such as these, necessary as they may be, tend to operate independently, uncontrolled and unchecked by democratically elected and legitimized institutions such as parliament or even the government.

Under the new "security package," the BFV has gained new responsibilities. It now includes the gathering and evaluation of information on any activities directed against the concept of understanding among peoples and the peaceful coexistence of peoples (Section 3,1). This provision of the law was strongly criticized as too vague, for "peaceful existence of peoples" is a veritably boundless term, opening the front door for persecution of unwanted political thought and political action. According to the Ministry of the Interior, these regulations aim to record any activities directed against political opponents abroad. It is often difficult, if not impossible, to prove the use of violence or that a person is actually involved in planning terrorist acts in Germany that could affect internal security.

Under certain circumstances, the Office is also granted the right to request information as defined by law from banks, financial service institutes, finance companies, aviation companies, and companies providing telecommunication services (Section 8,5), to the extent that this assists the Office in the framework of its preventive tasks. To facilitate the processing of data relating to telecommunication connections and the usage of telecommunication services, the provisions set forth in Article 10 of the Basic Law (on the privacy of post and telecommunications) shall apply. While a special parliamentary committee supervises the measures taken under these extraordinary provisions, these regulations have triggered much critique.

As part of its anti-terror measures, the Office has also been given the right to use technical means, under certain circumstances defined in Article 10 of the Basic Law, to locate mobile phones in order to establish the phone number and information on the phone-card. It is hoped these measures can reveal important information about the environment in which persons suspected of planning acts of terrorism are operating and help to identify other individuals or groups who might be involved in terrorist networks. The law also allows for information-sharing with other institutions such as the Federal Office for the Recognition of Foreign Refugees (*Bundesamt für die Anerkennung ausländischer Flüchtlinge*). Under certain conditions, this Office and the foreigner's authorities have the right to initiate transmissions of data relevant for protecting the political order against criminal and terrorist threats.

Internal Security and Antiterrorism Measures

The federal government responded very quickly to the events of 11 September 2001. Only eight days after the attacks on New York and Washington, the cabinet issued plans for a swift reaction to the threats posed by terrorist activities. This first "security-package" aimed at amending the regulations for private associations, making it possible to ban religious groups showing extremist tendencies, as well as any other ideological groups. A second, more comprehensive package proposed wide-ranging and far-reaching additional authority for the police and the intelligence administration and new regulations for non-German citizens, resident aliens, and asylum-seekers.

Even prior to the September events, the Government had been considering legal measures to outlaw fundamentalist religious groups pursuing radical political goals and supporting terrorism or planning other criminal acts. Hiding under the umbrella of a religious community, some of these groups were considered extremely dangerous by the security authorities. In practice this was primarily meant for fighting extremist Muslim "religious" groups even though all precautions were taken in order to avoid being perceived as biased against Muslims in general. In addition, with a mainly Turkish or Kurdish Muslim community Muslim extremism and radical Islamism are not as prominent in Germany as they are in France or in the United Kingdom. The government stressed emphatically that this amendment to the Law on Private Associations (*Vereinsgesetz*) was not intended to intervene in religious freedom. "It is merely a matter of preventing extremist groups from continually pursuing anti-constitutional goals that are allegedly based on religious beliefs" (BMI 2001). Only days after parliament's final approval, a radical Islamic group, the Cologne-based "Kalif-State," was banned under this law.

The second measure, which had already been considered for legislation before 11 September 2001, was the introduction of a new Section 129b of the German Criminal Code. This makes membership in and support of terrorist groups prosecutable, even if these groups do not have a relevant structure in Germany. A similar provision, the much disputed Section 129a of that code, was established to combat political groups supporting German terrorist groups like the Red Army Faction or the "Red Cells" in the 1970s. The new legislation closed the gap that previously existed in the prosecution of international terrorist organizations and is considered an important contribution toward fighting terrorism.

The new legislation also brought about an institutional shakeup of security agencies, extending to them new and far-reaching authority. The BND, which is responsible for espionage and counterespionage, has been granted the same right as the BFV. Under certain circumstances, it maintains the right to request information about accounts, account-holders, and other authorized persons, as well as about monetary trans-actions and investments (Section 2,1). The MAD, is now permitted to gather and evaluate information on any activities conducted by members of the Armed Forces or civilians working in the Ministry of Defense that are directed against the concept of understanding between peoples and against the peaceful coexistence of peoples (Section 2). However, unlike the BFV and the BND, the MAD shall not be entitled to request information on economic activities of members of the armed forces. But it has been given the right to request companies providing telecommunication services and teleservices as part of their business to divulge information on data relating to the usage of this equipment.

One of the most problematic provisions of the new law is the obliga-tion of social insurance institutions to provide information to the secu-rity authorities. The new security laws give law enforcement authorities access to general social data and to specific data necessary for conducting computer-aided profiling. On the basis of these provisions, all students of Arabic and/or Muslim origin have been screened and the universities have been compelled to provide the data from their student files. Attempts to challenge these regulations before the courts have failed. In practical terms, the results of these measures were extremely disappoint-ing for the security agencies. If they had resorted to the experiences of the 1970s, when extensive *Rasterfahndung*-measures were undertaken, they would probably have been more realistic about the actual outcome.

Apart from new legislation, other measures in the operational area were taken to respond quickly to the situation, with the BGS stepping up surveillance measures and controls along borders. Even before the United States launched military actions, the security authorities of the federal government and the *Länder* had already implemented security plans for areas considered at risk, especially American, British, Israeli, and Jewish facilities. The states implemented new computerized analy-ses of data and search measures based on the police laws of the *Länder*, with the goal of tracking down alien suspects living in Germany.

These and other operational measures, increased security measures at airports and nuclear power plants, and special investigative procedures conducted by the police, such as screening groups of people by means of computer-aided profiling and searches,[3] taken by the federal government in the immediate aftermath of 11 September were meant to achieve two things: to protect the public and to provide for a greater awareness and sense of security.

Amendments to the Foreigners Act and Asylum Procedure Act

Because some of the terrorists responsible for 11 September were foreign citizens, some of them students living in the FRG and one of them, Mohamed Atta, had entered the country with three different falsified passports, officials came to the conclusion that amendments to the Foreigners Act (*Ausländergesetz*) were inevitable. These changes introduced by law include the refusal to grant a visa or residence permit to any persons suspected of engaging or supporting terrorism or acts of violence. These persons shall be prohibited from entering and residing in Germany and if they are already in the country, they will be deprived of their tourist visa or their legal status as resident alien. Cooperation between diplomatic offices of the FRG and security authorities shall be intensified due to the security authorities' heightened need for information in the light of the security situation. German diplomatic offices are entitled by law to implement new identification measures (fingerprints) in the visa procedure and the introduction of forgery-proof identity cards when they issue long-term visas.

German consulates all over the world have to prove whether an applicant poses a threat to the free democratic basic order (*freiheitliche demokratische Grundordnung*) or to the security of the FRG and, if so, a visa is to be denied. Visas for those who have already entered Germany can be annulled and these persons can be expelled if they resort to violence or terrorist activities.

The protection of political refugees from possible deportation has also been limited by a much stricter use of the provisions set forth in the Geneva Refugee Convention of 28 July 1951. The Asylum Procedure Act (*Asylverfahrensgesetz*) has also been amended and stricter rules introduced to curb the "misuse of the right of asylum." New measures to identify persons have been established: fingerprints of asylum seekers will automatically be matched with those taken by the police at the scene of a crime and stored by the BKA. Voice-recordings as a technique were introduced to establish identity by determining which country or region they originate from, and documents obtained in connection with the asylum procedure are now to be stored for ten years.

Last but not least, the procurement of information from the Central Aliens Register has been enhanced by amendments to the Act governing the Central Aliens Register (*Ausländerzentralregistergesetz*). An encompassing visa file is to be established, in order to improve the clearance checks on persons entering the country, and police access to this data is to be improved. These measures and the newly established right of the police to retrieve all available data on an automated basis, are meant to enable legal authorities to determine immediately whether or not a foreigner is residing lawfully in Germany or not.

Taking into account all these measures concerning migration and asylum, one can hardly avoid the impression that the antiterrorism bill has created a convenient pretense for pushing forward restrictive regulations on asylum and immigration, which had been on the agenda for quite a long time and yet which had met with stiff resistance by a wider public and relevant groups within the governing coalition. The precautions taken immediately after the terrorist attacks, tighter security measures at airports, protection of nuclear power plants, and changes in the law of private associations and criminal law now seem to receive wide acceptance and have raised little serious controversy. The second security package, however, proved to be highly controversial. Parliament approved the law only after a fierce public debate and internal squabble within the governing coalition of Social Democrats and Greens.

The representatives for data protection (*Datenschutzbeauftragte*) strongly criticized the original plans of the federal government as going too far and as an attempt to introduce a permanent legal State of Emergency (*Ausnahmezustand*). While this critique was somewhat exaggerated, many of the measures taken after September 11 were not as precisely aimed at fighting terrorism as the government claimed. As a sideeffect, some restrictions were imposed which only indirectly have to do with terrorism—for example, measures to identify asylum-seekers and those who misuse the German welfare state.

Some of the regulations are in clear breech of established standards of data protection. According to the right of "informational self-determination" established by the Federal Constitutional Court in 1983, personal data can only be collected by public institutions, if and insofar they are absolutely vital for the public good (BVerfGE 65, 1–72). Security, without any doubt, is a public good. The question remains whether the political measures taken to defend it are adequate and produce effective results. One of the positive effects of the controversial debate in parliament was the institution of a time limit for the bill—it will have to be reevaluated and, if necessary, changed or not renewed in five years time. However, in comparison to the measures taken by other countries—the United Kingdom, for example—the German authorities have acted with much more restraint and caution.

More Security?

All these measures were taken not only to provide greater security against further terrorist attacks, but also aimed at safeguarding the "basic human right of security," which some constitutional legal scholars have interpreted into the German constitution (Isensee 1983; Robbers 1987). There is no doubt about the duty of the state to face threats to domestic and external security; it is a question of how to do so and how, in particular, the German government has reacted.

Trying to assess the politics of the German government, in general, and after 11 September, in particular, one would come to the conclusion that they reacted with some restraint on the continuum of a response model. This *response model* was prominent in the 1970s, when European (and other) governments had to react to a dramatic increase in crime and violence (Gurr 1989; Scheingold 1984; Waddington 1992). In this model, governments and politicians react to an anomalous situation in which the public perception of crime or other threats to security does not coincide with reality but is nevertheless successfully exploited by political opponents or by populist groups or parties to gain support for their cause. If mainstream politicians fail to respond to these sentiments, they are likely to suffer the "Dukakis syndrome"—punished for appearing to be "soft on crime" (Anderson 1995). As politicians learn from a number of similar experiences in Britain, Germany, France, and other countries, they are tempted into imitating these populist notions and by doing so, they contribute to a trend I would describe as the "Le-Pen effect." There was great risk following the terrorist attacks on New York and Washington that Germany would response to these challenges in a similar way. However, in Germany the first draft of the new security laws, proposed by the German Minister of the Interior, Otto Schily, (publicly given the label of "Otto catalogue" after a well-known retailer) was much more radical than the final version and tended to undermine basic civil liberties. A political controversy over these plans led to decisive changes of the wording and content of these laws. This demonstrates how consolidated the political system is today when compared with the 1970s, when terrorist attacks by the "Red Army Faction" nearly led to a state of emergency and drastic legal measures, and furthermore reveals how strong elements of a discursive political culture have become even in a time of manifested insecurity. Whether this trend would continue to hold if Germany, like other countries, were to become the target of massive terrorist attacks or massive civil strife, remains an open question.

Notes

1. In the state elections in Hamburg in 2001, a new "Party for a Law-and-Order-Offensive" (mostly called "Schill Partei" after its founder Ronald Barnabass Schill, a former judge and later Senator for the Interior in

Hamburg) ran a successful campaign on a law-and-order and tough-on-crime ticket.

2. Only in recent years have there been indicators of a cautious "revival" of empirical studies of security matters in German political science. To my knowledge, the only comprehensive empirical study on internal security in Germany in the Anglo-Saxon literature is by Peter Katzenstein (1990).

3. "The aim of computer-aided profiling is to exclude the vast majority of persons who have undergone computer-aided profiling from subsequent police investigations. Only if further data comparisons reveal other conspic-uous features of persons and relevant information has been supplied by other sources about these very persons, will police measures be implemented on these persons alone following a subsequent evaluation of the individual case which falls within the remit of the Federal *Länders'* police forces. These consolidated results of computer-aided profiling and search provide the basis for concrete investigations" (BMI 2001).

CHAPTER 9

From Taboo to Strategic Tool in Politics: Immigrants and Immigration Policies in German Party Politics

Oliver Schmidtke

If there were any notion of a Social Democratic–Green reform project for their last term in office the issue of the German Citizenship and Immigration Law would rank high on the list. Even though being very cautious about the degree of change that the new government promised to introduce in 1998, the outdated Citizenship Law (*Reichs- und Staatsangehörigkeitsgesetz*) was surely at the core of Federal Chancellor Gerhard Schröder's idea to "modernize" German society and politics. In his government declaration of 10 November 1998, Schröder (1998b: ch. 13) stated programmatically: "Realism teaches us . . . that the immigration to Germany which has taken place over the past decades is irreversible. We invited these immigrants to come and they are here to stay. And today we say these people in our midst are not strangers. . . . Far too long those who have come to work here, who pay their taxes and abide by our laws have been told they are just "guests." But in truth they have for years been part of German society. The Government will modernize the law on nationality."

As Schröder has stated, Germany has witnessed immigration on a mass scale since the early 1960s and now is home to 7.3 million foreigners—at 8.9 percent of the population as a whole it is the highest proportion of the population of any of the major European countries

(Münz and Ulrich 1997). And many of them—for example, almost two-thirds of all 2.1 million Turks—have already been living in Germany for over ten years. In stark contrast to this reality of postwar German society, the issue of citizenship, immigration, and nationhood has not played a prominent role in political discourse or policy-making until very recently. This can be widely attributed to the fact that there used to be a consensus among all major parties that immigration was not an issue that was critical to German society; rather, this issue was dealt with in terms of accommodating "foreigners" and, as it was commonly put in euphemistic terms, "guest workers" (*Gastarbeiter*). Most prominently, the liberal-conservative government under Helmut Kohl insisted on the idea that Germany simply was "not and cannot be a country of immigration."[1] Throughout the 1990s, however, with a massive influx of asylum-seekers and war refugees from former Yugoslavia, this perspective changed dramatically. As this chapter will spell out in some detail, there are a series of reasons why the new government under Schröder made it one of its key policy priorities to tackle the thorny question of immigration and citizenship.

Yet, this policy field and initiatives of the SPD–Green coalition developed a political dynamic with far fewer positive effects for the Schröder government than initially anticipated. In the following I will develop a hypothesis according to which the field of immigration and citizenship has moved to the center of party competition in German politics—however with implications that have often not been intended by party strategists. In interpreting recent political campaigns and the role that issues related to immigration have played in the September 2002 general elections, two aspects have to be taken into consideration that are related but still follow different political scripts. On the one hand the chapter will look into the policy process and the way the German polity has reacted to the challenges involved in the constant influx of immigrants into Germany. On the other hand it seeks to highlight the process whereby party competition has been a driving force in bringing immigration and related issues of xenophobia into the spotlight of political debate. In this latter respect the controversy over how German society should react to the challenge of an increasingly multiethnic and multicultural society has repeatedly been employed as an instrument of agenda setting designed to spur (antiimmigrant) political mobilization. This perspective will allow me to highlight the implications of the Red–Green policy initiative in this field both with respect to the public perception of the governing coalition's performance during the last four years and with regard to the actual achievements of the Schröder government in this field.

My basic hypothesis is that the policy field under investigation has shown two peculiar and seemingly incompatible dynamics in terms of its impact on recent political developments. On the one hand, issues of immigration are closely linked to the—rational—debate about Germany's future labor market and its aging society. Here the main parties in German politics show a surprisingly similar pragmatic approach to the issues and an articulated commitment to collaboration beyond partisan lines. On the other hand, however, this issue has been employed in a populist fashion designed to evoke emotional attachment to those allegedly defending national interests and identity. In times of an ever closer resemblance of the two major catch-all parties, the issue of immigration has repeatedly been used as an effective political device to polarize the electorate and to reinstate strong party allegiances. As a result, policy initiatives to formulate a new immigration law have been seriously hampered by a highly emotionalized campaign conducted by the parties involved. Given this peculiar dynamic of this policy field and the events preceding the general elections in September 2002 the Red–Green coalition could not capitalize politically from its lead in reforming the outdated Citizenship Law and introducing new legislation for regulating immigration. On the contrary, the Center–Right opposition could effectively exploit related issues for mobilizing consent for their political agenda mainly by playing the national(istic) card.

In the first part I will provide a historic perspective on how the issues of immigration and citizenship have been dealt with in postwar West Germany. This approach will allow me to provide an interpretative framework for conceptualizing the far-reaching transformations of the 1990s in this respect. In a second step, I will analyze related political campaigns of the last years in more detail, shedding light on the nature of the envisioned reforms in this policy field and the political debate surrounding them. In the last part I will lay out some conclusions about the role of immigration and citizenship politics in contemporary German party politics and how it is related to the structural change in politics in more general terms.

Immigration and "Guest Workers" as Nonissues in Traditional German Politics

In order to understand why the issue of immigration and citizenship traditionally played such a low-key role in German politics it is instructive to highlight briefly some distinct peculiarities shaping political culture in postwar West Germany relevant to the topic under discussion.

First, there is the historically specific tradition of nationhood and the much-discussed primordial base of its Citizenship Law dating back to 1913 (Brubaker 1992; Giesen 2001; Hailbronner 1989; Joppke 1999; Lepsius 1985; Weil 1996; Zank 1998). As Brubaker has pointed out so eloquently, Germany's notion of nationhood as the cultural base for defining inclusion and exclusion into its citizenship regime reflects a blood-based, ethnically framed tradition of the national community. As a result, immigrants or "foreigners," as they have widely been referred to, have traditionally been perceived as aliens. The term *Gastarbeiter* (guest workers) reflects how the early recruitment of foreign workers mainly in Southern Europe was widely seen as a transitory measure to address the shortage of labor in the booming postwar economy (Barbieri 1998). West German society perceived those who came to Germany throughout the 1960s and early 1970s primarily as a temporary work-force bound to return to their countries of origin once they completed their professional assignments. It is within this logic that labor recruit-ment (1955–1973) was stopped in 1973; immigration was meant to be a transitory measure to meet economic necessities. Yet this abrupt termi-nation of the recruitment of foreigners did not stop immigration to Germany: family reunions, asylum-seekers, and ethnic Germans from Central and Eastern Europe formed a continuous flow of people into a country that by this time had already become a country of immigration against its declared intention (Thränhardt 1995; 1996).

Conceptualizing these immigrants, who as a matter of fact decided to stay in ever-greater numbers, as "foreigners" shaped the political debate on related issues (Meier-Braun 1995). Immigration and policies of integra-tion were relegated to the margins of politics; they were simply not recog-nized as part of the society (Faist 1994). If they appeared at all in political discourse, it was mainly framed as a measure to deal with evident features of crisis (lack of control, crime, etc.). However, key issues such as the immigrants' structural underachievement in the education or professional sector or the insufficient integration into German society, never really became a relevant subject of public debate and policy-making. The under-lying rationale was simply to question whether Germany as a nonimmi-grant country by definition needs to deal with these issues at all. Reflecting this logic, policy initiatives with respect to immigrants and asylum-seekers were mainly designed to restrict their numbers, control their influx, and limit their access to basic citizenship provisions (such as the right to vote in Germany even after many years of residency, etc.).[2]

Second, as the labor force coming to Germany was mostly from Southern Europe, ethnic Germans in Central and Eastern Europe form another group that, albeit for entirely different reasons, was exempted from any controversial debate in German politics. Within the framework of the *jus sanguinis* tradition the German public used to make a categorical distinction between alleged transitory workers on the one hand and ethnic Germans residing in the formerly communist sphere of influence on the other hand. Whereas the former group was never really expected to become German citizens after a certain period of residency in the country, the latter group of ethnic Germans was immediately included into German society. They had, as migrants returning to their country of origin, a stationary right to become German citizens under the Federal Expellee Law of 1953.[3] Although substantive in terms of sheer quantity, the latter group was simply exempted from any political controversy; the Cold War reality made these people of German origin living in Central Eastern Europe a highly privileged and endorsed group supported by all major parties. Also until recently the so-called *Vertriebenenverbände* (expellees' organizations) played a critical role in German politics with a weighty clientele mostly loyal to the more rightist spectrum of the political scene. Their political influence and the climate of the Cold War confrontation made sure that the stark differences between the privileges of the ethnic Germans and the status of "denizens" (Hammar 1990) for immigrants from Southern Europe never really became subject of public controversy.

Third, until today German political culture with respect to immigrants and "foreigners" is strongly shaped by the moral imperatives resulting from the legacy of the Third Reich and the Holocaust. The horror of the Jewish genocide orchestrated by Hitler's National Socialist Party has generated a sensitivity for the concerns of migrants and refugees that translated into one of the most liberal asylum laws in Europe. The current generation in power has been strongly socialized into this post-Holocaust consciousness that provides some powerful normative responsibilities particularly when it comes to dealing with the requests of people exposed to political prosecution. Also, and equally important in shaping public debate and the political parties attitude to immigration and nationhood, this legacy has been a powerful device to prevent any openly racist or xenophobic sentiment to gain public or political prominence. Any attempt to challenge this consensus on categorically condemning racist or xenophobic approaches to "foreigners" has traditionally been met with uncompromising resilience by the German public and political elite (Levy 1999; Reutter, chapter 1 in this volume). As a result, and contrary to what has happened in other European countries over the course of the last two decades, in Germany there have been no really successful right-wing, anti-immigrant political parties.[4] This particular aspect of political culture in Germany restricts the opportunities of political organizations that hope to embark on an openly anti-immigrant, nationalistic form of political mobilization. In their desire not to be associated with these political forces in any respect there was a silent consensus among the mainstream parties to avoid the issue of immigration and the presence of non-Germans in contentious public debate altogether. For instance the decision in 1973 to stop the recruitment of guest workers never turned into a contested political issue among the major parties. Although the West German states formulated some policies for dealing with the massive influx of migrants there was an implicit understanding among the political elite to depoliticize the issue of immigration.[5]

Party Competition in the 1980s and the Pandora's Box of "Ausländerpolitik"

Under the conditions outlined here it is not surprising that political parties in the FRG widely refrained from employing issues related to immigrants in their political campaigns. Still rather constrained, the conservative CDU/CSU discovered the issue of "foreigners" and immigration as a promising tool for spurring (electoral) support only in the early 1980s. On different occasions representatives of this party have sought to capitalize on the widespread anxiety about immigrants in German society by accusing the social democrats of being unable or unwilling to handle problems related to immigration in an appropriate manner. Although the then SPD/FDP government stopped all active recruitment in 1973 it was accused of being too lenient in allowing too many immigrants to settle in Germany in times of economic crisis and rising unemployment. When Helmut Kohl came to power in 1982 he declared that *Ausländerpolitik* (policy framework for foreigners) would be one of the key priorities of the new government. However this claim never really materialized in concrete policy initiatives and the issue quickly disappeared from the political agenda after the elections.

The SPD on the other side was highly reluctant to make immigration a positive reference point in their political campaigns or programs. Reflecting on the SPD's decision not to ask for local voting rights for foreigners in 1980, Helmut Schmidt, former leader of the SPD and chancellor until 1982, said in retrospect that this issue went against the "instincts of our core electorate."[6] This statement is striking as it captures the traditional attitude of the Center–Left toward these issues.

Knowing, or at least assuming, that a more liberal policy approach toward immigration and the naturalization of foreigners would be hazardous with respect to the sentiments widely held in society, this party systematically sought to downplay this agenda in political discourse. It is not exploitable in terms of a Left–Right divide and allegedly not popular with blue-collar workers. This passive attitude of the Center–Left, and the lack of any challenging approach (beyond the general commitment toward integrating immigrants in Germany), has made the SPD vulnerable to the CDU/CSU's claim that their opponents on the Left are simply too "soft" on immigration control and thus indirectly responsible for the problems associated with "foreigners."

Against this background the issue of "foreigners" and immigrants gained considerable attraction to be exploited for strategic political purposes throughout the 1980s. On several occasions, yet still in a rather restrained manner, the CDU/CSU employed anti-immigrant sentiments and pleas for a more restrictive policy toward asylum-seekers when they needed confrontational and mobilizing topics in electoral campaigns. For example, during the general elections in 1987 and the Bavarian regional elections in 1986 the Center–Right sought to make this issue a crucial element of its aim to mobilize support. In particular the campaign of the CSU in Bavaria was shaped by the deliberate attempt to evoke fears about the allegedly unrestrained influx of asylum-seekers, portraying the party as the legitimate guardian of "German interests." Here a powerful narrative of the "the boat is full" and a demand for a law and order approach to the supposedly rampant crime committed by "foreigners" provided the base for challenging its Social Democratic opponent on a polarizing platform.

However, this political option proved to be a risky political strategy to embark on at the time. One politically upsetting lesson for the more conservative CSU was that this agenda had unintended consequences that proved to be rather ambivalent in terms of enhancing the attractiveness of the party. As much as this issue was able to steer public emotions and mobilize the conservative, nationalistically minded clientele (Ingenhorst 1997), it also involved the risk of strengthening the more radical Right and alienating the liberal fraction of the political Center.[7] As a matter of fact, the rise of the extreme right-wing, anti-immigrant party *Republikaner* in the late 1980s can be directly linked to the efforts of the established conservative parties in Germany to give weight to an agenda highly critical, if not outright hostile, to immigrants and foreigners. It is not by accident that the leader of the *Republikaner*, Franz Schönhuber, used to be a close collaborator of the former charismatic head of the CSU, Franz Josef Strauss, before establishing his own nationalistic and anti-immigrant organization. In this respect, it meant an incalculable risk to the more conservative wing of the CDU/CSU to play the antiforeigner card. On the one hand, it needed to stay within the narrow margins of what the German public was willing to tolerate in terms of an openly hostile attitude toward nonnationals, and on the other hand it was keen on keeping those votes from the far Right partly encouraged by its own nationalistic, anti-immigrant agenda.

One other strategic consideration that has shaped party competition with respect to the issue of immigrants is the perceived voting behavior of those groups that, in spite of their long residency in Germany, are not qualified to vote because of their citizenship status. The dominant perception has been that ethnic Germans (*Aussiedler*)—with their traditional value system and nationalistic mind-set—are a "natural clientele" for the conservative parties, whereas the mostly blue-collar "guest workers" are perceived to have a natural inclination to vote for the Social Democrats.[8] Still, the SPD remained very constrained about the issue of foreigners and immigrants throughout the 1980s and the demand to extend voting rights to this group. It was up to the then newly created Green party to promote the cause of liberalizing German citizenship regulations. They advocated the rights to citizenship for every individual who has resided in Germany for at least five years. In 1993 the Green party was partly responsible for a grass-root initiative in favor of dual citizenship that was able to collect more than one million signatures (Murray 1994).

The "Crisis of Immigration" and the Polarization of the 1990s

The 1990s mark a qualitatively new era in challenging the silent consensus of the political elite on issues of immigration and the lack of any substantial public debate on them. A series of factors contributed to this change.

It seems that the end of the Cold War and the new political realities in post-1989 Europe have radically changed the political environment in which issues related to immigration are dealt with in German politics. One element of this change is simply the sheer numbers of migrants and refugees coming to Germany in the early 1990s. With the borders to Central Eastern Europe becoming permeable, Germany became the destiny of the overwhelming majority of the asylum-seekers that were uprooted by the wars in former Yugoslavia. In 1992 alone there were 438,000 applicants for asylum. Furthermore, ethnic Germans from the former Soviet bloc decided to move to Germany on a massive scale.[9] Politically this was repeatedly framed as a "crisis of immigration" or as the then chancellor, Helmut Kohl, put it in dramatic terms, a "crisis of the state" (*Staatskrise*). In response to the perceived inability of the German state to protect its territory from excessive immigration the governing conservative–liberal coalition decided to push for a change in Germany's liberal asylum policy. Yet, for this step the governing coalition needed the support of the opposition in order to change the Basic Law and the right to asylum enshrined in it. The deliberations and public debate leading to this amendment of Article 16 of the Basic Law in 1993 was the first forceful indication of how the status of issues related to immigration had taken on a decisively different role in domestic politics. With the aim to force the SPD into the so-called asylum compromise, the governing coalition engaged in a massive campaign asking for tougher legislation to control immigration using manifest antiforeigner undertones (Koopmans 1996, 1999).[10] In particular the asylum-seekers were largely depicted as a threatening and destabilizing hazard to German society. Even the quality press repeatedly expressed concerns over "excessive immigration by alien cultures"(*Überfremdung*).

Along with the enormous influx of asylum-seekers, German society in the 1990s had to accept that a large and consequential minority of those migrants who were recruited since the mid-1950s settled in Germany (Böhning 1984). The transformation of the temporary workforce into permanent residents started already in the 1970s but it took some time for the public to acknowledge this fact. In many respects it has now become manifest that immigration is an irreversible trend of modern German society and that "foreigners" play an increasingly visible part in it. In particular, in West German cities the pluri-ethnic and multicultural makeup of daily life has become normality. Also, different immigrant groups have become far more active politically in recent times, emphasizing their claim to be an integral and gradually more self-conscious part of contemporary German society (Eder et al. 2003; Kastoryano 2002; Koopmans and Statham 1999; Radtke 1994; Soysal 1997).

Another factor contributing to the new prominence of immigration and asylum as agenda setting topics for political debate and conflict is the rise of xenophobic attacks against foreigners that surged in Germany in the early 1990s. It became apparent that modern Germany had indeed been transformed into a pluri-ethnic society (Leggewie 1994; Schmidtke 2001) and that the state could simply not be negligent of this fact in light of the manifest racism in civil society. Initially, the government under Helmut Kohl minimized this phenomenon by describing it in terms of the misguided marginal groups in German society. Yet, in spite of the constant diction that Germany is "not a country of immigration," the problems of how to integrate immigrants and how to approach the regulation of immigration became far too pressing to be simply neglected by this rationale. Issues regarding immigration and citizenship now moved to the center of the debate on the nature and course of German society, questioning established patterns of national identity and societal integration via citizenship rights (Halfmann 1997; Kurthen 1995).[11]

The Policy Initiatives of the Red–Green Coalition and the Reaction of the Conservative Opposition

In early 1999 the Red–Green government was able to submit a working draft for an act to reform Germany's nationality law by introducing "dual nationality" for foreigners who have lived in the FRG for a long time and, above all, for their children who have been born in Germany.[12] With the modernization of the outdated German nationality laws, the traditional ancestry principle has been supplemented by elements of a territorial tradition (*jus soli*) that facilitates the acquisition of German citizenship by birth. This step removed the strong reliance on an ethno-cultural understanding of nationality and aligns German citizenship law with the model commonly used in other European nation states.

The major thrust of this policy initiative was, as stated by Schröder in his government declaration, to modernize Germany's Citizenship Law in a way that would facilitate naturalization, integration, and participation for immigrants in Germany. Its principle idea of allowing dual nationality was that foreign fellow citizens should be able to identify with the state in which they permanently reside without being forced to renounce their traditional links to their original homeland or having to enter into lengthy legal conflicts to release them from their previous nationality. Moving away from the primordial base of defining membership, the territorial principle was to become the deciding factor for the acquisition of German citizenship and not ancestry. The key points of the suggested reform were to grant German citizenship to children of foreign parents at birth if one parent was born in Germany or had immigrated to Germany before his/her fourteenth birthday and has a residence permit. Also it sought to facilitate the naturalization of adults by shortening the period of residency needed to eight years (previously 15 years) and accepting multiple nationality.

The issue of dual citizenship became one of the most controversial issues in the domestic debate on this legislation. It provided a supreme opportunity for the ailing CDU/CSU after the devastating loss in the 1998 general elections to regain momentum and to overcome its manifest crisis. In February 1999, the SPD–Green government's proposed dual nationality law became the centerpiece of the CDU election campaign in Hesse. The CDU mobilized a massive signature campaign against the federal government's proposal to permit foreigners becoming naturalized Germans to routinely keep their old passports.[13] In exit polls of the time, opposition to the government's dual nationality proposal was second only to worries about unemployment. After only 100 days in office the Red–Green government had to accept a surprising defeat in this regional election, and the CDU victory caused the SPD–Green federal government to lose its majority in the 69-vote *Bundesrat*, which it needed to approve the dual nationality legislation. This forced the SPD–Green federal coalition to modify its proposal, under which babies born in Germany to foreign parents now would be considered German nationals as well as nationals of their parents' country until the age of 23, when they would lose German nationality if they did not affirmatively select it (Green 2000).

In light of this political success and reacting to the ongoing initiatives of the Red–Green coalition to complement this first legislation with a comprehensive immigration law the CDU/CSU provoked an enormous debate on the nature of national identity in light of massive immigration. In October 2000, CDU parliamentary leader Friedrich Merz said in a session of the *Bundestag* that immigrants to German society should conform to a German *Leitkultur* or guiding, hegemonic culture. And underlining the weight of this topic for the political agenda Merz said his party would not shy away from making tighter immigration controls a campaign issue in upcoming local polls and a general election due in 2002. Laurenz Meyer, CDU general secretary, followed and declared: "Ich bin stolz, Deutscher zu sein" (I am proud to be German). The CSU, the CDU partner party in Bavaria, released its own position paper on immigration, concluding, "Germany is not a classical country of immigration and must not become one in the future." The CSU endorsed the *Leitkultur* concept, and said foreigners living in Germany should share "values rooted in Christianity, the Enlightenment and Humanism."[14]

To understand why this term provoked such a heated public debate one has to be aware of the fact that it is somewhat reminiscent of Nazi theories of racial supremacy. Evoking emotive terms, such as "patriotism," "the nation," and "the Fatherland" meant reintroducing notions into public discourse that since the War, because of the discredited tradition of modern German nationalism, had been used only very reluctantly by Germany's intellectual and political elite. Against this background it is not surprising that the Left accused the Christian Democrats of using the term *Leitkultur* as an ill-disguised synonym for forcing immigrants into assimilation or, worse, promoting a new form of exclusionary nationalism (Rauer and Schmidtke 2001). After some weeks of heated public debate the CDU/CSU had to realize that they simply could not fill the term *Leitkultur* with any substantive meaning (in terms of defining what it actually means to be German). Also, because of the highly controversial narrative baggage of this notion it was dropped from its use in political discourse rather rapidly.

Yet, in light of the ominous debate on the German *Leitkultur* one could have expected the conservative opposition to refrain entirely from cooperating in drafting new legislation for citizenship and immigration. Here one has to be aware particularly of how ambivalent the position of the CDU/CSU on these issues actually is. This is well mirrored in another statement by Merz: "We have a problem integrating some of the foreigners in Germany. And we should not exacerbate that problem by more immigration. This is why we must talk about who should be allowed to immigrate to Germany. And that should then be governed by a law on immigration and integration."[15] In the following I investigate this ambivalence to, on the one hand, seeking to control and restrict immigration and, on the other hand, to acknowledge that the current legislation is simply insufficient in dealing with current challenges in this field.

The Fierce Political Battle over the New Immigration Law

It has been a key issue of the Red–Green coalition's agenda to supplement the overhaul of the citizenship provisions by the first ever law on immigration in Germany. At the beginning of their term in office the governing parties set into motion a lengthy process of deliberation with the opposition in Parliament. From the beginning Gerhard Schröder tried hard to achieve a cross-party consensus on the reform—partly because of the need to have the new law confirmed by the *Bundesrat*, partly because of the desire to keep this topic out of partisan politics. The Social Democrats and the Green party have become (painfully) aware of how vulnerable they are by a strong nationalistic opposition to their attempt to change the Citizenship and Immigration Law. No other piece of legislation has been drawn up in such close collaboration with opposition Union parties and the FDP over the last years.

The dynamic of the negotiations on this immigration law reflects the sensitivity of the issues as well as the complicated decision-making process of a law that needs to be passed in the *Bundestag* and the

Bundesrat, dominated by the government and the opposition respectively. This political constellation has led to the paradoxical situation that in the end the Red–Green coalition did not include the very moderate recommendations of its own commission of experts, headed by Rita Süssmuth (CDU). Just before the first year of its mandate this commission presented a number of proposals that were far more liberal than the current law that was eventually drafted. Instead, anticipating the opposition of the more conservative fraction of the CDU/CSU, Schröder's government decided to make the new law far more restrictive and water down its original proposal considerably. Stoiber and his Bavarian interior minister, Beckstein, demanded that the text of the law should expressly declare an intention to "limit immigration."[16] SPD–Green party politicians consequently changed Paragraph 1 of the draft law appropriately with the aim to win the compliance of the conservative CDU/CSU opposition and to fence off their plans to make the foreigners issue a central theme in their electoral campaign.

In spite of being so closely involved in drafting the legislation the CDU/CSU opted against the proposal that was brought into Parliament. The basic argument on the basis of which the conservative opposition—not, however, the FDP—challenged the government's draft was to argue that with over four million unemployed there would simply be no need for an immigration law. Irrespective of the pressure coming in particular from the business community and the churches the CDU/CSU insisted that immigration would have negative effects on the labor market and the society as a whole. On the surface their refusal to compromise was provoked by some unresolved problems with the draft version of the law (mainly related to the proposed point system for immigrants and the age of children with a right to join their families in Germany). However, considering how close the Schröder government moved toward the position of the opposition indicates that strategic considerations regarding the impending electoral campaign played a decisive role.

Still, after months of publicly staged disputes and an intense five-hour debate, the *Bundestag* passed the country's first-ever immigration law on 1 March 2002 with a 320–225 vote for the proposed SPD–Green immigration law, sending it to the upper house on 22 March. The law was designed both to allow more skilled workers to qualify as immigrants and to redefine the status of foreigners in the country in accordance with the new pluri-ethnic reality of German society. In essence, it was very similar to provisions in classical immigration countries in their attempt to control and regulate the flow of foreigners with respect to the needs of labor market and society as a whole. The new law was to shape immigration with an eye to Germany's integration capacities and its economic and labor market conditions, while continuing to fulfill the country's international humanitarian obligations. The law regulated entry, length of stay, employment conditions, and integration of foreigners.

In the end, the amendment of the law on immigration, which ought to have been a moment of triumph for the ruling coalition, has instead been overshadowed by legal challenges and controversy. In a highly disputed procedure the *Bundesrat* adopted the law with a 35–34 vote on 22 March 2002. The winning margin was supplied by the state of Brandenburg, yet the opposition immediately challenged its legitimacy, charging that voting was unconstitutional. Under Article 51 of the Basic Law, a state must cast its *Bundesrat's* votes uniformly. Yet as the SPD prime minister of Brandenburg and his CDU interior minister voted differently on the law it was up to Brandenburg's governor to clarify the state's vote and he registered a vote in favor, prompting leaders of the opposition-led states to walk out in protest (see also Kropp, chapter 4 in this volume). In a statement in the *Frankfurter Allgemeine Zeitung*, Angela Merkel, chairwoman of the CDU, immediately put pressure on Germany's president, Johannes Rau, who had to sign the bill if it was to become law: "If he signs it, we will have no other choice than to ask the constitutional court to determine the legality of the way in which this law materialized."[17] Eventually, President Rau signed the law on 19 June 2002 and invited the CDU/CSU to challenge this decision at the Constitutional Court. In December 2002 the Constitutional Court, ruling that the vote cast by Brandenburg in the *Bundesrat* was invalid, blocked the immigration law originally scheduled to take effect at the beginning of 2003.

In the end, in spite of all the caution with which Schröder has sought to win the consent of the liberal–conservative opposition, the procedure of amending the law shed a doubtful and highly controversial light over the whole legislative process. The focus in public debate shifted from the substantive issues of the law—on which all parties agreed in principle—to the dubious procedure to which the government had to resort in order to have this law pass the *Bundesrat*. The accusations of improper procedure and an arms-length deal by the governing coalition overshadowed what was set out to be one of the core legislative initiatives of the Red–Green government.

The Ambivalence of Public Discourse: Between Pragmatism and Populist Exploitation

Beyond the actual process of deliberating the law it is worth shedding some light on the broader political environment in which the partisan struggle over the issues involved unfolded. This perspective will help us to better understand the strategic routes on which the opposition embarked to challenge Schröder's government in this field. Reflecting the political debate surrounding the new law on immigration, two ways in which the issue of immigration has shaped public discourse over the course of the last decade can be distinguished. Although closely related thematically, they seem almost detached in the way they are employed in public discourse. The first is rooted in a rational reflection on the projected benefits and costs involved in attracting immigrants to Germany. The aging German society, the crisis of the social security system, and the need for qualified labor provide the thematic context in which this issue is being discussed. Interestingly there seems to be a convergence in the positions of the mainstream parties regardless of the traditional partisan divide. Even the conservative Christian Democrats have acknowledged the need for controlled immigration and have contributed to drafting legislation in this field. Given the prevalence of rather pragmatic concerns, the political elite has agreed to make some major concessions on how national borders define patterns of inclusion and exclusion into German society. Showing more flexibility with respect to processes of naturalization of foreigners, work permits for nonnationals (the so-called Green Card initiative), and dual citizenship status, the rigidity of rules for foreigners enshrined into the old Citizenship Law has been considerably relaxed. In essence, right across the political spectrum of the parties represented in the German Parliament the traditional rules of inclusion and exclusion appear to be outmoded and overly rigid.

Yet, at the same time the issue of immigration and national identity has recently been employed as a polarizing and mobilizing tool in party politics. One exemplary campaign in this respect was the discussion on the possibility of dual citizenship and the aforementioned debate on the *Deutsche Leitkultur*. In stark contrast to the CDU/CSU's willingness to be involved in modernizing Germany's Citizenship Law the conservative party engaged in a campaign designed to discredit any attempt to call into questions features of loyalty to, and identification with, the national community. National borders were portrayed as demarcating the fundamental allegiance of individuals to their collectivity. In their political campaigns the CDU/CSU repeatedly depicted (excessive) immigrants as a genuine threat to German society and employed a nationalistic rhetoric based on the idea of ethno-cultural homogeneity. This shifted the focus of public debate decisively from pragmatic concerns over the desirable form of immigration to a controversial discussion of the alleged vulnerability and integrity of the national community. As became manifest in the deliberation on the new immigration law, images of a national identity under scrutiny and fears of societal disintegration as the likely effects of immigration were deliberately used for strategic purposes.

It is with respect to these two narratives in particular that the CDU/CSU has challenged the initiatives to reform the German Citizenship Law and to introduce new legislation for regulating immigration into Germany. On the one hand, the CDU/CSU acknowledges the need for political action in the field of immigration considering the demographic stress on the labor market and the German social system. This is somewhat unexpected for the Christian Democrats as their former leader, Helmut Kohl, has overpowered any attempt to discuss issues related to immigration with the simple argument that this would not be an issue of concern to German society. It might be partly due to the pressure from the business community that the CDU/CSU has become far more open to the idea of a controlled and guided immigration policy. While insisting on the priority of German nationals on the labor market the liberal fractions of the CDU have embarked on a more cooperative approach to the initiatives in the field of citizenship and immigration.

Yet at the same time—and in remarkable contrast to this rational discourse—this issue has been employed widely to portray the conservative party as the true protector of national interests and identity. Repeatedly, in the 1990s, the CDU/CSU has embarked with great vigor on an agenda that deliberately uses fear of "foreigners" for purposes of political mobilization. During the years of the Red–Green coalition the conservative opposition has posed as the defender of national identity and national interests on several occasions. With this agenda it could rather successfully cover the lingering crisis of leadership and the severe effects of the corruption scandals of the late Kohl years. It has also helped to ease the political crisis of the contemporary conservative party, which, with the demise of communism, has lost its antidote in defining its own political identity. With the debates strangely detached from each other, the CDU/CSU could present itself as a party deeply committed both to internationalizing Germany and deepening the process of European integration while simultaneously playing the strongly nationalistic card when painting the allegedly devastating effects of "uncontrolled" immigration.

Conclusions: Immigration and the General Elections in September 2002

The general elections in 2002 are the first in the history of postwar German politics to be critically shaped by a controversial debate over immigration and citizenship. Several factors shaping political culture in postwar Germany had contributed to the fact that the political fight over the form and desirability of immigrants traditionally played a low key in competitive party politics or was even banned from public discourse. However, this has changed decisively over the last decade. What we have been witnessing is both that questions of immigration and its effects on German society have simply become too momentous to be ignored politically and that actors have increasingly discovered immigration to be an important cleavage and resource in competitive party politics (Hunger 2000).

Yet, it is difficult to stipulate the exact degree of influence on the outcome of the general elections that can be attributed to the field of citizenship and immigration. Given the prominence of related public debates over the course of the last years and considering the weight put on the related legislative initiatives by the Red–Green government it is not unjustified to claim that this issue has indeed considerably shaped the orientation and decisions of the electorate. Over the course of the last four years the issue of immigration, citizenship, and foreigners rank highest on the list of those things that concerned and divided the public along partisan lines. Also it is important to recognize the meaning given to citizenship and immigration policies as one of the core reform initiatives of the Red–Green coalition. In particular for the Green party it was a supreme opportunity to gain public visibility and to broaden its political identity beyond environmental concerns. It was with respect to the new law on immigration that the Green party hoped to portray itself as the motor of political reform in the governing coalition. Also, for the Red–Green government the immigration law was a critical, albeit in public perception barely successful, test for its ability to materialize their political goals in terms of competent policy initiatives.

Considering how majorities were formed to amend the legislation in this field and how the whole process was handled, one can surely argue that, although the reform of the Citizenship Law and the attempt to formulate a new legal base for immigration have constituted a prime opportunity for the government under Schröder, the coalition never received the potential political credit for it. In particular, with respect to the way in which the Schröder government sought to obtain a majority in the *Bundesrat* by striking arms-length deals with single regional representatives of the CDU left a negative mark on the whole process. It gave the opposition the opportunity to call it foul play and to threaten the legislation in the courts. Its original goals and achievement of introducing legislation on immigration for the first time ever in Germany is widely lost for the governing coalition, due to the fierce debate on whether the procedure of passing the bill was constitutionally sound. In public perception the whole process led to the image of a murky deal between elite politicians in which the subjects of the reform itself took a back seat to the quarrel between the major parties.

Along the same lines, it is questionable whether the strategy of the Schröder government to gradually water down the draft version of the immigration law in order to achieve the consent of the opposition was politically very successful in the end. Indirectly acknowledging the vulnerability of the government in this policy field and anxiously aiming to prevent the opposition using this issue in an emotional campaign, the Red–Green government was very clear from the outset that it wanted to see new legislation in the field of immigration and citizenship to be based on a broad consensus of all major parties. The lengthy process of compromises and backroom deals consumed much of the initial enthusiasm that at least the more liberal part of the German public showed. With a law that has integrated so many alterations demanded by the Conservative opposition, the boldness of the initiative—as evident in the above cited government declaration by Schröder—was lost too. As a result, the government is hardly able to portray the new law on immigration as a genuine achievement of the Red–Green government—if and when the law will eventually be approved.

One related observation, which however exceeds the reflection on the direct electoral effect of this policy field, is how the Left–Right divide as the decisive reference point in voting behavior has undergone a major transformation. The classic battleground for the two major forces in German politics has been the issue of redistributive politics and the welfare state. As this conflict is widely tempered by the competing, yet rather pragmatic claim over which party has more competence in the field of managing the economy, other issues have been moved to the forefront in defining the political identities of the moderate Left and Right.[18] In this respect it is not simply the changing social reality of Germany as a multiethnic society or the demographically driven need for immigration but also the resonance that related political issues find in the electorate. In times of ever closer resemblance of the two major catch-all parties the issue of immigration can effectively be employed as a political device to polarize the electorate and to reinstate strong party allegiances. The features of party competition in recent German politics reveal how attractive the rejection of "foreigners" as a "weapon of last resort" (Thränhardt 1993: 354) has indeed become.

Against the background of de-nationalization and a breath-taking path of European integration the issue of immigration and citizenship is one prominent field in which fears, concerns, and frustration with the current political realities can be articulated. Invoking strong symbolic patterns of national community and identity promises stability in a world undergoing radical transformation. Considering the most recent public debates, the myth of ethno-cultural homogeneity has proven to still be a forceful element in determining interests and articulating anxieties about communal belonging. As a result, policy initiatives to formulate a new immigration law have been seriously hampered by a highly emotional campaign conducted by the parties involved (the debate on granting the right of dual citizenship and the more recent discussions surrounding the new immigration law represent a vivid illustration of this effect). A nationalistic rhetoric might still come from the margins of these societies. However, what is alarming is that their emphasis on exclusionary nationalistic feelings and antiforeigner sentiments resonates with beliefs and representational practices that are not alien to mainstream society and politics.

The CDU/CSU is highly divided over the question as to whether it is a promising and legitimate idea to use the issues related to immigration for domestic political purposes. Some consider these issues—partly for tactical reasons—to be too risky a strategy for political mobilization as they are prone to alienate the more liberal voters in the Center and to provide indirect support for more right-wing anti-immigrant groups. The more conservative wing of the party, however, sees this issue as a prime opportunity to create a political climate favorable to the Center–Right. It forms an agenda that allows the CDU/CSU to reestablish a mobilizing political identity and to embark on a highly productive agenda in a world in which the differences between the major parties in classic fields of partisan politics such as the economy have become decisively smaller. In this respect, the logic of party competition and the need to reinvent political identities in times of fading traditional ideological cleavages might be a significant driving force behind the new struggle over issues of immigration and nationhood. It is the seductive power of a polarizing and emotionally forceful agenda that makes attractive the use of these issues for strategic purposes in politics. Still, as successful as this might be for political mobilization, this strategy is prone to promote a nationalist agenda with strong exclusionary undertones that fundamentally contradict what the reform of the German Citizenship Law set out to achieve, namely a more successful inclusion of immigrants into German society.

Notes

1. Helmut Kohl quoted in: Rick Atkinson, "Top U.S. Envoy in Berlin Criticizes Germans," *The Washington Post* (16 April 1994).
2. These measures were complemented by state-driven attempts to enhance the integration of immigrants into German society. Yet, compared to similar patterns in immigrant societies such as Canada, these policies were perceived and institutionally enshrined as at best secondary issues for the German polity.
3. Münz and Ohliger (1997) estimate that since 1945 ca. 15 million refugees, expellees (*Vertriebene*), or ethnic Germans (*Aussiedler*) have fled to Germany.
4. These parties and organizations—such as the *Nationaldemokratische Partei Deutschlands* (NPD, National Democratic Party of Germany), the *Republikaner* (Republicans), or the *Deutsche Volksunion* (DVU, German People's Union)—have always remained marginal to the political establishment, obtaining some minor and mostly highly transitory success in regional and local elections (for a comparative perspective see Betz 1994). This however did not prevent groups in civil society from engaging in the openly violent attacks that became so shockingly rampant in the early 1990s.
5. Discussing the British and French case, Freeman (1979: chapter 4) came to a similar hypothesis.
6. *Münstersche Zeitung* (8 November 1993).
7. The CDU/CSU had to realize how restricted the opportunities are to employ this agenda in a political culture shaped by the taboo on any kind of racism. For instance, when the now chancellor candidate Edmund Stoiber spoke of the tendency of a racially mixed society (*durchmischte und durchrasste Gesellschaft*), the public outcry over using a language reminiscent of the Nazi period made him rescind his comments immediately.
8. As strongly as this consideration preoccupies strategists in the parties it might actually be rather misleading. *Aussiedler* put a high degree of emphasis on integration through work and the state, whereas the family and religious orientation of most migrants from Southern Europe does not seem to work in favor of parties that champion a more postmaterialist orientation.
9. This number peaked in 1990 with almost 400,000 *Aussiedler* coming to Germany. Reacting to this figure the government under Kohl introduced significant procedural restrictions in the Ethnic Germans' Reception Law in 1990. As a result the number of new arrivals dropped dramatically.
10. The government spoke about a "threshold of tolerance" that German society would endure with the influx of so many asylum-seekers. Presuming the "unassimilibility" of these immigrants, the SPD was accused of nurturing xenophobia by not allowing for stricter rules for asylum-seekers (Blanke 1994).
11. Here the work of the German sociologist W. Heitmeyer is quite intriguing (1994, 1997).

12. This law was amended in May 1999 by simple majorities in both chambers of the German Parliament. For an account of previous debates on this issue see Blumenwitz (1994).
13. The CDU/CSU was able to gather more than five million signatures against the proposal (Koopmans 1999).
14. See the Homepage of the CSU at www.csu.de (date of downloading: 20 October 2000).
15. Radio Interview, Deutschlandradio, 3 November 2000.
16. Other significant concessions concern the already difficult legal situation confronting foreigners and refugees. Also the age limit of children who are allowed to follow their parents as immigrants was lowered from 16 to 12 to ensure that they are better able to integrate into German society.
17. *Frankfurter Allgemeine Zeitung* (23 March 2002).
18. This point is also intimately linked to the recent transformation of social democracy in Europe. The underlying conflict over the social distribution of resources and power in a society is no longer the reference point for the political cleavages that Third Way social democrats consider of primary importance (see Schmidtke 2002).

CHAPTER 10

Red–Green Environmental Policy in Germany: Strategies and Performance Patterns

Kristine Kern, Stephanie Koenen, and Tina Löffelsend

Environmental policy is considered a cornerstone of Red–Green politics in Germany because it is integral for party identity and a measure of performance for the Greens (Bündnis '90/Die Grünen). In 2002, after four years in office and at the beginning of the new legislative term, it appears that environmental policy may be one of this government's few success stories. After the elections in 1998, the Greens faced a dual challenge. On the one hand, party members as well as their voters had high expectations, particularly regarding the realization of the phase-out of nuclear energy and the ecological tax reform (SPD and Bündnis '90/Die Grünen 1998). The opposition to nuclear energy was one of the central features of the environmental movement of the 1970s and has remained crucial for the Green party since then. On the other hand, their general ability to govern was still questioned by their critics (Roberts 1999: 151; Rüdig 2000; Rüdig 2002: 78, 92).

In 1998, the Green party acquired its first opportunity to influence environmental policy directly at the national level as part of the ruling coalition. This changed their situation fundamentally because certain issues—for instance, the phase-out of nuclear energy—fall under federal-level competence. Thus, the 1998 elections opened a policy window for the Green party. Radical policy changes had to be expected at least in some areas. Because such changes are rare in Germany, which generally prefers a "policy of the middle way" (Schmidt 1987) and tends toward continuity and stability (Katzenstein 1987; Goldberger 1993; Lees 2000: 111), one has to ask (and try to substantiate empirically) whether this opportunity structure has indeed changed Germany's environmental policy fundamentally. Whereas comparative studies show that there is no evidence that established parties make a difference in environmental policy (Kern and Bratzel 1996: 292–293), it is still an open question whether Green parties in power can initiate fundamental policy changes.[1] The underlying question of this chapter is whether radical policy changes are possible in such a situation. Does a Green party make a difference when it comes to power? How are national strategies influenced by the path dependence of national policy and the tendency toward global policy convergence?

Types of Strategies Between National Path Dependence and Global Policy Convergence

Any assessment of the Red–Green coalition's environmental policy must be based on the legacies of the Christian–Liberal government that preceded it. Thus, the situation faced by the Red–Green government, when it came to power in 1998, must be given due consideration. Moreover, it is crucial for an overall evaluation to determine the position of Germany from an international standpoint. In 1998, Germany was considered a pioneer in some policy areas but lagging behind in others. For instance, Germany had pursued an ambitious climate protection program but, at the same time, it had not yet decided on some issues closely related to Agenda 21, although most of the other OECD countries had already met their obligations in this respect. Consideration of the legacies left behind by the Christian–Liberal government form the background of our analysis. We take two analytical dimensions into account: the scope of policy change and Germany's international position. Based on a combination of these two dimensions, four possible types of policy strategies and performance patterns can be outlined (table 10.1).

Table 10.1 Types of policy strategies and performance patterns

International position	Scope of policy change	
	Radical change	*Moderate change*
Pioneer	(1) Moving first strategy	(3) Staying ahead strategy
Laggard	(2) Catching up strategy	(4) Lagging behind strategy/policy

(1) A situation in which radical policy change occurs and a country has the international position of a pioneer before this process starts can be described as a *moving first strategy*. Since no internationally acknowledged models exist, this kind of change-of-path is not facilitated by international developments, but rather has to be based primarily on national innovations and initiatives. Therefore, high innovational capacities are necessary, and policy entrepreneurs with sufficient resources to influence the national policy agenda are needed. However, to take the first step ahead of other countries not only carries the risk of failure, it also offers the chance to become a global pioneer. This strategy pays off when other countries follow and a diffusion process is initiated by the policy innovation—especially if new technologies are developed that can be exported to other countries.

(2) When policy changes radically, but a country's starting point in the specific policy area is an international laggard position, the underlying motivation can best be characterized as a *catching up strategy*. In this situation, a change-of-path is easier to accomplish because other countries have already taken action. Transaction costs can be reduced if internationally acknowledged models already exist. Although such models cannot always be transferred easily from the national context where they were developed to other countries, the diffusion of policy innovations is certainly facilitated by this arrangement. Foreign models can be used in the policy process as an important argument by policy entrepreneurs; that is, the introduction of new policies is supported and accelerated by "best practice" developed in other countries, as well as by the recommendations of international or intergovernmental organizations like the OECD.

(3) If a moderate change occurs but a country has already achieved an international pioneer position prior to the policy change, this combination can be labeled as a *staying ahead strategy*. In this case the legacies of the former government resulted in the country's having a good international reputation in this specific policy area. Because of a good reputation, policy entrepreneurs might set their priorities in different areas and prefer only minor changes to the originally successful policy. Radical changes could involve the risk of failure, while minor changes might be sufficient to maintain the reputation as an international forerunner and push other countries in the same direction. The policy follows the same path, and the risks of a change-of-path are avoided.

(4) Finally, there is a fourth combination: namely, an international laggard position that nevertheless results only in moderate change. The reason for such a *lagging behind* might be the low salience of the issue on the national political agenda, or the lack of strong policy entrepreneurs that support innovative strategies and radical change. A reason to pursue such a policy intentionally is the expectation that, in this specific field, a race to the bottom is likely to occur and, therefore, moving ahead and becoming a pioneer might not pay off in the long run.

In a situation where a Green party comes to power for the first time—depending on a country's international position, the legacies of its old government, and the salience of the issue on the agenda—moving first, catching up, or staying ahead might, at any time, become dominant strategies. At least in certain areas of concern that are high on "Green" political agendas, radical change is expected by party members and voters alike. Whether such changes actually occur is finally determined by the bargaining processes within the governing coalition and the development of the policy process. By contrast, lagging behind other countries demonstrates a lack of an intentionally taken strategy. However, even if a Green party is in power, the bargaining processes for a controversial black and white issue, combined with personality and political conflicts between specific party members may result in the country's lagging behind.

Environmental Policy in Germany Before 1998

While the first 20 years of the FRG were characterized by strong engagement in the reconstruction of the German economy, with environmental issues playing only a marginal role, the Social–Liberal coalition in 1969 marked an important turning point. Through the implementation of a quick-start program (*Sofortprogramm*) in 1970 and the adoption of an environmental program containing the three principles of precaution (*Vorsorgeprinzip*), cooperation (*Kooperationsprinzip*), and the polluter-pays principle (*Verursacherprinzip*), the German environment became important enough to be considered as an independent and programmatically profiled policy field for the first time (Hartkopf and Bohne 1983; Weidner 1999: 429).

Given the favorable conditions at the outset, for example, the generally positive public opinion toward reforms, widespread optimism regarding the organizational and regulatory capacities of the state, and the satisfactory state of the economy at the end of the 1960s, a number of pieces of federal legislation could be enacted (e.g. the Waste Act in 1972, the Federal Immission Control Act in 1974, and the Nature Conservation Act in 1976) (Müller 1989; Pehle 1997). The legal-institutional extension of these new policies was promoted through the establishment of a German Council of Environmental Advisors (*Rat von Sachverständigen für Umweltfragen*, SRU) in 1971 and the establishment of the German Federal Environmental Agency (*Umweltbundesamt*) in 1974. With these initiatives, the Social–Liberal coalition started an ambitious program of environmental policy, which must be considered extremely positive, considering that the main impulse for these initiatives came from within the government coalition and only to a small degree from external demands.

With the oil crisis and the subsequent world recession, the government began to shift its main priorities to the economic and employment sectors. This negative development, however, was not reflected among the German society. Interest as well as demands for a more offensive environmental political strategy grew steadily and led to the establishment of numerous citizens' initiatives, new environmental organizations, and, in 1980, the founding of the Green party. With the support of growing interests among the media, public pressure on economic interest groups, trade unions, and the party system as a whole increased (Malunat 1994: 7).

As in other countries, German environmental policy, in its initial phase, was characterized by a command-and-control approach consisting mainly of instruments such as licensing and standard setting (Jänicke and Weidner 1997: 139). In the first phase of environmental policy in the early 1970s, the German approach was primarily oriented toward the modification of already existing legislation; new approaches developed in other countries were not supported by the relevant actors. For instance, policy innovations such as the introduction of an environmental framework law, a constitutional amendment, an environmental impact assessment, or the class action suit (*Verbandsklage*) for NGOs had not been decided upon in Germany. Although German environmental policy was institutionalized in the early 1970s, Germany did not really belong to the group of countries who were environmental pioneers. A single important exception to this, however, can be seen in the launch of the "Blue Angel" (*Blauer Engel*) system in 1978—the first eco-labeling system worldwide. Such voluntary instruments became very popular in other countries in the 1990s. The German system served as a model and was imitated and emulated by many countries all over the world (Kern et al. 2001b).

The number of initiatives taken by the Christian–Liberal coalition during their 16-year government (1982–1998) resembles, in their general course, a curve with a strong upward trend, peaking between 1987 and 1992, when Klaus Töpfer was environmental minister. A strong downward tendency can be observed for the period after the 1994 elections, when priorities shifted mainly toward the economic reconstruction of the new German federal states (*Neue Länder*) in the former GDR (East Germany).

The environmental protection activities of the Christian–Liberal government, when measured against the criterion "improvement of environmental quality," led to considerable progress, making the overall balance of their initiatives look better than that of the Social–Liberal coalition. However, it has to be taken into consideration that the external demands for problem-solving and the economic, political, and social framework conditions changed in the course of the 1980s. Increasing environmental awareness within the German society and the rising expectations of the citizens for a more proactive environmental policy resulted in better opportunities for the implementation of stricter standards (e.g. in the area of pollution control, or with the program on the reduction of CO_2 emissions,). It can be stated that, for the period during which Environmental Minister Klaus Töpfer was in office, the capacities for environmental policy were widely expanded, making Germany a pioneer in many areas. During this period, the German government also played a very active role in formulating international agreements (Weidner 1989; Jänicke and Weidner 1997; Jänicke et al. 1999: 32–33).

Despite the generally positive balance resulting from the policies of the Christian–Liberal coalition, at least prior to German reunification, deficits still existed in the areas of nuclear energy, nature conservation, land use, and the regulation of chemicals. Especially after the elections in 1994, no significant progress had been made in these policy areas. Moreover, by the time the Red–Green coalition started its initiatives in 1998, Germany had not yet developed a national sustainability strategy, although most OECD countries had already adopted such plans. Regarding the establishment of environmental strategies and policies, the Christian–Liberal coalition primarily followed the same path as their predecessors. Although the debate on economic instruments in environmental policy had been going on for years (following a number of ideas raised by Töpfer), it did not result in the introduction of new policy instruments like eco-taxation, which, by this time, had already been introduced in several other European countries, especially in Northern Europe. Flexible economic instruments were still missing and German environmental policy was far from being based on an integrative strategy aiming at all relevant policy areas.

In the long-term evolution of environmental policy paths, there are marked differences between countries. Germany was not among the pioneers (the United States, Sweden, the United Kingdom, and Japan) in the initial phase of environmental policy in the early 1970s, but adopted many approaches from other countries such as the clean air standards. In the 1980s, this situation changed fundamentally, when Germany became a pioneer in several policy areas and an influential player in the international environmental policy arena (Andersen and Liefferink 1997; Jänicke and Weidner 1997: 142). In the 1990s, German environmental policy generally lost momentum after reunification, because economic and social problems were given higher priority than environmental issues.

After the 1998 elections, when a new government with a different policy agenda came to power, Germany had the opportunity to become an international pioneer again. After more than four years in office the questions to be asked are: What strategies have been chosen and how can different outcomes be explained? What difference did the Red–Green coalition make for Germany's international environmental policy position? Furthermore, have there been any radical changes in Germany after 1998 that are of general interest for other countries?

Analysis of Select Initiatives of the Red–Green Government

The following section analyzes four cases of Red–Green environmental policy from 1998 to 2002. Since not all environmental policy initiatives of the new government can be examined here, we have chosen the following four examples: energy policy, the introduction of ecological taxes, climate protection policy, and the development of a national sustainability strategy.[2] These particular cases were selected because they represent central environmental policy projects of the Red–Green government. The phase-out of nuclear energy and introduction of the ecological tax reform were the two most essential issues for the Greens, ranking high on their political agenda since the founding of the party. Special focus will thus be placed on innovations in the form, content, and style of this new government's environmental policy vis-à-vis that of former governments. The crucial question for the analysis of the case studies is how the different types of strategies and output of the policy process can be explained. Together, the four policies form the background for an overall assessment of the environmental performance of the Red–Green government (Zahrnt 2001; Bundestagsfraktion Bündnis '90/Die Grünen 2002; Flasbarth and Billen 2002).

Energy Policy—Germany Moving First

The phase-out of nuclear energy has always been one of the fundamental demands of the Green party. In their coalition agreement with the SPD, the Greens finally succeeded in making this demand a concrete goal for the upcoming legislative period. Both partners concurred that the phase-out of nuclear energy should be laid down by law, and that this would settle the issue of nuclear energy once and for all. A 100-days program was developed with a few measures: revision of the existing nuclear law in a number of areas, and an invitation to the main energy companies to create a forum for discussion on the future steps toward the phase-out of nuclear energy and the development of a new energy policy. One year after the beginning of the talks, a consensus was to be reached and a law drafted (SPD and Bündnis '90/Die Grünen 1998).

During its four-year legislative term, the Red–Green government initiated a number of successful energy policy projects. The two main projects were:

- The termination of nuclear energy use as approved by the cabinet in September 2001 (Act on the Structured Phase-Out of the Utilization of Nuclear Energy for the Commercial Generation of Electricity),[3] focusing on three points: (1) a ban on constructing new commercial nuclear power plants and the restriction of the residual operating time of existing nuclear power plants to 32 years from the time of the plant's start up; (2) a maximum permitted residual electricity volume for each individual nuclear power plant; and (3) as of 1 July 2005, prohibition of the delivery of spent fuel elements for reprocessing and restriction of nuclear waste disposal to final storage.
- The Renewable Energy Sources Act (*Erneuerbare-Energien-Gesetz*) in March 2000, regulating feed-in tariffs, in combination with the so-called 100,000 Roofs Program promoting the use of solar and photovoltaic systems.

These initiatives, however, were not brought to fruition without problems for the Red–Green coalition. Concerning the phase-out of nuclear energy, the SPD and the Greens started from very different positions. While the Greens at first made the immediate phase-out one of the main goals to be achieved within a Red–Green government, the SPD was much more careful in the formulation of its preferred policy. In the course of the government's term and during the consensus talks with the energy companies, differences in opinion about certain elements and also about the preferred level of compromises became obvious, not only between the two parties, but also within each of the parties themselves. This gave the energy companies more bargaining leverage and led to a number of additional discussions. In the end, the Greens had to give in on a number of important points in order to guarantee the acceptance of the agreement as a whole.

The reactions to the deal eventually hammered out between the energy companies and the federal government have been ambivalent. Most comments from environmental science experts have been positive. According to the experts, the agreement to abandon nuclear energy as one source of energy production marks a radical policy change indeed. For almost three decades, nuclear energy has been a central point of conflict within the German society, which, thanks to the new agreement, seems to be resolved. The agreement also offers the advantage that, because of the compromise with the nuclear industry, protracted legal quarrels and potential compensatory payments (as was the case in Sweden) can be avoided. Despite the legitimate criticism that the phase-out could have been achieved faster, the federal government has nevertheless paved the way for a change in energy policy (Jänicke et al. 2002: 52; Reiche 2002).

In contrast, the major environmental organizations in Germany strongly criticized the government for its failure to achieve an immediate, environmentally sound discontinuation of nuclear energy. "We expected the Red-Green government to follow a clear and unambiguous path towards abandoning nuclear energy instead of looking for compromises with the nuclear industry. Thanks to the agreement, nuclear energy has been legally approved to continue at least until 2023, which will have severe consequences for a real energy change" (BUND 2002: 21; our translation).[4] Effectively, the agreement allows the generation of nuclear power in the future totalling about the quantity produced up to this point in time. This long-term perspective delays—at least in the short run—the diffusion of innovative power-plant technology, because such a deferral mitigates pressure for modernization on the industry's side. Further, the problem of finding a central location for the final storage of nuclear waste is not yet tackled—it is merely postponed (Mez 2001: 430).

The project to phase-out nuclear energy faced renewed criticism immediately after the German elections in the fall of 2002. Because of earlier concessions made by the chancellor to the nuclear industry, the government eventually had to give in and allow the oldest and most insecure German power plant in Obrigheim to operate for two years longer than originally scheduled (i.e. up to 2005).

The process of phasing-out nuclear energy has been mainly triggered by domestic factors. The potential for conflict is very high in this policy area because vested interests are directly affected. These conflicts are difficult to solve, especially when a coalition government is involved. Although not all actors are content with the results of the German version of phasing-out nuclear energy, judging from an international standpoint, it was a far-reaching decision.

Nevertheless, the process of phasing-out nuclear energy in Germany parallels a general trend in the EU: to date, half of the eight member states with nuclear units (i.e. Belgium, the Netherlands, Germany, and Sweden) have decided to phase-out nuclear power. Out of the total of 15 EU countries, three take a proactive approach in nuclear energy policy: namely, Finland, France, and the United Kingdom. Spain has placed a moratorium on the construction of new nuclear power plants since the Chernobyl catastrophe (Reiche 2002: 15–16). Some countries, for example, Denmark and Italy, decided against nuclear energy during an earlier phase.

Regarding the initiatives of the Red–Green government in the broader field of energy policy, the Renewable Energy Sources Act, as the core of the Red–Green energy and climate protection policy, can be regarded as particularly successful. This piece of legislation is assessed as being extremely positive by environmental experts as well as all stakeholder groups. It has led to a boom in renewable energies, not anticipated by the government itself. The share of renewable energies in the electricity market grew to almost 7.5 percent by the end of 2001, and the investment rate in this sector expanded by 1.6 percent. Wind-powered electrical energy grew three times, also creating 60,000 new jobs. With a steady increase over the past few years, Germany has become one of the major exporters of these technologies. Furthermore, it received exceptional international recognition for this novel approach (Hirschl and Hoffmann 2002: 8–9; Reiche 2000). The act now serves as a model for countries like France and the Czech Republic, who have adopted essential portions of the German legislation (BMU 2002b: 7).

Although the photovoltaic solar power share of Germany's total energy supply is still below 1 percent, it is worth noting that the German government succeeded in nearly doubling the capacities in this sector and thus putting the country in the lead in Europe and second (after Japan) worldwide. Concerning wind power, Germany expanded its leading margin and holds the top position internationally, providing about a third of the world's wind energy capacities and half of Europe's (Bundesregierung 2002b).

Despite its success, Germany may experience difficulties in trying to meet its international obligations. The reference value for Germany in the respective EU directive demands an 8-percent increase in the share of renewable energy on the electricity market, in the period from 1997 to 2010; this is equivalent to a target of 12.5 percent share for renewable energy. Experts say that the target will not be an easy one to meet (Reiche 2002: 16–17), but the German government is obviously more optimistic. The new coalition agreement of October 2002 set the goal of doubling the proportion of renewable energy consumption (*Primärenergieverbrauch*) by 2010 (compared to the ratio for 2000). Accordingly, the funding of the programs to raise the share of renewable energies is assured and will even be gradually increased.

The leading position of Germany in this area was underlined during the discussions at the World Summit in Johannesburg. At that summit, which took place just a few weeks prior to the German elections in 2002, the German government presented itself as the driving force behind EU environmental policy. Germany received international attention for its proposals in the area of renewable energy. Among other initiatives, Germany will sponsor an international conference on this issue in 2004. It intends to provide support to developing countries; and it is promoting the establishment of an international agency for renewable energy.

In the international arena Germany effectively combines pioneer strategies (Liefferink and Andersen 1998) to maintain its leading position; it convinces others to catch up, pushes its own solutions, and strives for international institutionalization. Recent developments show that Germany may become an international pioneer in energy policy, because the German version of phasing out nuclear energy is already being discussed as a model in several other countries. Moreover, in the area of renewable energy sources, Germany has already achieved forerunner status and is pursuing its proactive policy with an internationally oriented objective.

Ecological Modernization of the Economy via Ecological Taxes—Germany Catching Up

The consideration of ecological aspects within the tax system has been a very important element in the current government's strategy of ecological modernization. The basic idea behind the ecological tax reform was to shift the main share of taxes from the "labor factor" to the "environment factor" (as they are referred to in German government jargon) by continuously, but moderately, raising the price of environmentally harmful energy supplies, accompanied by an annual decrease of the costs for the social security system (Bundesregierung 2002e). Increased energy prices are designed to reduce energy consumption and to improve resource productivity in general; lower labor costs aim at improving conditions for maintaining and creating employment.

Focusing on the idea of an ecological tax reform as one of the main tools to ecological modernization in Germany, the new government agreed to set the goal of reducing the contributions to the social security system from 42.3 percent in 1998 to at least 41.1 percent of the taxable income. At the same time taxes on gasoline, heating oil, natural gas, and electricity were to steadily increase, being linked to potential results of negotiations over EU-wide energy taxation, and price developments on the global energy markets. In this way, it was intended that moderate increases in energy costs (introduced with a view to help reduce costs to employers) would ultimately contribute to an overall reduction in labor costs. A major part of the revenues from the eco-tax was supposed to flow into the general pension fund. This was designed to reduce contributions to the fund in the first stage (1999) from 20.3 to 19.5 percent and in a second and third stage to 19.1 percent (0.6 percent reductions for both employers and employees) (SPD and Bündnis '90/Die Grünen 1998, see table 10.2).

Table 10.2 German ecological tax reform

Petroleum products and electricity[a]	Apr. 1999	Jan. 2000	Jan. 2001	Jan. 2002	Jan. 2003
Gasoline (low-sulphur)	+6 Pf/l	+6 Pf/l	+6 Pf/l	+3 cents/l	+3 cents/l
Diesel (low-sulphur)	+6 Pf/l	+6 Pf/l	+6 Pf/l	+3 cents/l	+3 cents/l
Heating oil	+4 Pf/l	—	—	—	—
Natural gas	+0.32 Pf/kWh	—	—	—	—
Electricity	+2 Pf/kWh	+0.5 Pf/kWh	+0.5 Pf/kWh	+0.26 cents/kWh	+0.26 cents/kWh
Contribution to the national pension fund (percentage of chargeable income)	19.5	19.3	19.1	19.1	18.8[b]

[a] Pf/kWh, Pfennig per kilowatt hour; Pf/l, Pfennig per liter (2 Pfennig ≈ 1 eurocent); figures for the tax rates in euro have been rounded.
[b] Originally projected estimate.

Sources: BUND 2001b: 6; Bundesregierung 2002f.

Despite strong opposition to the ecological tax reform, the Red–Green government finally succeeded in passing the bill in the German parliament. Its implementation constitutes significant progress in explicitly integrating environmental concerns in fiscal policy. The eco-tax was to be implemented in several steps up to 2003, beginning in 1999, with an increase in mineral oil tax by 3.07 cents per liter. The same year an increase in heating oil tax by 2.05 cents per liter would occur, and an increase in natural gas tax by 0.16 cents per kilowatt hour was implemented (for the following years see table 10.2). Additionally, a general electricity tax of 1.02 cents per kilowatt hour was introduced.

The Greens and the SPD finally succeeded in implementing the ecological tax concept in Germany but, again, it is apparent that the Greens could not stand up to many of the SPD's demands. Compared to the initial concepts worked out by the Greens, they finally approved an increase of taxes on heating oil, mineral oil, and electricity, which differed markedly from what they had originally demanded. The same applies to the special provisions for the coal industry (especially hard coal). Where the Greens did succeed was in tax reductions for the public transportation sector and tax exemption for heat-power cogeneration plants. Generally speaking, however, it was primarily the SPD whose concepts were successfully pushed through.

Nevertheless, the ecological tax reform is one of the outstanding achievements of the Red–Green government. Energy resources have become more expensive, promoting energy conservation and contributing to global climate protection. Although the environmental benefits of the new tax system will take time to evolve, some positive effects are already visible: decreased gasoline sales in the transportation sector (minus 3 to 4 percent in 2000 and 2001), positive effects on CO_2 emissions (a reduction of about 2 to 3 percent compared to a counterfactual scenario), increased usage of public transportation or car sharing, and increased sales of low-fuel-consumption automobiles (only 3 to 5 liters per 100 kilometers) (DIW 2001: 221; BUND 2001b; Greenpeace 2002: 13–14; Trittin 2002: 39).

Criticism mainly revolves around the time frame of the eco-tax project, namely its termination of tax increases after 2003. Friends of the Earth, Greenpeace, and the German Council of Environmental Advisors (the SRU) urge the federal government to continue the moderate increase of taxes beyond 2003, to guarantee planning security and to safeguard the positive and sustainable effects that this new initiative can generate. Therefore, it is also necessary to reconsider the many special provisions and exemptions for industry. The concessions made here constitute one of the important reasons why the potential of the tax reform cannot as yet be fully realized and, in effect, an overall ecological change of the economic structure is hampered (DIW 2001: 225; SRU 2002: 359). Initial fears concerning negative effects on employment and economic development (competitive disadvantages through additional taxes) so far have proven groundless. As the eco-tax is part of a larger (income) tax reform package, private households are (in sum) not additionally burdened. However, positive effects on the labor market—one of the major pro-arguments of the German eco-tax concept—are determined by other economic factors such as oil prices and wage development (DIW 2001: 222–25).

The ecological tax reform was one important step in the process of sustainable structural change in the economy. A future challenge will be to integrate eco-taxation into a comprehensive reform of the whole system of finance and taxation. Ecological taxes can then serve as a useful instrument in those areas where tax incentives are more flexible than legal regulations or bans. At the same time, environmentally harmful subsidies—for example, for the hard (anthracite) coal or the airline industry—need to be cut back, and the national budget aligned in accordance with ecological criteria (Massarrat 2000; Loske and Steffe 2001; cf. Meyer and Müller 2002; Burger and Hanhoff 2002).

Regarding the development of eco-taxes, the picture looks different than it did in the case of the innovations in energy policy already discussed. Although in both areas radical policy changes were initiated, in eco-taxation Germany has not been an international pioneer.[5] The years-long debate on eco-taxation in Germany influenced other countries, for example, Austria, where an eco-tax was introduced earlier than in Germany (Reiche 2000). Despite these indirect spillover effects from an international standpoint, Germany had become a laggard in this policy field. As early as 1990, Finland introduced a carbon tax on fossil fuels, followed by Norway and Sweden in 1991, and by Denmark and the Netherlands in 1992. The Nordic countries introduced this policy innovation almost simultaneously (Kern et al. 2001a: 20; Tews et al. 2002). The diffusion process slowed down between 1992 and 1999 when only three countries introduced energy/CO_2-taxes (Belgium in 1993, Austria and Slovenia in 1996). Both Germany and Italy introduced such taxes as part of an ecological tax reform in 1999, and the United Kingdom introduced a "Climate Change Levy" in 2000 (Tews 2002: 4–5). Although Europe as a whole proved to be the most innovative in international comparison, this did not have any effect on Germany until the Greens came to power in 1998.

Nonetheless, in the 2002 coalition negotiations, the Greens were not able to assert themselves against the will of the Social Democrats and achieve an unconditional continuation of eco-taxation beyond 2003. The continuation will be contingent on a review of overall economic performance and emissions development in 2004. Because of large deficits in the national pension fund, generated by continuously high unemployment, the German government was forced to raise contributions to the fund to 19.5 percent for 2003, although this met with strong external as well as internal opposition from the Green coalition partner. However, without the additional eco-tax revenues, the national pension fund contribution rate would have risen even higher. Nevertheless, large segments of the German public viewed this increase as a failure of the eco-tax concept, which was originally designed to help stabilize the national pension fund contribution rate and, ultimately, to decrease it. In terms of other socioeconomic considerations and for the sake of public acceptance of ecological taxation, it would probably have been better had the German government sought an alternative method of refueling its flagging national pension fund.

Although the question remains open as to whether the reform will be successful in the long run, the government did succeed in catching up to other more advanced countries in this field. Successful models of forerunner countries were decisive as positive reference points for the acceptance of ecological taxation in Germany. A concept that had been discussed for years was finally introduced—the Red–Green coalition had eventually initiated a change of path.

Climate Protection Policy—Germany Staying Ahead

Since the ratification of the Framework Convention on Climate Change, international negotiations in the field of climate protection have gone through a very difficult process. The Kyoto Protocol did, however, lead to a commitment by the industrialized countries to reduce their greenhouse gas emissions by at least 5 percent from 2008 to 2012, compared to the respective levels for the year 1990. Among the group of industrialized countries, individual states have committed themselves to different targets: the EU to −8 percent, the United States to −7 percent, Japan to −6 percent, and Russia to ±0 percent. Within the EU, Germany set its goal to reduce its CO_2 emissions by 21 percent by the 2008–2012 period, compared to 1990 levels (Brouns and Treber 2002; Reiche 2002: 17).

In their coalition agreement of 1998, the SPD and the Greens stress the national climate protection target to reduce CO_2 emissions by

25 percent by the year 2005, compared to 1990 levels (SPD and Bündnis '90/Die Grünen 1998). One main impetus toward fulfilling this goal was the decision to launch a national climate protection program in October 2000 (Trittin 2000). This program confirms the ambitious 25-percent reduction target, and divides the responsibility for the remaining reduction among the following sectors: private households, buildings, energy, industry, and transportation.[6] Further projects include a new Energy Saving Regulation (*Energieeinsparverordnung*) for buildings, and a voluntary agreement on climate protection between the German government and the German business sector. In this agreement, business committed itself to reducing its own specific CO_2 emissions by 28 percent by 2005, compared to 1990 levels, and its specific emissions of all greenhouse gases by 35 percent by 2012, compared to 1990 levels. The government also made a commitment to reducing its own CO_2 emissions by 25 percent by 2005 and 30 percent by 2010 (BMU 2000).

As a result of the aforementioned initiatives, coupled with economic decline and a different energy mix in the new *Länder* following German reunification, greenhouse gas emissions in Germany declined by more than 18 percent in the 1990s (SRU 2002: 335). This makes Germany one of the few countries likely to achieve the emission goals set out in the Framework Convention on Climate Change and the Kyoto Protocol. Accordingly, this development is welcomed by almost all sources: "The German federal government has been able to keep and extend its international role as a pioneer in the field of international climate protection. Especially with regard to the Bonn negotiations on the Kyoto Protocol in July 2001, the German delegation took a leading role in guaranteeing that the negotiations would finally come to a successful conclusion" (BUND 2002: 33–34).

However, both the German Council of Environmental Advisors (SRU) and the German Institute for Economic Research (DIW) strongly criticize the ongoing subsidies for the coal industry—the most CO_2-intensive energy source. The current policy to secure the coal stores is not compatible with the ambitious German national climate protection program, which requires a fundamental review of the energy supply system, focusing ideally on the long-term phase-out of fossil energy sources (Böckem 2000; DIW 2000: 5–6; Bundesregierung 2002a; SRU 2002: 393–97).

Additional criticism articulated by Friends of the Earth—with Greenpeace and the SRU both agreeing—is that it is crucial for Germany's long-term development to finally incorporate into its national climate protection strategy the mid-term goal of reducing CO_2 emissions by 40 percent by 2020. This would show Germany's sincere commitment to its international responsibility in this area. The opportunity to establish an ambitious European-wide climate protection target would increase, and other European countries would be more willing to accept a common reduction policy.

A third point of criticism, particularly emphasized by environmental groups, refers to the lack of concepts for environmentally friendly mobility in the transportation sector, and reducing emissions generated through the renovation of old buildings in the construction sector. According to the respective NGOs, both areas contribute a high share of CO_2 emissions, and neither are given due consideration in the current programs (Greenpeace 2002: 12–13). The transportation sector, in particular, needs to be given stronger attention, because its share of national CO_2 emissions has grown steadily from 17 percent in 1990 to 21 percent by 2000 (Brouns and Treber 2002: 13).

In climate change policy Germany was active internationally prior to the 1998 elections. As early as 1990, an ambitious CO_2 emissions reduction program was introduced, and a voluntary agreement between government and industry was negotiated. The national CO_2 reduction target of 25 percent by 2005 was the highest among the pioneering countries (the Nordic states plus Germany). From an international perspective, Germany was the most successful country regarding the reduction of CO_2 and the other five greenhouse gases (although it must be noted that almost 50 percent of this reduction owed itself to so-called wall-fall profits, meaning that the collapse of the East German economy after reunification accounted for a large portion of the decrease in emissions, particularly by the mid-1990s) (Scheich et al. 2001: 364, 378).

In the 2002 coalition agreement, the SPD and the Greens agreed to carry forward their efforts in climate protection and in maintaining Germany's pioneer position. There is mutual consent within the coalition that environmentally harmful subsidies be subject to revision or removed altogether (e.g., the value-added tax exemption for inner-European flights). Nevertheless, and despite vigorous critique, the coalition partners agreed to ensure continued funding of the hard coal mining sector up to 2010 (although this will go hand-in-hand with further restructuring of the sector and steadily decreasing federal subsidies).

Responding to the claims of NGOs and environmental experts mentioned earlier, the new coalition agreement contains a commitment to a 40-percent reduction target for greenhouse gas emissions in the 1990–2020 period. Albeit this commitment is tied to a simultaneous concession by the other EU countries, Germany insists that the other EU member states agree (in the framework of the Kyoto Protocol) to an

EU reduction target of 30 percent within the same period. Thus, in the new Red–Green legislative term, Germany once again presents itself as an international and EU forerunner in climate protection; at the same time Germany is also pushing for European solutions.

National Strategy for Sustainable Development—Germany Lagging Behind

The concept of sustainable development has its origins in the 1987 report of the Brundtland Commission. In this report sustainable development was defined for the first time as development that meets the needs of the present without compromising the ability of future generations to meet their own needs (World Commission on Environment and Development 1987). Based on different international conferences and agreements sustainable development was made the guiding principle for all future efforts in these fields and since then serves as the basis for all measures to be taken. Following the Rio agreement, the UN General Assembly passed a resolution in June 1997 in which all signatory states were requested to complete a national sustainability strategy by 2002 (Stephan 2001; Umweltbundesamt 2002).

As only initial steps toward a national sustainability plan were taken by the former coalition government, the new Red–Green government formally integrated "sustainability" as a goal in its coalition agreement. The agreement states that the primary aim of "ecological modernization" is to be based upon the principle of sustainability, with Agenda 21 serving as the main guideline. It was agreed that the government would work out a national sustainability strategy with concrete goals and practices by the end of the legislative term and, in this way, it would create an instrument to promote ecological innovation and the implementation of Agenda 21 (SPD and Bündnis '90/Die Grünen 1998).

In the course of four years, the new government has taken definitive steps toward this goal, including the establishment of a "Green Cabinet" within the government and the German Council for Sustainable Development (*Rat für Nachhaltige Entwicklung*, RNE). The 16 members of the Council represent industry, environmental NGOs, trade unions, consumers' rights groups, the churches, and the scientific community. In December 2001 the first proposal for a national sustainability strategy was presented; after some modifications the final version was adopted in April 2002 (Bundesregierung 2002h).

The German national sustainability strategy contains three main elements, namely, an underlying concept upon which strategy is based, a management concept for sustainable development, and a set of programmatic priorities. The *underlying concept* is the core of the strategy determining the political and societal actions necessary to guarantee sustainable development. Four aspects of this concept are of fundamental importance: (1) justice between generations, (2) quality of life, (3) social cohesion, and (4) international responsibility. The *management concept* for sustainable development consists of management rules, a number of specified and, in part, also quantified goals for sustainability in different sectors, a number of indicators to measure progress by continuous monitoring, and review of performance. The *programmatic priorities* encompass eight areas in which goals and measures were further developed than elsewhere. In the field of environmental policy, the following four areas receive special attention: (a) climate protection, (b) environmentally friendly mobility, (c) agriculture, environment, and nutrition, and (d) land use.

In examining the final outcome of the process of formulating a national sustainability strategy in Germany, from the perspective of the two coalition partners, the results are not as positive for the Greens as they are for the SPD. By considering the position of stakeholders who explicitly point to the equal value of the three dimensions—economy, social issues, and environment—within the concept of sustainability, the SPD, with a hard focus on the economic dimension, functioned as broker and sought to strike a balance between various positions. A number of elements of the new strategy reflect the differing approaches: for instance, the establishment of indicators and goals for a review of performance was a concession to the ecological proponents in the coalition, while the importance attached to improving efficiency clearly reflects the main argument of the economic proponents in the coalition.

The general tenor of the discussion on the impact of the new national sustainability strategy is ambivalent. Despite some innovative elements in its overall approach, the national sustainability strategy has failed to deliver a comprehensive plan of action with the potential to steer future development in the direction of sustainability (Jänicke and Volkery 2002). The evaluation by the German Council of Environmental Advisors emphasizes some positive aspects—for instance, the convincing institutional design, the positive role of the management rules, and the formulation of quantitative goals that can be directly controlled. Nevertheless, it has also been shown that the strategy lacks several important elements and fails completely in other aspects. One important point here is that the few formulated concrete goals concerning the status of the environment are by no means sufficient. Additionally, the integration of the recommended 40-percent reduction in greenhouse gases by 2020 into the strategy was not taken into consideration. Also, raising environmental awareness among polluters has only just begun and needs to be developed further. In addition, the selection of indicators is not always appropriate, because some do not meet the requirement of representativeness; some goals are far too ambitious in relation to existing capacities for implementation of the management concept within the government (SRU 2002: 220).

Friends of the Earth, one of the leading German environmental organizations, argues, for example, that the government has failed altogether to produce an integrated approach; they claim that the government has instead merely proposed a catalogue of measures in the areas of energy consumption, agriculture, and mobility, reflecting only the specific interests of particular departments. Moreover, so Friends of the Earth claims, the measures indicated are composed almost exclusively of initiatives already incorporated into official government policy and do not represent any new or innovative long-term concepts (BUND 2002: 5–6).

In sum, the Red–Green government has fulfilled its goal of formulating a national sustainability strategy by the end of its legislative period, but it has not presented an approach that really offers any new ideas or that demonstrates its sincere commitments to initiating far-reaching reforms toward comprehensive sustainability in Germany. Nevertheless, it is positively recognizable that a start has been made, which can be built upon.

Looking at the introduction of national sustainability strategies in OECD countries, the conclusion to be drawn is that Germany has never been within the group of pioneers in this field. Although first steps to establish such a strategy were taken under the Christian–Liberal government, no strategy was approved in Germany until the Red–Green government came to power. In contrast, the approach of strategic, goal-oriented environmental planning spread very rapidly in the 1990s among the industrial countries, but also in newly industrialized and developing countries. Within a decade of the adoption of the first national environmental plans in Denmark, Sweden, Norway (1988), and the Netherlands (1989), more than two-thirds of OECD countries had adopted national environmental plans or sustainability strategies (Jänicke and Jörgens 1998; Kern et al. 2001a). Thus, only future development can reveal whether Germany will eventually take a proactive approach to sustainability policy or remain a laggard in this area.

Types of Strategies in Red–Green Environmental Policy

Following our indepth look at four different policy issues in Germany and the Red–Green initiatives undertaken in these areas, we now turn to table 10.3, which shows how the selected policies can be placed in the scheme developed here (see table 10.1). Starting from the legacies of the Christian–Liberal government and based on (1) the scope of policy change and (2) the position of Germany as a pioneer from an international perspective, we can draw the following conclusions.

In the case of a radical policy change, the policy window provided by the last elections finally resulted in a change of policy path. Although the overall impact of such radical changes cannot be estimated within a single legislative term because the implementation of the decisions takes much longer than four years, what we can say is that radical changes did occur in energy policy and ecological taxation policy. In contrast, for climate protection policy and the introduction of a German national sustainability strategy, only moderate policy changes could be observed. In addition, Germany's international position vis-à-vis environmental policy underwent a shift, and this shift is relevant for both cases where radical changes occurred (in energy policy and ecological taxation).

In the area of energy policy Germany is considered a pioneer today. Radical policy change helped Germany attain an international pioneer position. Although innovative approaches in the area of renewable energy resources existed before the Red–Green government came to power, these initiatives were systematically pursued and resulted in an extremely dynamic development. The phase-out of nuclear energy as well as the initiatives to support renewable energy sources have already had impacts on the policy of other countries.

Regarding eco-taxation, a radical change was facilitated by the fact that this issue was part of the election manifestos of both parties (Lightfoot and Luckin 2000: 165). Although Germany cannot be placed in the group of pioneers in the area of eco-taxation, Germany's international position

Table 10.3 Selected Red–Green government initiatives

International position	Scope of policy change (1998–2002)	
	Radical change	*Moderate change*
Pioneer	Energy policy	Climate protection policy
Laggard	Eco-taxes	National sustainability strategy

has certainly improved due to a successful strategy of catching up to other comparable countries.

In climate protection the legacies of the Christian–Liberal government are decisive for the leading role of Germany in the international arena. In this area, a staying-ahead strategy could be observed and Germany has managed to maintain its leading position in climate protection policy.

Finally, a national sustainability strategy was developed and decided upon during the first legislative term of the Red–Green government. However, the legacies of the Christian–Liberal government combined with the policy of the Red–Green government have ultimately resulted in Germany lagging on an international level. In contrast to its forerunner status in climate protection policy, Germany still lags behind many other countries such as the Netherlands, who have introduced more innovative approaches within the last few years.

To sum up, during the legislative term of the Red–Green government in Germany, radical change in environmental policy occurred in several areas, particularly energy policy and eco-taxation. This development was most likely to take place in these areas, as both issues were always high on the Green agenda and, therefore, became part of the coalition agreement. The phase-out of nuclear energy especially can be considered as one of the main goals of many Greens to be accomplished within their legislative term (Lees 2000: 112).

Conclusions

In their first legislative term, the Red–Green coalition set the coordinates for a new priority to environmental policy. The role of the Green coalition partner as the "driving force" and "watchdog" in this field shows the importance of the innovative capacities provided by Green parties in governments. Despite all—yet justified—criticisms, the Red–Green government's performance in the environmental policy field remains remarkable, especially in light of the strong and stormy opposition the German Ministry of Environment and its head, Jürgen Trittin, faced in the first years of the new government. Such developments, combined with the high priority of certain issues on the "green" agenda, triggered radical path changes. It seems that such changes are only possible if national driving forces are strong enough. The case studies do not provide evidence that such changes can be initiated by international factors alone. Although several countries had introduced eco-taxes, Germany did not adopt such innovations prior to the 1998 election. It does not seem likely that a Christian–Liberal government would have supported such policy changes.

There are different types of global policy convergence: It can be the result of harmonization processes within the EU or internationally binding agreements. Besides such "hard law" there are also the soft mechanisms of policy diffusion. Path changes are facilitated by innovative strategies of other countries because foreign models can be used by policy entrepreneurs as a point of reference.

Furthermore, a pioneer can influence the policy of other countries. In this respect, a striking feature of Red–Green environmental politics is their striving to achieve multilateral arrangements and international agreements, as evidenced by their efforts to push for national and international solutions. This international orientation is a tribute to Germany's status; its purpose is to defend the top position the country has achieved in some areas of environmental policy. By pressing other countries to commit to similar policies and implement comparable standards, Germany increases acceptance for its approach and thus avoids the risk of isolation and competitive disadvantage on international markets. In certain fields Germany serves as a catalyst for the diffusion of advanced environmental policies.

Regarding the perspectives of the Red–Green government, it can be stated that fundamental changes were brought about in formerly neglected areas, yet successful policies continued and expanded. Judging from recent developments, the government seems determined to proceed on the path that they have taken. Since the main environmental projects were launched in the last legislative term, the government will now have to deal with mainly safeguarding and expanding the policies, moving toward the "ecological modernization" of Germany. While in 1998 radical policy changes could be expected in at least some areas, it can be assumed that the second legislative term of the Red–Green government will be characterized by a period of stabilization. Therefore, in contrast to the previous four years, similarly vociferous public controversies are less likely; but, as a side effect, public and media attention given to environmental issues may decline. Despite their success in the 2002 elections, the Green party will have to struggle to secure its influence in the coalition. It has already become apparent that Germany's poor economic performance will alter the political agenda to the disadvantage of Green policies like eco-taxation or new environmental regulations.

Notes

We are grateful to Manfred Binder, Helge Jörgens, Claudia Koll, Stefan Niederhafner, Danyel Reiche, Werner Reutter, Kerstin Tews, and Helmut Weidner for helpful comments.

1. Besides Germany, there are only four other countries where Green parties became part of a governing coalition: Finland (1995), Italy (1996), France (1997), and Belgium (1999); on the impact of Green parties on coalition negotiations and governmental policy in general see Müller-Rommel (2002: 9).

2. Although the introduction of renewable energy sources and eco-taxation can be considered as part of the German climate protection program, they are separately analyzed here, because of the marked differences regarding the scope of policy change as well as Germany's international position.

3. *Gesetz zur geordneten Beendigung der Kernenergienutzung zur gewerblichen Erzeugung von Elektrizität* (Bundesregierung 2001, 2002a).

4. The indication of the year 2023 as the first year in which realistically all nuclear power plants will be phased-out, refers to the agreement on the amount of electricity still to be produced at each nuclear plant. The average productivity of each power plant was estimated at 95 percent, while the data for 2000 show that the average productivity was only about 86 percent. This lower percentage is also confirmed by the data of the preceding years. Since 95 percent served as the basis for the calculation of the amount of electricity still allowed to be produced, the operating time might be extended to 34 or 35 years (BUND 2001a).

5. The amendment of the Nature Conservation Act is a similar case and falls in the same category of "catching up." The instrument of the class action suit for associations (*Verbandsklage*) had been introduced in many other countries before an equivalent decision was taken in Germany.

6. By 1999, CO_2 emissions in Germany had decreased by 15.3 percent, compared to 1990 levels. All six greenhouse gases mentioned in the Kyoto Protocol had decreased by 18.3 percent, again compared to 1990 levels.

PART FOUR

Germany and the World: European Politics and Foreign Policy

CHAPTER 11

From "Tamed" to "Normal" Power: A New Paradigm in German Foreign and Security Policy?

August Pradetto

The following analysis discusses central aspects of the foreign and security policy of the Red–Green government in Germany between 1998 and 2002. I begin by addressing efforts by the Red–Green coalition to strengthen common European Foreign and Security Policy (EFSP) within the framework of European integration. Second, I assess the transatlantic dimensions, and finally, the policy vis-à-vis the UN and the Organization for Security and Cooperation in Europe (OSCE).

For decades Germany has regarded European integration as the focal point of its foreign and security policy. Since the conclusion of the Maastricht Treaty in 1992, the implementation of a Common Foreign and Security Policy (CFSP) has acquired primary importance. Based on the Amsterdam Treaty, which came into effect in May 1999, the Red–Green coalition attempted to advance these goals according to decisions drawn by the EU at the Cologne (June 1999) and Nice (December 2000) summits.

Since the very inception of the FRG, special ties with NATO and the United States of America have played into this European effort. While the significance of these ties had already began to diminish even prior to the dissolution of the Cold War and concomitant unification of Germany, they remained a constitutive element of German foreign and security policy after 1990 as well. In this regard, the first Red–Green coalition, as the first German government run by Social Democrats since

Germany underwent unification and gained full sovereignty, raised both distrust and new expectations among various constituencies. The Greens did not have a reputation as being amicable with either the United States or NATO, and a Green party member was to become foreign minister. Yet both NATO and the United States played a special role in German foreign and security policy during the 1998–2002 term of office. It is intriguing to research this role, which conflicted with Germany's previous political intentions and—in contradiction to the governmental party's agenda—contributed to the most dramatic transformation in German foreign and security policy and its military instrument, the *Bundeswehr*.

With these considerations in mind, it becomes particularly urgent to explore how the politics of the Red–Green government developed vis-à-vis the UN and the OSCE. It is not only the Social Democrats and the Greens, but also the conservative parties in Germany—namely, the CDU, CSU, and the more liberal FDP—which have cultivated the tradition of multilateralism and juridification in international relations. Given the catastrophic history of German foreign policy until 1945, the foreign and security policy of the FRG remained focused upon the realization of objectives established by the international community in the Charter of the United Nations in 1945. Germany's foreign and security policy thus sustained an "institutionalist" orientation that contrasted with the more "realistic" or pragmatic tradition pursued in British and U.S. foreign policy. However, Germany's participation in the 1999 Kosovo and the 2001/2002 Afghanistan war created dilemmas for the Red–Green government. I, therefore, focus not only upon how Red–Green politics have played themselves out within the UN and the OSCE, but also on the general course of German foreign and security policy.

European Foreign and Security Policy

In determining strategic and operational tasks, the Red–Green coalition gave top priority to European integration, stressing that the incorporation of Germany into the EU was "of central importance to German politics" (Coalition agreement 1998: ch. XI, item 2). Emphasis was also placed on Germany's future willingness to join the integrative-multilateral sphere of the EU, despite its increased power potential and its considerably more important position in Europe and the world since unification in 1990. While Federal Chancellor Gerhard Schröder invoked the term "national interests" more often than other politicians and sought cross-party legitimacy for his political platform by more strongly emphasizing "German interests" (Schröder 1999b, 2002c), this has by no means undermined an accentuation of integrative-multinational orientation in German foreign and security policy. The federal government regarded European integration as essential to the realization of national, European, and international security, and the Red–Green coalition was fully cognizant of the fact that Germany's power and influence primarily rested in Europe (Fischer 2001b). Foreign Minister Joschka Fischer, in particular, devoted himself to drawing up a European basic rights charter (Fischer 2000c). The EU enlargement policy progressed to the level of concrete accession negotiations and dates for a whole series of Central and East European as well as Mediterranean countries (Schröder 2000).

The coalition agreement proclaimed that the CFSP created through the Amsterdam Treaty was empowering the EU to act in international politics and to further the safeguarding of common European interests. The federal government would continue to strengthen the "communitization" (*Vergemeinschaftung*) of the CFSP, since the intent behind the CFSP was to increase the EU's capacity to prevent civil crisis and resolve conflicts peacefully. The Red–Green coalition would therefore support majority decisions, more foreign authority, the strengthening of the European Security and Defense Identity (ESDI), and would work toward further developing the Western European Union according to the terms of the Amsterdam Treaty. The coalition would furthermore exert its influence within the EU to strengthen the OSCE and UN through "joint action" (Coalition agreement 1998: ch. XI, item 3).

Common Foreign and Security Policy, the Nature of European Security and Defense, and the European Forces

After four years of Red–Green government, progress on the issue of security and defense has been minimal and accompanied by much ambivalence. Despite partial rapprochement with the European Community (EC) regarding the overall institutional framework, and in particular, the incorporation of the European Parliament (EP) and Commission, the CFSP is still divided into an intergovernmental "2nd pillar" distinct from the supranational "EC pillar." This means that, for the time being, each member state is still responsible for its own foreign policy. The intergovernmental nature of the CFSP is also reflected particularly in the decision-making procedures that are subject to the principle of unanimity while majority decisions have already become a common feature in other areas of the EU.

When the EU took more radical steps and deliberations with regard to the CFSP, it was not just in response to the negative experiences encountered by the Europeans amidst the warring factions in Kosovo and/or Yugoslavia in the spring of 1999 (Pradetto 1999) and later, but in response to unilateral actions pursued by the United States following the 11 September 2001 terrorist attacks—actions that the Europeans felt were self-serving. At the same time, the lack of consensus in European foreign policy became particularly evident during these crises in 1999. France, Great Britain, and Germany vacillated between different positions, undermining the spirit of cooperation in foreign policy among Europeans. Joint projects such as the formation of European crisis reaction forces were motivated more by the fear of a possible withdrawal of U.S. forces from Southeastern Europe than by any coherent political strategy. This resulted in the decision that Europeans should have operational joint forces. The reasoning was that the Europeans should be able to act independently in accordance with their own security and defense policies, in the event that the United States withdrew from European crisis regions such as Southeastern Europe or commit insufficient forces (Arnold 2002).

The Red–Green coalition's attitude toward this issue was variously characterized as unbalanced, ambivalent, double-strategic, coherent, or complex. Within the framework of a further "Europeanization" of Europe, it sought to strengthen common politics and common institutions, especially in the deficit-ridden area of foreign and security policy. Yet for both financial and political reasons, the SPD–Green government also sought to avoid the possibility of competition between the European forces and NATO that had surfaced under former governments. Given the limited resources available for defense in Europe, the doubling of force and command structures would be most imprudent. It was reasoned that the European forces should be linked to the NATO structure in terms of forces and policy-making, and be available as modules for deployment by the EU (Volle and Weidenfeld 2000).

The Red–Green government thus more or less continued what has become a tradition of European political ambivalence about foreign and security policy. On the one hand, the government wanted considerably more "Europeanization," but by no means as much as France, resulting in the pursuit of more independent EFSP while also supporting the U.S. presence and NATO. The perception of the necessity for greater European independence intensified during the Kosovo War, as the German government and the minister of defense felt not just poorly informed, but even ignored and duped by decision-makers in Washington. Yet the government was also anxious not to jeopardize close ties with the United States as it engaged in debates on a Europeanization of the EFSP.

Of course, German diplomacy also had to contend with Great Britain, a country that had traditionally exerted strong support for the predominance of NATO in European security and military issues and continued to do so following the radical continental changes in 1989/90. All London governments regarded the United States as a safeguard for maintaining a balance of power in Europe. That a mutual social-democratic rapprochement was able to take place between Tony Blair and the Schröder/Fischer team is historically unique, but the British position never went so far as to reduce the importance of NATO in favor of European security policy and European forces.

While some may feel that the Red–Green government implemented the Maastricht, Amsterdam, and Nice decisions at "a snail's pace," some progress in controlling the CFSP was made under the Schröder/Fischer term of office. The further development of the CFSP is now essentially the responsibility of the General Affairs Council, in which all foreign ministers of the 15 EU member states hold representation. The Council normally meets once a month, and now has some tools at its disposal for exerting control over the CFSP as defined in the Amsterdam Treaty. So, in summary, following implementation of the Amsterdam Treaty and the peaking of the Kosovo War, an attempt was made to stimulate the progress of the development of both the CFSP and the European Security and Defense Policy (ESDP).

The Kosovo War had a catalytic effect on the common EU foreign policy formulated in the Amsterdam Treaty, and the 11 September 2001 attacks became a litmus test for the procedures thus far established. Following the terrorist attacks on New York and Washington, the EFSP witnessed a major throwback to nationally oriented foreign policies, with member countries of the EU largely acting independently and/or in bilateral consultation with the United States. The EU had to confine itself to internal crisis management—very much in contrast to the original intention of giving the CFSP a face and voice in serious crises. The task now became one of trying to minimize the consequences as Great Britain, France, and Germany lapsed into nation-state patterns of crisis management.

In a special session in Brussels on 21 September 2001, the European Council adopted an action plan aimed at strengthening judicial cooperation, preventing funding of terrorism, increasing flight safety, and incorporating the fight against terrorism more effectively into the CFSP, in particular, and the EU, in general. At the same time, the member states disavowed common foreign policy measures and no signs of uniform action pursued by the EU could be discerned. For example, Britain's foreign Minister Straw traveled to Pakistan, Saudi Arabia, and Syria immediately following the terrorist attacks without consulting with other EU members. It also became evident during this crisis that among all the EU member countries, France, Great Britain, and Germany would be the major decision-makers in determining the CFSP (Algieri 2002: 597), once again evincing the discrepancy between programmatic definitions and real politics within the federal government when it came to military crisis management. It fits perfectly well with this overall assessment that the coalition agreement made no reference to the military components of a CFSP and that respective ideas were summated only via very brief and vague statements on "civil crisis prevention," "peaceful conflict settlement," and "strengthening of the OSCE and UN." Concrete developments, then, went far beyond the problems identified and intentions expressed in the coalition treaty; as mentioned earlier, the Kosovo War in particular had a catalytic effect in this area.

Civilian Crisis Prevention and Peaceful Conflict Settlement in Southeastern Europe

After the Balkan region had been stabilized with the leadership and support of the United States, the EU indicated with its Stabilization Pact for Southeastern Europe that it considered itself the political authority qualified to determine the future of the Balkans, premised on the conviction that prospects for peaceful coexistence and the prevention of further violent conflict could only be secured through a long-term commitment and the establishment of civil structures. That the Europeans would have to bear the major portion of the burden was self-evident. Following the Kosovo conflict, Germany's government actively worked to ensure that the EU would address these challenges.

The decision-making process within the Union aimed at placing Kosovo—for several years, if not decades—under an international administration formally supervised by the UN, but, in practice, funded and organized by the EU. In this respect, the German presidency during the Red–Green tenure made a major contribution toward defining at least the conceptual framework for such a solution (Krause 2000). The Germans had initiated the Stabilization Pact for Southeastern Europe even before the end of the Kosovo War, and under their leadership, the EU accepted a political role that complemented the military one carried out by NATO in the settlement of the conflict (Katsioulis [n.d.]).

In January 2000, the EU Agency for Reconstruction officially took up its work in Kosovo and thereby became the successor of the TAFKO (Task Force Kosovo), which had initiated immediate relief measures such as demining, restoration of housing and power supply, as well as setting up local governments immediately following the end of the hostilities.

The EU has taken over a leading role in the implementation of the Stabilization Pact for Southeastern Europe and represents one of its financial pillars. Between 1991 and 2000, it made available more than 5.1 billion euro in relief funds, not including the bilateral payments made by individual member countries. An estimated 80 percent of the Kosovo Force (KFOR) personnel came from EU countries, with a contingent of 800 European police officers that is subject to increase. The EU has managed to maintain its high level of aid during the new decade as well, making available approximately 852 million euro for the five Western Balkan countries, with Germany contributing the largest individual share. In addition, the EU and Germany participated in a number of NATO-led operations like "Essential Harvest" that was seamlessly followed by operation "Fox." Apart from protecting the international observers with approximately 1,000 security personnel, the EU has agreed to also bear the expense of 38 million euro per year needed to station 500 police officers from EU countries, including 115 from Germany, in Bosnia Herzegovina. In conclusion, I would note that EU and NATO success in reducing economic, social, and political problems in Southeastern Europe was due not in the least to substantial contributions from Germany. These tasks could be tackled only by a historically unprecedented institutional and military commitment whose end remains nowhere in sight.

The interrelationship of civil and military crisis management should be discussed in this context. In the early 1990s, the federal government under Kohl/Genscher had promoted the dissolution of Yugoslavia by recognizing Slovenia and Croatia. However, the Yugoslavian wars confirmed concerns traditionally harbored by France and Great Britain about the need for a territorial status quo policy to guide German and European politics. But this approach confronted both the German government and the EU with the dilemma of continuous military commitment as a precondition for civil crisis management in Southeastern Europe. They faced opposition from political elites on the Balkan who did not want to relinquish their claim for *nation-building* (and, thus, for change of the territorial status quo and existing borders), and to date the situation has improved only incrementally. The civil and military commitment extended by Germany and the EU to Southeastern Europe is fraught with complications, having inspired a chain reaction among other political elites also seeking to exploit the Western military conflict settlement to enforce their own interests.

Military conflict resolution has thus become caught up in the whole dilemma (Pradetto 2002a). While NATO and the EU understandably wanted to maintain the territorial status quo, large portions of the elites in Southeastern Europe tried to capitalize on the collapse of Yugoslavia and to complete their own nation-building. This implied either rectifying territorial borders along ethnic boundaries or maintaining the territorial borders in those instances where ethnic minorities demanded autonomy or even independence. NATO and the EU, in contrast, placed their hopes in public policy to install properly functioning multicultural and multinational societies in Southeastern Europe (Pradetto 1998b).

To the extent that one regards Western policy appropriate, the means, the objectives, and the consequences of military crisis settlement are legitimate. Conflict settlement by NATO and by military means are justified to the extent that the priority lies in maintaining a condition of nonwar and maintaining the territorial status quo while establishing multinational societies. If, however, the peoples' right of self-determination is regarded as a precondition for the internal legitimization of existing states and thus, also for maintaining peace, cooperation, and security in the region, military conflict resolution will perpetuate the type of renewed struggle for nation and territory endemic during the past decade in the Balkans.

Western military crisis settlement has thereby become nearly a precondition for effecting more far-reaching public policy needs resulting from the Western status quo policy. The divergent interests put forth respectively by the western guardians of military conflict resolution and by many elites in the former Yugoslavia have confronted NATO and the EU with an extremely difficult task, namely, *state-building*. The situation is most dire in Bosnia-Herzegovina, where military conflict settlement has resulted in a constitutional situation requiring allocation of unprecedented resources to establish a properly functioning state, even as these measures have not yet met with much success. Furthermore, it has become particularly evident during the Red–Green term of office that the political strategies applied in Southeastern Europe resulted in expansion that went far beyond the aim of containing violence.

NATO and the United States

The coalition agreement stipulated: "The new federal government considers the Atlantic Alliance an indispensable instrument for stability and security in Europe and for the establishment of a lasting peace order" (Coalition agreement 1998: ch. XI, item 4). The government also declared that—in continuity with the policies of its predecessors—U.S. involvement in the Alliance and its presence in Europe remained "preconditions for security on the continent." In the next sentence, however, the Red–Green government stressed the particular desire to incorporate Russia and to cultivate partnership with this country in the interests of European security. They also promoted blending other countries of the postcommunist region with "western structures" such as the Ukraine, and with "the other participants in Partnership for Peace," and with NATO. The federal government also stressed that "the door to the Alliance" would remain open for other democracies, as it aimed for a stable pan-European peace order. Already agreed upon were the admission of the three Eastern Central European postcommunist countries, Poland, the Czech Republic, and Hungary, and the date of their official membership, namely, the Alliance's Jubilee Summit on the occasion of its fiftieth anniversary in April 1999. Thus, the government's programmatic statements on NATO politics could be interpreted as being institutional in nature, with the intention to contribute to a pan-European security and peace order through increased incorporation of the postcommunist region into NATO. The description of the relationship of NATO with the other European security institutions could be understood in this sense as well. The federal government vowed to promote "close cooperation, effective coordination, and reasonable division of tasks" between NATO and other institutions responsible for European security (Coalition agreement 1998: ch. XI, item 4).

Otherwise, there was nothing else in the coalition agreement—let alone in the election programs of the two parties—indicating a special commitment to the further development of NATO or to limiting NATO's eastward expansion. NATO was identified as an "indispensable instrument" of European security; its real meaning in the government parties' thinking became relative by the other statements made in this context. This stood in clear contrast to the U.S. government's intentions to give NATO a greater political and military significance and a more global sphere of activity. The brief statements issued by the Red–Green government about the Alliance and its inclusion in an overall context of security political organizations effectively countered the U.S. government's plans for the Alliance.

At the same time, the brief remarks contained in the coalition agreement seem to accept that NATO was evolving from a defense community to a security and interest organization prepared to deploy its military for more than merely defensive purposes. Of course, by asserting that the federal government would make efforts within the framework of a forthcoming NATO reform toward "binding the tasks of NATO outside Alliance defense to the rules and standards of the UN and OSCE" (Coalition agreement 1998: ch. XI, item 4), the Red–Green coalition moved toward a further "juridification of international relations." At first glance, this would seem to be a redundant declaration of the terms of the original NATO Treaty of 1949, which explicitly refers to the Charter of the United Nations and regards itself as an organization operating within that framework. However, the need to reassert this declaration is more understandable in light of the heated debates in 1998 regarding NATO's future tasks, in which the United States pressed for a decoupling of the Alliance from the UN and possible military involvement in tasks going beyond Alliance defense and the original restriction within the Alliance area of NATO.

In the coalition agreement, the United States was identified as "the most important non-European partner of Germany" and as an "indispensable constant of German foreign policy." Another expression of mild enthusiasm asserts, "a close and friendly relationship with the USA (is based) on common values and common interests" (Coalition agreement 1998: ch. XI, item 4). The wording about NATO gave the impression of a compromise between Red and Green, with the Greens accepting the Alliance as "indispensable" and thus "foreign policy-capable," on the condition (stipulated by the SPD, as well) that Alliance policies would be bound to international law and the UN. It was furthermore assumed that NATO would engage in "coordination" and "reasonable division of tasks" with other institutions responsible for European security, such as the UN and OSCE. In practice, however, the Red–Green government had to completely reorient its NATO policy very swiftly when the international political environment changed in fundamental ways and other key players attached more importance to Alliance policy than the two ruling parties had originally assumed and expressed in the coalition program.

This reorientation started before the new government was even sworn in. The turning point was arguably evinced in Germany's agreement to participate in NATO military action under U.S. leadership, in the event that Milosevic refused to comply with the ultimatum issued by U.S. Special Commissioner Richard Holbrooke requesting removal of the bulk of the Belgrade troops and militia forces from Kosovo. The decision was announced on 16 October 1998 under the Kohl interim government, which conducted business until the election of the new government by the *Bundestag* at the end of October, in close cooperation with SPD and Green leaders. Thus the Red–Green coalition *nolens volens* gave preference, first, to military threats rather than the preferred "preventive policy" and, second, to NATO Western military Alliance rather than to a pan-European multinational organization such as the OSCE. Third, the incoming government parties (in accordance with the opinions of SPD and Greens) abandoned their previous request for a mandate by the UN Security Council, which at that time held exclusive power under international law to adopt such measures.

Committing NATO to Rules and Standards Established by the UN and OSCE

Similar tendencies could be observed in Germany's support of the U.S. negotiations at Rambouillet. Here, too, the expressed war threat was intent upon ignoring the UN, against valid international law. Participation in the Kosovo war against the mandate of the UN represented the most flagrant violation of highly valued principles. Although the authorization of NATO missions was controversial in Germany, the lack of a mandate for the Kosovo mission was tolerated in the Red–Green coalition with the exception of a few Green MPs and even fewer SPD members of the *Bundestag*.

An analogous change of course is amplified in the approval of the new Strategic Concept adopted by NATO at the Washington Summit on 23/24 April 1999, which established principles for determining objectives, tasks, and future operational actions of the Alliance. Beforehand, three controversial issues needed to be clarified (Pradetto 1999; Alamir 2000). First, the future core function of NATO was in question: originally, back in 1991 it had been agreed that security, the transatlantic alliance, and collective defense would remain NATO's focal tasks. While this still remained valid, it is true that collective defense had assumed center stage. There were diverging opinions regarding whether to uphold these central tasks or whether to assign equal significance or even higher priority to new tasks pertaining to international crisis management. Closely linked with the dispute over core function was, second, the question of geographic range and/or responsibility. Should NATO become an instrument of worldwide crisis management, or should it, as advocated by a majority of European countries and Germany in particular, be confined to its previous treaty area, that is, crises and conflicts within Europe? Third, there was the problem of mandating NATO for non-Article 5 operations; that is to say, administering crisis management tasks outside the realm of collective defense. Here, particularly France (and in the beginning Germany) took the view that non-Article 5 activities should be strictly contingent upon authorization by the UN Security Council. The United States, on the other hand, regarded such a legal binding of *out-of-area*-operations restricting the Alliance's ability to act effectively.

In other words, the issue came down to the future tasks and powers of NATO in three aspects: its functional parameters (for defense or, beyond that, for military crisis management), its geographic parameters (as limited to the treaty area or unlimited to surroundings of the "transatlantic area"), and finally, its duty to international law (whether bound by the mandates of the UN Security Council or considered "self-mandating"). As the new Strategic Concept indicates, a decision was made in favor of canceling previous restrictions in the three areas outlined. While the UN is still regarded as a "primary agent" in the preservation of international security and peace, an exception was made permitting military action outside these parameters, that is, outside the established treaty area, outside the state of defense, and outside the jurisdiction of the UN Security Council.

Efforts were made to camouflage the manner in which this decision contradicted earlier principles (and the foreign policy credo of the SPD and Greens) by emphasizing the "exceptional character" of, for example, the measures taken in Kosovo and of the programmatic statements made in NATO's new Strategic Concept. In effect, it was asserted that principles were not being abandoned and European and world peace remained the "responsibility" of the OSCE and UN. In addition, they consulted formulations of international law and suggested that there was agreement between the previously shared principles and the new contradictory measures; the latter were simply "further developments" of international law or "new adaptations under customary law" (Hippler 1999). In reality, however, even as NATO underwent reform it had not been committed to the rules and standards of the OSCE and UN reform. Instead, the earlier rules and standards were retroactively adapted to the new principles and policies of NATO laid down in the new Strategic Concept.

The United States was also successful in implementing the new Strategic Concept because nobody else had ever thought to demand such a reorientation. The consent of the Red–Green government is especially remarkable in this regard. The Kosovo War that started five months after the election of the Red–Green government was an example of the application of those new principles. The federal government justified participation in the Kosovo War as the need to become active *out of area, out of UN*, and *out of defense*. Both the war itself and the definitions in the doctrine were declared an exception, with the Alliance's defense function remaining the main task. But in reality, given the existing balance of power and the changed political and military conditions, only a non-Article 5 and out-of-area operation was conceivable in the foreseeable future. Defense against an attack on the countries of the NATO Alliance became an unlikelihood.

This reorientation was evident in the deployment of the *Bundeswehr* in the operation "Enduring Freedom," aimed at repelling al Qaeda attacks and bringing about regime change in Afghanistan—again, by circumventing the UN (Pradetto 2002c). In this instance, the federal government referred to the *casus foederis* (Art. 5 of the Washington Treaty) invoked by NATO, even though this clause was itself of dubious legitimacy, given the legal issue of self-defense until the UN Security Council takes the required measures (Bruha and Bortfeld 2001). But an "emergency case" was declared in light of the international problems and the complaints at the grass roots level of the two government parties, herein forcing an "adaptation" rather than a change of the rules.

However, the government and particularly the Green foreign minister vigorously tried to bring the UN (and the OSCE, if necessary) "back into the game," inviting the UN to end the military conflicts and bring about a "political solution," as had happened following the first bombings supervised by NATO in the Federal Republic of Yugoslavia in late March 1999 and also after a brief period of war in Afghanistan. An effort was made to reverse the marginalization of the UN for which Germany had been in part responsible during the pragmatic search for compromises and multinational solutions to violent situations, and also in the interest of internationally distributing the tasks that still needed to be accomplished in Kosovo and in Afghanistan after the war. However, the SPD and Greens abandoned this approach when faced with poor opinion-poll results for the federal elections on 22 September 2002, reverting to their platform of foreign policy principles and harshly criticizing the Bush administration's declaration of a war against Iraq. Widespread domestic and international rejection of an "Iraqi adventure" gave the SPD and Greens as antiwar parties the license to attack politicians of the opposition parties who had not unilaterally ruled out *Bundeswehr* participation in a U.S.-led war against Iraq.

NATO Enlargement to the East

The Alliance decided in July 1998 to permit the enlargement of NATO and received the nations of Poland, the Czech Republic, and Hungary in

April 1999. This was the first enlargement to take place since the end of the Warsaw Pact, the Cold War, and the East–West conflict. Discussions about the war in Kosovo and evident disagreement within the Alliance about the use of military technology pushed other security issues into the background and lent urgency to the need to develop a common ESDP. Germany, in particular, sought to exert decisive influence on the development of the ESDP. Attempts among some postcommunist countries, especially the Baltic States, to put the issue of enlargement back on the agenda were unsuccessful. The Schröder government was very reserved about the Baltic States because of the deteriorating relations between NATO and Russia during the war in Kosovo and because of the general reluctance of the United States to engage more actively in NATO and Eastern European matters. This reserved stance was prevalent not only among the parties in power but also among the opposition parties, which were not interested in any measures leading to the inclusion of other countries into NATO.

The situation did not change until George W. Bush became president of the United States. While differences in opinion in Washington and Moscow were growing increasingly divergent on topic of the American enlargement plans, the German government remained skeptical about a new round of NATO enlargement, barely reacting to the Baltic States' increasingly vociferous requests to accede to NATO. The Baltic States were considered a "sore point" because their accession to the Alliance would create a direct border between NATO and Russia. Whereas when Poland joined NATO, the Alliance had only had to contend with bordering the Russian exclave of Kaliningrad, if the Baltic States were acceded into NATO, Kaliningrad would be surrounded entirely by NATO territory and cut off from Russia proper. During his visit to the Baltic States in October 2001, Rudolf Scharping, then German defense minister, declared it was still too early to discuss the possibility and procedures for a second round of NATO enlargement, but that decisions about possible enlargement of the Alliance should be made during next year's NATO summit. Only Slovenia's possible membership in NATO did not involve any points of contention.

It was only after the terrorist attacks of 9/11 and the subsequent improvement (virtually instantly) in relations between the United States and Russia, did circumstances seem fertile for German politicians to resume this security-related integration strategy—all the more so, as the unilateralization of U.S. policy and concomitant marginalization of NATO became evident. Inclusion of new members into the Alliance promised the continuation of the security-related stabilization policy by means of a NATO-enlargement already pursued by a growing number of the political elite in Germany since 1993/94. In addition, it was hoped that including new members would strengthen NATO's institutional-political dimension, which had been strengthened under Germany's then-chancellor Helmut Kohl and particularly emphasized by the Social Democrats throughout the 1990s. It was moreover hoped that accepting a fair number of states would compensate for the Alliance's growing loss of status. The Red–Green coalition also considered such a development advantageous for the pan-European security policy because it dovetailed with the efforts in Washington and London to include Russia more extensively in the Alliance.

Thus, what the SPD and the Green party share in their fundamental attitudes is a conviction that NATO should be utilized as an institution. Through intensified cooperation with the former communist countries in Eastern Europe and their increasing integration into the Alliance, NATO was to contribute to a pan-European security structure and, in so doing, provide an institutional basis for the earnestly desired security-related multilateralism. Only the future will reveal how much can really be achieved. Efforts to draw former communist countries closer to NATO represent an important basis not only for European security but also for a geographically extended multilateralism reaching across North, Central, and Southeastern Europe. However, cooperation between Russia and NATO is largely contingent upon the relationship between Washington and Moscow and therefore on the respective policies and situations of the top political echelons in both capitals.

Now, the transformation of the Alliance from a collective defense organization to a selective organization of intervention among participating nations is being advanced. If the former communist states were included in NATO, this would result in a general strengthening of the American position within the Alliance, since the postcommunist countries tend to have a strong affinity with the United States. Unlike the majority of the "old" NATO members, they would likely support a unilateral intervention-oriented global policy as currently pursued by the United States and act as their partner in case of an intervention. This is probably one of the reasons why Washington pursued its pro-enlargement policy, giving high priority to "national interests" when pursuing foreign policy, and engaging in an intense struggle in recent years to maintain dominance in NATO, so as to retain influence on European security policy and avoid competition with an increasingly independent Europe.

It is simultaneously evident that NATO is (and will remain) an "apparatus of consultation and consent." Even during the Cold War, all efforts to convert the organization into an instrument serving particular interests remained unsuccessful. The marginalization of NATO in the worldwide U.S. military campaign following the terrorist attacks of 9/11 confirms that it is impossible to use NATO as an instrument if important members disapprove. This was also evident in spring and summer 2002 during the debate pursued by the Bush administration on regime change in Iraq by means of military intervention.

The United States

The relationship between the German Red–Green coalition and the United States has been fraught with contradictions from the very beginning. Although statements issued by the SPD and the Green party in their election manifestoes and in their coalition agreement did not explicitly correspond with views in Washington, decisions made by the German government were quickly brought into line with the stance taken by the U.S. administration. This was, in part, attributable to the affection many Social Democrats and Greens felt for President Clinton as someone whose manners and political vision seemed agreeably different from the American cliché. More importantly, the new German government, as the first Left-oriented constellation of leaders, felt obliged to demonstrate its loyalty. Indeed, it sought to demonstrate particularly to the United States but also to all other partners as well as neighbors and countries in Eastern Europe that it would adhere to the principles of "continuity" and "reliability." Both these key terms were assigned a central position in the foreign policy rhetoric employed by the Red–Green coalition during the initial stage of their term of office (Fischer 2001b).

Yet, the government maintained that it needed to break away from traditional principles in foreign and security policy due to the extreme violation of human rights taking place in Kosovo, which was similar to a civil war and which resulted in refugees entering Central Europe and eventually also Germany. This was also the explanation for the Red–Green government's approval of an approach that, while it did not have the consent of the UN, was adopted by the United States, Great Britain, and eventually also by NATO. Even before the Red–Green government was elected by the *Bundestag* and sworn in by the federal president, they were "caught on the hop" by the Clinton administration, which firmly requested Germany's participation in NATO military actions in the event that Milosevic should fail to meet the aforementioned demands stipulated by U.S. special envoy Holbrooke. In contrast to the protests of the Green party, the coalition parties regarded this political move as a means to prove their loyalty and reliability.

Newly elected Green Foreign Minister, Joschka Fischer, contributed to the discussion of a new Strategic Concept for NATO by pushing one of the few concrete points of the Red–Green coalition agreement: specifically, the right of first use of nuclear weapons, which the Alliance had claimed in all military doctrines since its foundation because of the Soviet Union's conventional superiority in relation to Europe. Fischer sought to rescind this part of NATO's military strategy in light of the radically changed international environment since the end of the Cold War, and reasoned that this could represent the first step in the international disarmament policy proclaimed by the Red–Green coalition.[1]

However, not only the United States but also other nuclear powers became annoyed with this proposal, so Fischer had to quickly abandon this unique effort to formulate alternate strategies. It also became clear that the insistence on first right to use nuclear weapons was aligned with the U.S. global commitment and its goal of further globalizing its military capabilities and therein engaging in *power projection*. Since any U.S. or NATO troops would be quite vulnerable if deployed to areas outside Alliance territory, the threat of first use of nuclear weapons could serve as deterrence to potential enemies. In this context it is worth noting that the interpretation of military power involved only marginal references to "defense" as understood in the Cold War era. Indeed, during this debate the concept of defense was revoked and replaced by the idea of "security" and the interests of the Western Alliance (Lovelace and Young 1998).

Of course, the Red–Green government's participation in formulating these adaptations and strategy definitions for the NATO should not be understood to imply that the German armed forces will regularly participate in missions such as that in Kosovo or in Afghanistan. Nor will Germany's government or the NATO completely reverse their general foreign, security, and military policy. As stressed earlier, the debate about the consequences of the war in Kosovo and the events of 9/11 indicates that NATO has essentially remained an organization poised to take action only with the consensus of a majority of its members. While this was the case with the "Essential Harvest" mission in Macedonia in late summer 2001, it did not apply in the reactions to the terrorist attacks of New York and Washington. The war in Afghanistan effectively made clear that the differences between the United States and the Western European NATO members have increased. It also revealed that the United States remained completely uninterested in making decisions on NATO-level because it might restrict how the United States could conduct war.[2] From the point of view of American policy, NATO's significance could essentially be compared to that of the UN.

However, NATO's new strategy within the framework of the globalization of U.S. military power and its attendant doctrine of power projection may create new challenges for NATO and its members. With the increasing global presence of American or other national NATO forces, the vulnerability of these forces deployed to other countries will increase, too. It is difficult to predict the ramifications for the Alliance's defense capabilities, but the strategy of military expansion has already inspired the United States to terminate the Anti-Ballistic-Missile Treaty and to draft alternate plans for a regional missile defense system.

Fischer's initial suggestion to abandon the right to first use of nuclear weapons represents the only attempt to define alternatives to U.S. policy within the framework of NATO. Thereafter, the German government made every effort to foster cooperative transatlantic relations with the United States. Simultaneously, however, CFSP and ESDI became even more central to the security considerations of the Red–Green government. This ambiguous political orientation toward the United States was variously interpreted within the government. A minority, particularly within the Green party, complained that Germany was submitting to Washington's wishes, while others regarded Fischer's conduct as clever, realistic, and flexible. The latter contingent felt that the foreign minister was quick to recognize that opposition to the United States would not result in a larger scope of action but, on the contrary, cause difficulties and problems.[3]

Relations between the Red–Green government and the United States suffered a setback when George W. Bush assumed the presidency in November/December 2000. Politicians among the Green party publicly expressed their negative impression of the new president, and a majority of the German media and the German public shared these views. Among the first changes enacted by the new administration were an acceleration of missile defense plans (while accepting the termination of the ABM Treaty), stepping back from any attempts to interfere in the Middle East conflict, and threats to withdraw most of the U.S. troops from the Balkans. These first steps caused uproar and annoyance particularly in Germany. The generally confrontational military foreign and security policy pursued by president Bush left many Europeans with the impression that the United States intended to utilize its superior weapons to fight the enemy and then leave to Europe the costly, long-term, and hardly prestigious task of restoring peace to the region in the next decades (Bastian 2002).

As for the ESDP, the German government regarded its increased commitment as a real opportunity to draw conclusions from the war in Kosovo, and further sought to strengthen Europe's position to make it an equal partner in negotiations with the United States. The relationship between the Red–Green government and the United States was therefore characterized by: (1) a desire to maintain the transatlantic relationship and keep the U.S. armed forces in Europe; (2) efforts to increase European independence, foreign and security policy, and military capacities; (3) conflicting sentiments about either pursuing multilateral "European" structural aims or alternately charting the unilateral approach pursued by the Bush administration. With such a mixed agenda, the Red–Green government's policy toward the United States was virtually destined to lead to conflict, and an already difficult situation deteriorated even further as a result of disagreements about the role of the United States and NATO in the future ESDP, U.S. missile defense plans, the Bush administration's rejection of the Kyoto Protocol, and the International Criminal Tribunal, as well as their expansion of the war on terrorism waged against the so-called axis of evil.

The OSCE and the UN

In the coalition agreement, the OSCE was designated as the "only pan-European security organization" and therefore regarded as irreplaceable. The new federal government was thus compelled to promote and expand the legal basis of the OSCE and to enforce "mandatory peaceful concil-iation of conflicts." This involved strengthening instruments and compe-tences of the organization and improving its ability to prevent crisis and settle conflicts in nonmilitary fashion. The new federal government championed the design of infrastructure for crisis prevention and civil-ian conflict resolution that would include financial support of peace and conflict research (Coalition agreement 1998). However, these objectives were pushed into the background as the Kosovo conflict worsened and recourse to a more *Realpolitik*-oriented approach to events in the Federal Republic of Yugoslavia became necessary. Meanwhile crises surfaced in other regions of Southeast Europe and, finally, the United States revised its foreign policy after 11 September 2001, and NATO pursued its eastward enlargement policy. This trend was supported by political elites in Eastern Europe who regarded not OSCE but rather NATO as the primary means to achieve stabilization and democratization in postcom-munist areas of Europe (Pradetto 1998a; Pradetto and Alamir 1997).

However, an issue that had not even achieved resolution within the coalition program was the status of the OSCE as an "irreplaceable" instrument of European security vis-à-vis other security instruments and organizations such as NATO. The OSCE was to have a status similar to the UN. The new federal government therefore deemed it a "special task" to reinforce the OSCE politically and financially and to transform it into a body able to effectively solve international problems. For the purpose of UN missions, "stand by forces" were promised as "independent units" for peacekeeping measures. The new federal government would actively support the preservation of the monopoly of force at the UN and the reinforcement of the role of the secretary general of the UN. Germany would retain the option of becoming a permanent member of the United Nations Security Council if: (1) the reform of the Security Council was completed as part of a greater regional balance and (2) the European seat on the Security Council, which Germany in principle would have preferred, could not yet be obtained. The federal government would make sure that the means to enforce economic sanctions were extended and supported by sanction assistance funds (Coalition agreement 1998). However, despite a brief flurry of extensive debates, little progress was achieved on any of these issues during the Red–Green's coalition's term of office.

As mentioned earlier, these intentions and objectives failed not only as a result of broader international transformations taking place at that time. It was primarily the Kosovo War and the attendant revision of principles and international law that undermined the authority of the UN and the secretary general. The UN monopoly of force was challenged and denied, both implicitly and explicitly, and beginning in late 1998 a clear loss of jurisdiction was measurable in relation to other alliances, regional organizations, and ad hoc coalitions. However, Germany's financial support to the UN has been consistently high: next to the United States (with 22 percent) and Japan (with 19.7 percent), Germany is the third-largest contributor to the UN (9.8 percent of the regular budget in 2002), covering US$109 million in 2001. Mandatory contributions were also paid to various UN special organizations, with total German contributions in 2001 being in the area of 646 million euros (Auswärtiges Amt 2002).

The UN request for more autonomously available military capacities was not met despite promises made in the coalition agreement. But during the Red–Green term of office, the FRG, or more precisely, the *Bundeswehr* participated to an increasing extent in UN peace missions, with Germany contributing on average 10 percent of the mandatory contributions to every UN peace mission. Even prior to 11 September 2001, Germany was directly involved in 6 out of 18 UN missions/UN-mandated missions (UNIKOM/Iraq, UNMIBH/Bosnia-Herzegovina, UNMIK/Kosovo, UNOMIG/Georgia as well as SFOR/Bosnia-Herzegovina, and KFOR/Kosovo) and provided about 7,600 military personnel, some 450 policemen, and various civilian specialists. Early in 2002, about 900 troops from the *Bundeswehr* participated in the International Security Force in Afghanistan (ISAF); these units were later reinforced to a strength of 1,400. Germany was thus one of the leading countries in contributing personnel employed under a UN mandate. Since joining the largest UN peace force so far, UNAMSIL in Sierra Leone, which includes a civilian technical support team from the Federal Technical Emergency Relief Service, the German balance of services has been increased by another 20 troops. Germany has also financially supported individual missions (e.g., UNAMSIL, ECOMOG, MONUC) with millions of euros and provided donations in the form of equipment.

With the war in Afghanistan following the terrorist attacks of 11 September 2001 on the United States, the importance of the UN further declined; not only legal experts but even the UN secretary general felt that the system of international law standards had been further undermined. In the struggle against terrorism, the United States downgraded the UN to the task of nation-building, relegating it to the task of follow-up care upon completion of warfare and the change of regimes (Pradetto 2002b).

Concluding Remarks

Initially, the Red–Green government paid only scant attention to foreign policy. The Red–Green "project" was ultimately more oriented toward solving domestic problems, with foreign policy at best a "tail light"[4] of the coalition pact. It therefore comes as no surprise that the coalition was afflicted with a serious crisis when faced with foreign policy "adjustments" such as the wars in Kosovo and Afghanistan. The Red–Green coalition simply was not prepared for such contingencies. While it had been clear even prior to the election that the most sensitive issue for a future Red–Green government would indeed be foreign and security policy, no one—especially not in the Green party—anticipated such a dramatic and cumulated need for decisions on global issues conflicting most particularly with the Green platform on foreign policy.

This process of reorientation started even before the new government was sworn in. As mentioned earlier, on 16 October 1998, the *Bundestag* voted in favor of Germany's participation in a potential military operation of NATO against Belgrade—even without a UN mandate. Of course, many hoped anxiously that the operation would not need to be implemented and that the mere threat of military measures would cause Milosevic to give in. But after the failed peace negotiations in Rambouillet and Paris, Germany was to join the ultimatum presented to Milosevic, which involved the threat to militarily enforce an agreement on Kosovo. On 25 February 1999, the *Bundestag* agreed to the possible participation of the *Bundeswehr* in such an operation and, in the process, to contribute 6,000 troops in a military intervention in Yugoslavia not approved by the UN. However, the federal government was still convinced that Milosevic would give in, as he had done in earlier instances. Unfortunately, after several ultimatums had failed, NATO had to face its first war since its initial founding, and on 24 March 1999, hostilities began against the Federal Republic of Yugoslavia. Now stakes were laid on the assumption that Milosevic would surely give up within days, yet even this assumption proved fallacious. The first combat operation of the German air force dragged on much longer and turned out to be much more extensive than anyone could ever have expected.

During the Kosovo War the federal government agreed to NATO's new Strategic Concept of April 1999, which had been a controversial issue right up until its adoption. This involved establishing general conditions for the employment of German armed forces, as well as mapping new standard foundations for the deployment of NATO armed forces involving the option of out of defense, out of area, and out of UN operations.[5]

In the course of determining the current and future function of the *Bundeswehr*, the first Red–Green government negotiated a drastic transformation of paradigms. From 1998 until 2002, the parameters of the *Bundeswehr*'s task in preserving national and collective peace, as postulated within the scope of the coalition agreement, were exceeded in a manner unprecedented in the history of the FRG. Even during the discussion of NATO's new Strategic Concept in the spring of 1999, the principal task of the *Bundeswehr* was considered to be national defense and the defense of the allies. Three years later, the revision of the doctrine had been largely concluded and the transformation of the *Bundeswehr* into an "operative army" was fully underway.[6]

Just as striking was the contrast between an earlier lack of clarity about foreign, security, military policy principles, and strategies of action prior to the assumption of office and the later political practice.

The vast discrepancy between the Red–Green government's earlier theory and later policies were negatively perceived, particularly because expectations among major groups of the electorate and party members of the SPD and (most especially) the Green party were so completely different. The Red–Green government, and above all the Green political leaders, was burdened with constantly having to justify its specific foreign, security, and military policy to the electorate. Such explanations were all the more necessary under paradoxical circumstances that compelled individual representatives of the CDU/CSU and of other opposition parties to warn against accommodating Washington's wishes and strategies too extensively with regard to, for example, the Kosovo War; they, furthermore, raised the issue of independent German interests in the field of security policy. In the course of the so-called war on terrorism, the federal government was also subjected to reproaches from conservatives who argued that dispatching forces to Kuwait, where the United States was preparing for war against Iraq, would risk involving German armed forces in military activities that the government did not even condone.

In the aftermath of 11 September 2001, the discussion of public security policy suffered further setbacks as the federal government sought to balance the strategy of "unrestrained solidarity" with the United States, which involved military support, while trying to allay widespread unease about and criticism of a unilateral U.S. approach. This balancing act resulted in a policy of denial of knowledge: in spring and early summer of 2002, the federal chancellor, the foreign minister, and the defence minister persistently denied that there were U.S. plans to proceed militarily against Iraq.

During the close of the term of office and amidst the most intense phase of the election campaign beginning in late August, as sinking poll results raised doubts for the Red–Green government about its prospects of reelection in September 2002, the SPD and the Green party chose to return to the programmatic positions held prior to 1998. They vehemently criticized U.S. plans for military intervention against Iraq with the objective of toppling Saddam Hussein, and stressed that it was the responsibility of the UN Security Council to impose sanctions.

This change of German foreign and security policy is also remarkable in so far as a liberal–conservative coalition would have found it more difficult to implement such a policy. The coalition agreement represented a compromise between Red–Green principles of foreign policy and the pretense of "continuity" of German foreign policy and a continuing "close relationship" with the United States. None of the radical changes that took place during the term of the Red–Green government had been projected in this earlier agreement. Both the party programs of the SPD and the Greens and the coalition agreement suggest that the same foreign and security policy pursued by a Liberal–Conservative government would have raised massive protests and opposition from the very same parties that put this policy into practice.

One could say that within the history of the FRG the first Red–Green government has set a new precedent in reorienting foreign and security policy in Germany and the operational conditions for German armed forces. But one must also recognize that the transformation in security policy described here is part of a development already initiated in the late 1980s and early 1990s. German foreign, security, and defense policy were no longer threatened either by the Warsaw pact, or by a rapid increase in the Soviet arsenal, or by a withdrawal of nuclear protection by the United States. Instead, Germany wrestled with the collapse of the Soviet Union, the transformation of Eastern Europe, civil war in Yugoslavia, and the issue of how to respond to and ultimately prevent crises. Thus, the outbreak of civil war in Croatia, Bosnia, and Serbia, the ensuing acceleration in transnational migration, and the increasing number of UN peacekeeping missions led Germany to conclude that the use of military force was indispensable. In that regard, the German mission in Kosovo was almost an inevitable consequence. The missions of the *Bundeswehr*, first in Bosnia-Herzegovina, then in Kosovo, and finally in Macedonia, radically posed the question of the goals and agenda of an army confronted with new tasks and challenges. After the Kosovo War, with increased responsibility in KFOR, the Red–Green government had little choice but to pursue reforms initiated under the Kohl governments.

Both the changes in foreign policy and the Federal Armed Forces represent a change in paradigms most especially against the background of the Red–Green foreign policy program, which contrasted sharply with ensuing practices in Kosovo and in Afghanistan. These actions constitute a break with the doctrine of German troop deployment valid until then. However, the war in Kosovo and the mission in Afghanistan do not represent a change in foreign and security policy in the sense that the army was ascribed a completely new role as an instrument of German policy. Instead, the government was confronted with exceptional cases (i.e., first, the escalation of civil war and failure of diplomacy, and second, military support for the U.S. campaign "Enduring Freedom" following the terrorist attacks of September 11), cases not explicitly intended to establish a new foreign policy approach. This became evident not only through the ongoing emphasis placed on the "exceptionality" of the situation, but also through the stance of the German political elite during the dispute about a possible war against Iraq in 2002, which was not exclusively motivated by the ongoing election campaign. The approach of the Red–Green government is better explained by differently interpreting their "interests" as expressed through a refusal of the Bush administration's strategy of preemptive war in summer 2002, escalating risks in the Middle East, and a weakening of the international anti-terror coalition—arguments also brought forward by many Democrats in the United States.

Moreover, one can ascertain a strong degree of continuity within the Red–Green coalition with regard to many areas of foreign policy, including the very important issue of European policy pursued by Schröder/ Fischer in the spirit of enlargement and deepening of the EU, and Germany's commitment to European and global institutions. This stance is also evinced in Gerhard Schröder's formulation of pursuing a "German way" in its relationship with the United States, as postulated during the debate on Iraq and the German election campaign in August and September 2002. This phrase was retracted days later in Foreign Minister Fischer's remark, "Forget it!" and by Schröder himself who claimed to have invoked it only to refer to the domestic agenda.

Under the Red–Green government there was an undeniable change in paradigm for German foreign and security policy and for the use of the Federal Armed Forces. However, this change should primarily be understood as a means of adapting to a highly volatile environment and the resulting need for crises management. The first offensive deployment of the Federal Armed Forces in Kosovo and Afghanistan made apparent that transformations in German foreign policy and in the conditions for troop deployment had been underway for quite some time. Essentially, the FRG adhered under the Red–Green government to the foreign policy principles it had maintained since the end of the Cold War, principles that were and remain directed at integration, multilateralism, and the institutionalization of international relations on the basis of law.

Inasmuch as the FRG—to the extent that it is possible for contemporary nation states—has been able to act in full sovereignty since unification, it has mutated from a "tamed" to a "normal" actor in international politics. Germany continues to justify the particularity of German foreign policy—which stresses integration, multilateralism, and the institutionalization of law in international relations—through reference to the past and the responsibility for the course of history, and herein evinces that the nation does not fully regard itself as a "normal" power. But what exactly is "normal"? Acknowledging an awareness of historic mistakes and of historic responsibility can only enhance the integrity of national foreign policy.

Notes

1. "Scharping distanziert sich von Fischer. Irritationen um atomaren Erstschlag. Widerstand Albrights und Cohens. Besuch in Washington," *Frankfurter Allgemeine Zeitung* (25 November 1998): 1.
2. *Frankfurter Allgemeine Zeitung* (29 September 2001): 2.
3. "Scharping und Fischer finden eine Kompromissformel. Doch der Außenminister fordert weiter, die Nato-Strategie anzupassen," *Frankfurter Allgemeine Zeitung* (3 December 1998): 2.
4. U. Albrecht, "Neuer Anlauf in der Außenpolitik: Wo bleibt die rotgrüne Farbe?" *Frankfurter Rundschau* (6 December 1998): 9.
5. The coalition was faced also with a crisis by the debate about the issue of providing Turkey with a Leopard 2 Main Battle Tank for test purposes (with a view to subsequent procurement), which was accepted; critics argue, the position of the Red–Green government thus hardly differed from the position held by the conservative–liberal predecessor governments, which had been vigorously criticized for such arms exports. The de facto consent was justified by referring to the minority position of the German foreign minister at the Security Council.
6. "Die letzte Chance der Nato," *Die Welt* (25 July 2002): 3.

CHAPTER 12

European Politics of the Red–Green Government: Deepening and Widening Continued

Barbara Lippert

E uropean politics represented a challenging policy area for Germany's first Red–Green coalition. The new government had to confront the long shadow of Kohl's overwhelmingly positive record in European politics, as well as the widespread bipartisan recognition of his successful policies. Indeed, there was effectively no compelling demand for change. Notwithstanding Kohl's reputation as "Mr. Europe," some concern had developed about the late Kohl government's commitment to a stronger and more integrated EU following the disappointing results of the treaty revision in Amsterdam in 1997. This spurred the Red–Green government to equip Germany as an engine for European integration by means of a government prepared to pursue a deepening and widening of policy against the background of structural changes taking place internationally.[1]

Continuity and Change: EU Policy-Making and Policy-Makers

The first Schröder/Fischer government sought to maintain continuity for European politics at the level of political orientation as well as in policy-making. While Chancellor Schröder and Foreign Minister Fischer were new actors on the EU scene central to policy-making, those who had followed Fischer's writings and his speeches in the *Bundestag* and on other public occasions were already familiar with his views on foreign policy and European politics (Fischer 1994, 1999a,c, 2000a,b,d, 2001a). Considered somewhat of an eccentric within the Green party until 1998, Fischer leaned heavily on mainstream foreign policy convictions in Germany. He adhered to the *raison d'être* of instinctive multi-lateralism, pro-integration politics, prudent self-confinement (Fischer 2000d; also Fischer 1998a: 13), pre-eminence of Franco-German relations, and importance of transatlantic relations. In accord with the Green party's program,[2] he emphasized the civilian and peace-promoting nature of the EU and a post-national identity for Germany that would be compatible with a supra-national Union. Fischer later addressed these issues in speeches and statements about the *finalité politique* of the EU. When taking over the foreign ministry, he talked about a "liquefaction of conditions" (Fischer 1998b), which would carry risks but also reap opportunities for further shaping the course of European integration (Fischer 1998b, 1999a).

In contrast to Fischer, Chancellor Schröder was an unknown quantity with regard to his views on foreign and European policy. He shared the complaints expressed by many prime ministers of the German *Länder* with regard to "Brussels' centralism" and criticized the euro-project (Bulmer et al. 2000: 95; also Schröder 1997). External factors and the realities of the EU decision-making process drew Chancellor Schröder onto the EU stage and compelled him to seize opportunities available in this domain for shaping domestic and foreign policy (Janning 1999). His political stature expanded considerably during his first term, as did the attention he devoted to EU issues. Overall, however, the SPD assumed control of the government with a comparatively limited record of engagement in European politics (Hrbek 1972; Link 1986: 241–57; Link 1987: 277–90; Müller-Roschach 1980) and was possessed of an even poorer number of experts in this policy field (Bulmer et al. 2000: 33). Chancellor Brandt (1969–1974) had actively advocated the accession of the United Kingdom to the EC and recognized the political value of the EC as a political arena serving to balance *Ostpolitik* during the late 1960s and early 1970s. Chancellor Schmidt (1974–1982) figured as a proponent of European summitry: together with Giscard d'Estaing he initiated the regular meetings among heads of state and government under the banner of the European Council (Bulmer and Wessels 1987) and the World Economic Summit, and also initiated the European Monetary System (EMS) during the 1970s. Under his chancellorship, intergovernmental procedures and cooperation in foreign (European Political Cooperation, EPC) and economic policy were introduced and extended to the EC.

However, there were few initiatives and reforms of a polity dimension that originated specifically among the Social Democrats. Aside from strengthening the democratic legitimacy of the Community through direct elections among the EP, the overall SPD approach to European integration found expression through an agnostic view toward "constitution-making" and the overhaul of the political system of the EC/EU. Indeed, European policy was far less controversial than the politicization and polarization that characterized aspects of foreign and security politics in the FRG (nuclear arms policy, "Star Wars," etc.) until 1989. After carrying the status of opposition party for 16 years, it was difficult for the SPD to achieve a specific EU policy profile. Even today it is not easy to find qualities of excellence, political clout, and popularity among SPD elite with regard to EU politics. But the Red–Green government nevertheless pursued a rigid personnel policy whenever filling EU-related posts; proposals to nominate politicians from the CDU or FDP (e.g., Schäuble or Genscher as second commissioner in 1999 or as representative of the chancellor in the Convention) were consistently rejected by the Red–Green government, which preferred to pursue a low-key personnel policy of not sending political heavyweights to Brussels.

Only limited reorganization was introduced into EU policy in 1998. Traditionally, the foreign ministry has the primary role of coordinating European politics and shares it with the Ministry of Economics (Bulmer et al. 2000: 22–28; Rometsch 1994). Upon assuming office, the Red–Green government transferred powers from the Federal Ministry of Economics to the finance ministry under the direction of Mr. Lafontaine, who was chairman of the SPD party at that time. There is long-standing controversy in Germany about whether to concentrate responsibilities for European politics either in a special Europe ministry or in the chancellery in the form of a state minister, with the aim in either instance of streamlining efficient and coherent decision-making (Bulmer et al. 2001; Janning and Meyer 1998). Within the complex and multilayered German decision-making system there are many opportunities for vetoing EU policy, a feature only further reinforced by the strengthened role of the *Länder* and the *Bundesrat* following the Maastricht Treaty. So far, the realities of the federal system as well as of coalition governments in Germany have hindered any radical shifts toward a concentration of powers. The, however, limited change in 1998 is also attributable to the personality and political clout of Finance Minister Lafontaine, together with the expanding role of the Finance Ministry in European policy, although the function of the foreign ministry in coordinating the three pillars of the EU was actually strengthened (Bulmer et al. 2001: 245).

The chancellor's office, another key player in EU policy-making, has few resources. Its strategic importance lies in preparing European Council meetings, conducting bilateral relations with EU partners and respective joint initiatives, supporting the chancellor's initiatives in EU affairs, and resolving interim ministerial conflicts over concrete positions in the cabinet. Chancellor Schröder's office was therefore actively involved in the Agenda 2000 negotiations, in the Cologne summit during the German presidency, in the Nice summit to complete the Inter-Governmental Conference (IGC), as well as the series of German/French, German/British (Schröder and Blair 2002), and other bilateral initiatives (Bulmer et al. 2001: 242–61). However, EU policy-making did not fundamentally change under the first Red–Green government, which means that its weaknesses with regard to decentralization, institutional pluralism, sectorization, and complex coordination were also sustained.

Continuity of structures, interests, goals, and *Leitbilder* of German EU policy were widely documented in the coalition agreement and in successive policy statements (SPD and Bündnis '90/Die Grünen 1998; Fischer 1998a: 14). However, during the election campaign of 1998 and during the first weeks in office, the Red–Green government did try out several new formulas; for example, applying new realism in enlargement policy (Fischer 1998b), no checkbook diplomacy (e.g., Schröder 1998b), and standing up for the national interests of a matured country—which naturally caused some irritation within Germany and among partner countries.[3] This period of experimentation did not last long, for both the takeover of the presidency within the EU in January 1999—only three months after the general elections—and the Kosovo bombing on the eve of the special Berlin summit in March 1999, accelerated learning processes for the Red–Green government and upgraded the importance of European policy. Working through the crowded EU agenda demanded leadership as well as strategy; Schröder expected hard work in the trenches after the strategic heights had been occupied, particularly after the launch of the euro/EMU.[4] Although the goals of the Schröder/Fischer government were humble, insofar as they sought to complete projects, particularly that of enlargement (Fischer 1998b), Foreign Minister Fischer's talk of the "completion" (Fischer 2000a) of European integration as a task for his generation was very ambitious, indeed.

Deepening and Widening: Challenges to the Status Quo

Kohl/Kinkel had left the government during a downswing period with regard to both deepening and widening the EU. The successor government had to cope with many loose ends, most notably policy reforms, financing enlargement, leftovers of Amsterdam, and an uncertain timetable for enlargement that made German promises for a swift enlargement increasingly implausible.

Reform of Policies and the Net Payer Problem (Agenda 2000)

The settling of the Agenda 2000 was a key interest for Germany and the priority for the German presidency during the first half of 1999. The special summit on Agenda 2000 in Berlin (March 1999) focused on money and the reform of policies within an enlarged EU. These sensitive issues had to be remedied within a very short time frame. It was expected that within the period of the new financial perspective 2000–2006, new members possessing large agricultural sectors and a GDP well below the 75 percent threshold of EU GDP would join and demand transfers over decades to come. So old certainties of distributive policy were challenged. In summer 1997 and spring 1998 the EC tabled proposals for a seven-year financial perspective and the reform of regional policy and Common Agricultural Policy (CAP), which together comprise nearly 80 percent of the EU budget (European Commission 1997, 1998). The proposal included a special "ring fenced" budget for up to six new members that would—as working hypotheses—join in 2002 (Lippert 1999; Becker 2000; Caesar and Scharrer 2000). Conflicts immediately arose with regard to the financial perspective for the EU 15 and, more specifically, the reform of policies.

Germany played a central role in finding substantial solutions and, by assuming the presidency of the EU it also took on the task of moderating potential conflicts. At the same time it sought to distribute the burden fairly and maintained that simply extrapolating the status quo into the near future would not be acceptable. The German government's ambitious goals were threefold: to reduce its net contributions to the EU budget, to instate systematic and fundamental reforms on expenditures (CAP, regional policy), and to save money for incoming new members. This position posed a challenge to net recipients of transfers (e.g., Spain, Portugal, Greece), but also to France (because of CAP) and to the United Kingdom (because of the special conditions of the "rebate"). The big question was, would Germany, which benefited the most from enlargement and which was a self-styled advocate for the Central and Eastern European candidates, relinquish its solidarity and endanger enlargement or provoke a crisis of the EU 15?

Germany under Kohl held a fine record of applying financial incentives and financial commitments as a means to achieve overall political agreements (e.g., the Delors II-package in the 1990s) or to win support for its specific goals of shaping the EU polity and politics (Political Union, European Central Bank, Economic and Monetary Union, Stability Pact). However, the high level of unemployment in Germany together with the straightjacket imposed by the Maastricht criteria and the costs of unification considerably narrowed the nation's ability to extend financial compensations and incentives during the last years of the Kohl government. Moreover, since the era of Chancellor Schmidt, complaints seemed to surface recurrently about the so-called net payer position of Germany.

The Red–Green coalition adopted the notion of fair burden sharing from the Kohl government. Whereas former Finance Minister Waigel had favored changes on the income side of the budget through the definition of thresholds for maximum contributions (*Kappungsmodell*), the new government pushed for thorough changes on the expenditure side. The Schröder government's proposal to introduce cofinancing of direct income transfers for farmers through national budgets immediately led to a severe conflict with French President Jacuqes Chirac, a former agricultural minister. The German government ultimately had to give up these ambitions because its role as presidency did not allow for a hardliner strategy and because Germany did not want to risk blocking or slowing down the accession negotiations. Agenda 2000 was ultimately not so much a triumph as rather a hard earned and expensive compromise that secured the functioning of the EU 15 for the next years. However, it spoiled relations between Schröder and Chirac, and without the external challenges of the start of the Kosovo bombing and the crisis resulting in the resignation of the Santer commission, the antagonisms could easily have outweighed the imperative to get the act together.

The results of the Berlin summit reflect German interests in establishing a resources ceiling (1.27 percent of the EU GDP) and introducing a moderate reduction in the country's budgetary contribution. As a consequence of the Agenda 2000, Germany's net payer position improved: in 1995, Germany's share of contributions to the EU budget was 30 percent, while in 2002 it was only 23 percent. Agenda 2000 represented at least a partial progress in the fiscal and political sphere, insofar as it put a halt to the trend toward big budget. When compared with Southern enlargement, new members from Central and Eastern Europe will now receive fewer transfers from the EU budget.

However, the costs of the Berlin agreement were also considerable for Germany and the EU. The quarrel over the extension of direct payments to farmers in the Central and Eastern European (CEE) candidate countries in the final hours of accession negotiations in 2002 was grounded in Berlin's shallow decision to deny any such subvention to CEE farmers. The Berlin summit used postponement strategies wherever possible, avoiding a realistic assessment of the implications of enlargement for budget, policy reforms, and modernization of the EU economies. In the final analysis, the unashamed style and spirit of negotiations—matched only by the Nice European Council—led to many unsystematic, expensive, and short-lived solutions.

The "Leftovers" of Amsterdam: Power Games at Nice

"Nice" was about the preparation of the EU for enlargement through institutions and decision-making procedures and revealed both the strengths and the weaknesses in European politics under the Red–Green government. The Schröder/Fischer government was successful in setting an agenda for the intergovernmental conference (IGC) which opened in February 2000 and which led to the Nice Treaty in December. This agenda was basically restricted to addressing unsettled business from Amsterdam, that is, re-weighting of votes in the Council, establishing the size and composition of the Commission, and allocating seats in the EP for member states for an EU 27. The government wanted to limit the agenda to these points so that the IGC could be completed by the end of the French presidency, enabling the EU to continue and complete the ongoing accession negotiations without further delay. In the process of fighting for a straightforward agenda, the government also succeeded in loosening the foothold claimed by the German *Länder*, which sought to convey their assent via the *Bundesrat* to ratify the results of Nice with regard to the distribution of power between the EU and national level. This downturn of linkage policies by the federal government was mainly achieved through the "declaration on the future of the Union" in the Nice treaty, which contained target dates and measures for continuing the process of reform and constitutionalization, including the question of distribution of power. The disadvantage of pursuing such a narrow agenda was that there was little room for package deals and compensation of interests.

While the Red–Green government pursued well-established German positions, namely, double majority voting (of countries and population) in the Council to take account of demographic facts, extension of majority voting and the co-decision procedure, strengthening the EP and the Commission, and a more practical formula for enhanced cooperation, it also had to come up with concrete preferences and choices at the IGC. The Red–Green government sought better representation in relationship to the demographics of the Council and the EP. Given the size of the German population (82 million compared to 59 in France, 60 in the United Kingdom, 57 in Italy), this was not only a crucial point of contestation between small and large countries, but also a sensitive issue between the big countries, most notably Germany and France. Equal votes among the Big Four countries in the Council had been the norm in the Community. The German government reasoned that differentiated distribution of votes in the Council of the enlarged EU would also allow for differentiation between the Big Four. This suggestion for deviating from the historic parity between Germany and France alarmed Paris and led to severe disagreement and an all time low in relations (Guérot 2000: 181–82; Guérin-Sendelbach and Schild 2002: 43–45). Eventually Chancellor Schröder dropped this option in return for a so-called demographic safety net. He explained to the *Bundestag*—just as he had after the Berlin summit on Agenda 2000—that Germany was putting its legitimate national interests last for the sake of an overall compromise and in order to not block enlargement (Schröder 2001a: 1).

Completing the IGC in Nice was an accomplishment in itself because it paved the way for enlargement and it required the minimum in institutional adaptation and reform to accommodate the accession of new members (Lippert 2001b). Schröder's trip to Warsaw just prior to Nice underscored the importance of enlargement and of Poland as a future member, but it also appealed to the Social Democratic tradition of Willy Brandt's *Ostpolitik* (Schröder 2001a). Nice could be regarded as a platform from which the EU could govern effectively and efficiently with twenty-five or so members. However, it is difficult to speculate on how the revised rules of Nice will affect the dynamics of decision-making. The desire to install as many security nets and checks as possible resulted in more complex rules for qualified majority voting, that is, majority of weighted votes (73.4 percent) and of states and people (62 percent of the EU population). This scenario has the potential to result in deadlocks because it increases opportunities to block majorities (Giering 2001; Lippert and Bode 2001). The Nice results secured parity between the Big Four in the Council, but Germany became the only big country that can—because of the size of its population—block decisions together with two more countries. However, Germany has always sought to shape politics by creating coalitions and majorities rather than by blocking decisions.

The summits of Berlin and Nice became a forum presenting a German government that pursued traditional *Realpolitik* and framed its goals in terms of money, status, and power. But the attempts to embed these goals within an overall strategy for reforming policies and institutions to achieve a more effective, efficient, and legitimate EU failed. Like the Kohl government before them, Schröder/Fischer were unable to make substantial reforms a precondition for enlargement and so use enlargement as leverage for reforms. They came to realize that there was no solid majority inside the EU for enlargement that would reach a consensus on burden-sharing and depth of reforms. The horse-trading, rough style of negotiations, and inconsistent solutions led many to conclude that the method of convening IGCs for treaty revision was inadequate (Jopp et al. 2001; Lippert 2001b). In that regard, the call for a Convention on constitutional issues was a reaction to the failures of the Nice summit.

Finalité: *From the Humboldt Speech to the Convention*

Despite some initial reservation vis-à-vis grand European visions and the details of institutional engineering that have characterized the functionalist tradition of European integration, the Red–Green government gave fresh impetus to reflections on the *finalité* of an enlarged EU and improved its capacity to act. Fischer set out the *Leitbild* for a *federation of nation states* (Fischer 2000a) and Chancellor Schröder declared the necessity of *l'Europe puissance* (Schröder 1999b). Together, they provided a setting for the realization of a "renaissance of questions that tackle the future order of Europe" (Jopp 2001: 830).

While Fischer initially regarded issues about *finalité* as of minimal operational importance, he nevertheless stimulated a EU-wide debate (Joerges et al. 2000) on the further constitutionalization of the EU (Fischer 1998c). In a speech at Humboldt University Berlin in May 2000, he outlined his idea that "enlargement will render imperative a fundamental reform of European institutions" (Fischer 2000a: 16) and presented the alternative of either "erosion or integration" (Fischer 2000a: 22). Although Fischer delivered his Humboldt speech not in his capacity as foreign minister but explicitly as German parliamentarian, this programmatic speech was carefully prepared by diplomats of the Europe department and planning staff in the foreign ministry. It offered a stimulating blend of both unorthodox ideas and proposals together with traditional German thinking on European integration. Fischer furthermore tried to establish a parallel track for talking about the future of Europe in a wider and more fundamental sense than had been permitted by the tough bargaining over money (Berlin) and institutional power in the enlarged EU (Nice).

Fischer first of all offered a new *Leitbild* or at least a formula— "federation of nation states"—to replace the outdated "United States of Europe" *Leitbild*, which had envisioned some sort of *Bundesstaat* for the EU, preferably modeled on the FRG (Piepenschneider 2001: 329). It was recognized that it was unrealistic to ever hope to achieve this final stage of exporting institutions and designs to the EU level, especially after enlargement to a Union of twenty-five and more countries. However, Fischer focused upon the necessity for institutional reform not from a bureaucratic point of view but rather in the context of the *finalité* and a constitution for the EU ((Marhold 2001: 132–51; Rau 2001).

Second, Fischer managed to offend those who adhered to a functionalist approach when he declared the end of the Monnet method of constructing the Community by inching forward incrementally without a blueprint. In practice, however, the Red–Green government was following precisely this path at the summits in Berlin, Nice, and also in Laeken. But Fischer encouraged more visionary and less minimalist thinking and thus established some points for a debate on the EU system that would complement the intentionally narrow agenda of the IGC 2000 (Nice). This created a double track approach and instigated lively reactions within the EU (Jopp et al. 2001; Joerges et al. 2000).

Fischer essentially opted for a two-chamber legislature (EP and Council) with a strengthened EP; when he raised the idea for a second chamber of parliamentarians in addition to the EP, he was adopting French thinking that pursued a stronger role for national parliaments. Of course, this was anathema for federalists. The proposal has lingered on in current ideas for a subsidiarity committee composed of members of the EP and/or national parliaments and the installation of an early warning system (Göler 2002; Wessels 2002). Fischer did not restrict future executive powers to the Commission but conceived of a bigger role for the European Council. This was closer to French and also British thinking (Chirac 2002; Parker 2002; Aznar 2002) in stressing the role of an intergovernmental and superseding institution. Fischer was initially ambivalent about who should elect the president of the Commission, that is, the EP—in line with a clearly parliamentarian EU system—or the citizens directly, which would install a key feature of a presidential system and cause shifts in the institutional balance between Council, Commission, and the EP.

In defiance of federalist aspirations, he stressed his belief that nation states are here to stay and are unlikely to be overcome in the further process of integration. He demonstrated strong skepticism about the extent to which one can rely on spillover effects, herein heeding a caution drawn from his experience in EU foreign and security policy-making. Fischer's insistence on the importance of the nation state also made him more open to tackling questions about how to reorder competencies horizontally between the EU institutions and vertically between the EU and nation state levels. He emphasized the two sources of democratic legitimacy of EU institutions—direct legitimacy via the EP and indirect legitimacy via the Council—and herein underlined the *sui generis* character of the EU. He stressed that the EU should not be satisfied to muddle its way through and that enlargement would press the EU to maximize and improve its capacities on the international stage. The latter was indeed necessitated through the shock of 11 September 2001.

Thus, Fischer identified the crucial points for a debate that continued after Nice and Laeken. He displayed a pragmatic, constructive, and also strategic approach to issues, presenting arguments that went beyond the doctrine of pure integration and building bridges toward French thinking.[5] The coalition's successes included both the agreement to start a post-Nice process and the Laeken declaration (European Council 2001), which comprises mention of the need for a constitution and which enacted a Convention dominated by parliamentarians. The IGC 2004 can be traced back to a joint German–Italian initiative at the Nice summit. With Chancellor Schröder exerting his influence to back an SPD draft on European integration (Schröder 2001b), the Red–Green government demonstrated its keen interest in the future of the EU and in initiatives of the EU. For Schröder, improving the democratic legitimacy and general functioning of the EU system has become a stronger priority in light of recent policy-making in the EMU and challenges to international security. Schröder has used the expression *l'Europe puissance* (Schröder 1999c) in a gesture of solidarity with France but also because the term reflects the notion of "self-assertion of Europe" traditionally supported by the SPD. The idea of "Europe as a power" involves a vision for Europe as embodying a certain notion of civilization and a special type of welfare state, and the perception that European integration is a viable response to globalization, and furthermore upholds the ambition for Europe to serve effectively among the key international players.

Despite such leadership on the *finalité* of European integration, Germany initially maintained a low profile at the Convention in personnel and concrete contributions. Following the general elections of 2002, Foreign Minister Fischer replaced Mr. Glotz as representative of the chancellor at the Convention, herein underscoring the massive German interest in rendering the Convention a success. This produced the hoped for bandwagon effect, with member states, most notably France, followed the lead. Maintaining an understanding with France on key questions about future EU polity, including institutional reforms, will remain a keen concern. The German government furthermore seeks a strengthening of the president of the Commission, as a post held through elections of the EP, and probably tasked to also preside over the European Council. While France would prefer a president who can operate more independently of the European Council it is open to Fischer's original proposal to "merge" the roles of the High Representative for CFSP and the external affairs commissioner. Solutions of "big and small double hatting" will remain central in the endgame of the Convention, and an agreement between Germany and France could represent a major breakthrough.

EU Enlargement as a Political Project

The Red–Green government has shared the creed of the Kohl government to the effect that enlargement is in Germany's best interest and central to establishing democracy, welfare, and stability in the neighboring regions. Because of Germany's geographic location, its history, and its willingness to shape a peaceful continent, the Red–Green government declared itself prepared to serve as an engine for enlargement. Many social democrats understood enlargement as a timely continuation of *Ostpolitik*, one of the traditions and myths with which most SPD members and adherents strongly identify. The Greens also emphasized the need for eastward enlargement and the pan-European dimension of European integration.

This positive approach to enlargement was evident in the coalition agreement of 20 October 1998 (SPD und Bündnis '90/Die Grünen 1998) and the first general policy statement of Chancellor Schröder of 10 November 1998 (Schröder 1998b). While Schröder tended to highlight German economic interests in enlargement while also stressing the need to protect labor markets and uncompetitive sectors, Fischer referred to both the history and the future of the European project as defined through the ambition to secure peace and pursue civilized conflict resolution. As leader of the Green party group in the *Bundestag*, Fischer had declared: "Peace and freedom in Europe in the next centuries will depend on the question of eastward enlargement and the role Germany will play" (Fischer 1998b quoted in Lippert 2001a: 348), herein recalling Kohl's dictum at the University of Leuwen that "European integration is a question of war and peace" (Kohl 1996: 130). Given Germany's history and the sense of moral responsibility for Central and Eastern Europe, ·eastern enlargement was framed as a matter of the EU's political identity at the end of the Cold War (in general for the

EU: Schimmelfennig 2001; for Germany Lippert 2001a). From the start, Fischer made it clear that enlargement would be a central priority and pursued this line of reasoning throughout his time in office.

The Kosovo crisis of spring 1999 induced acceleration in broader thinking. Apparently, the foreign ministry had always tended more toward a geopolitical paradigm of enlargement while Schröder (and also Kohl) preferred a more restricted and controlled process that took into account the specific interests of the German economy. But after the Kosovo War, even Schröder realized the strategic importance of enlargement and the ceded "acknowledgement of geopolitical realities" (Fischer 2000a: 15). In his Humboldt speech, Fischer pointed out the dichotomy in continental developments: on the one side, we have the Europe integrated into the West and, on the other, the Europe oriented toward the East with the "old system of balance with its continued national orientation, constraints of coalition, traditional interest-led politics and the permanent danger of nationalist ideologies and confrontations" (Fischer 2000a: 12). Fischer feels that Germany would be the "big loser" (Fischer 2000a: 12) in a constellation that would fall back into nineteenth-century foreign policy. The German government therefore took the initiative to launch a specific Stability Pact for South-Eastern Europe. In light of the Balkan turmoil the Schröder/Fischer government also changed the German position on Turkey's candidacy for membership; together with Commissioner Verheugen, they supported the decision of the Helsinki summit in December 1999 to grant Turkey the political status of a candidate for membership and correct the "mistake" (Fischer 1999c) of the Luxembourg summit. This new position was assumed independently of the divide that still existed within public opinion, parliament, and political parties in Germany on this specific issue, herein proving that the geopolitical paradigm was winning ground in enlargement policy.

While the Red–Green government strengthened the German commitment to enlargement as a strategic goal of German foreign and European policy, it was also assertive about the terms of accession. From the beginning, the new government operated under the slogan of "new realism," seeking a restrictive approach in negotiations about, for example, the migration of labor and EU budget expenditures. In this regard, the Social Democrats were more assertive than the Greens, although the Green party loyally supported this course. The transitions agreed upon with the candidates with regard to the free movement of labor reflect the essentials of Schröder's proposals and claims of December 2000 (Schröder 2000).

However, Germany and other net payers (the Netherlands, Sweden, the United Kingdom) did not succeed in introducing reform elements in CAP before enlargement. On the contrary, the upgraded offers to the candidate countries (phasing-in of so called direct payments) place extra burdens on Germany. In regional policy, Germany favors a concentration of transfers within the poorest regions, that is, the new member states. This will, over the next years, also lead to reduced transfers from the EU budget to eastern Germany. In return, the Red–Green government expects more room for national regional support and subsidy schemes financed by national budgets. Here the key word is decentralization and less administrative intervention from the Commission. However, some fear a hidden agenda about watering down EU competition policy, which in many cases threatens Schröder's industrial policy (Schröder 2001b; Clement 2001).

In substance, there is much justification for the demand to limit the costs of (overly ineffective) EU policies and to use enlargement as a wake up call for policy reform, and grasp every opportunity to implement a reform. Moreover, at the Brussels summit of October 2002 the Red–Green government repeated the experience of Berlin 1999 in concluding that postponement of reform decisions is the only way to reach an agreement (most notably with France) and complete negotiations within the calendar year in December 2002. In any case, eastward enlargement turned out to be one of the strongest points of the Schröder/Fischer government. Given the haphazard rate of institutional reforms under the Amsterdam and Nice summits, enlargement could even be said to be moving in the fast lane. It remains to be seen whether the Convention and the successive IGC in 2003 will keep pace with the demands of an enlarged EU.

Germany—A "Normal State"?

In reforming policies and institutions and in negotiating the terms of enlargement with candidate countries, the Red–Green government followed a foreign and European policy regarded as a course of "enlightened self-interest" (Schröder 1999a: 575). A more self-confident and assertive style of policy-making was particularly attributed to Chancellor Schröder: "My generation and those following are Europeans because we want to be, not because we must be . . . That makes us freer in dealing with others . . . I am convinced that our European partners want to have a self-confident German partner which is more calculable than a German partner with an inferiority complex. Germany standing up for its national interests will be just as natural as France or Britain standing up for theirs."[6] This was understood as the preparedness to pursue a more "realistic" approach in maximizing so-called national interests and thus become more "normal" with regard to German foreign policy that is not essentially determined by rationality and self-interest but rather by collective memory (Markovits and Reich 1997). Fischer did not use this rhetoric, of course, but was more sensitive toward the power of collective memory, notably in relation to EU partner countries. He realized the double-bind situation of unified Germany: if Germany denies a leadership role it will be criticized, but if it accepts this role, distrust and fear of a hegemonic German position, "a German Europe," will also ensue (Fischer 1998a: 12 f.).

At the European summit in Nice, the German government neither claimed a hegemonic position nor a leadership role. But Nice revealed shifts in the relationships between member states and their individual standing, most clearly with regard to Paris and Berlin. Principles and rules that had never been questioned during the last 50 years of integration were discussed more openly and directly. The German government, in particular, raised demands with regard to its status, formal power, and national interests. Notwithstanding ignorance toward history and the politico-psychological disposition of France, the Red–Green government argued for a re-weighting of votes in the Council mainly on the basis of demography, arguing for formal terms of power without clear reference to a further political vision or a stimulating project. The non-convergence between Germany and France on the *finalité* questions, on the importance of enlargement, and the next steps toward a political union, made the German position difficult to sell and hard for partner nations to swallow. The German behavior in and around Nice was seen as a sign of *Geschichtsvergessenheit* typical for both the Berlin Republic and the post-Kohl generation of German politicians (Janning 2001: 321–22).

The power games in Nice seemed to echo Chancellor Schröder's assertion that Germany should behave like any other "normal country."[7] As on other occasions, he touched upon the idea of Germany stepping out of the shadow of history to stake the same claims as other countries. However, in substance, the German government neither sought for nor achieved a singularly powerful or hegemonic position in EU institutions. This is why the German government is still prepared to redefine the rule for double majority (majority of votes or states and majority of population) at the next IGC. In Nice it was difficult to see how Germany could capitalize on its traditional approach to shape the regional milieu, that is, to design compatible institutions, rules, and policy-making frameworks at the EU level, rather than seek plain power currency or possession goals. The Red–Green government offered little with which the partners could make sense of its recent behavior, indicating that the

German government needs to improve its ability to argue with member states and win their support for its ideas and preferences. Germany needs to adapt its EU strategy to its increase in formal power as well as its capacity to achieve *Realpolitik* goals with regard to national interest, status, prestige, and the like. At Nice the German government did not play a coherent and convincing role, instead alternating between conventional *Realpolitik* demands and the reflexes of self-confinement.

Conclusions

The four-year term of the Red–Green government was full of important incidents and decisions with regard to the deepening and widening of the EU: introduction of the euro, revision of the treaties in Nice, endorsement of a charter of fundamental rights, opening a Convention for a European constitution and perspectives for the IGC in 2003, agreement on a financial package for an enlarged EU (Agenda 2000), initiating accession negotiations with another six countries, and declaration of Turkey as a candidate for EU membership. Thus, the Schröder/Fischer government both continued with the integration path set out by its predecessors and made also some original contributions. This government differed from that under Kohl/Kinkel primarily in style and rhetoric. Other innovations and new accentuations were mainly induced from changes in the relevant framework for EU politics, which can be summed in the changing structure of the international system (Link 2001) after the end of the Cold War (multilateralism in a uni/multipolar international system), new security challenges, and shrinking socioeconomic resources after unification.

All in all, the record is mixed. The government succeeded in core decisions with regard to the deepening and widening of the EU. The first term of Schröder/Fischer will be memorable for Fischer's Humboldt speech that stimulated a Europe-wide debate on the *finalité*, as well as for reinforcing the civilian power of the EU with military capabilities through an upgraded ESDP, and for the near conclusion of accession negotiations. It was, however, less successful in coalition building with key EU partners. Attempts at strategic cooperation did not carry over from a series of efforts to revitalize the Franco-German tandem. Occasional coordinated steps with the United Kingdom or with Italy could not compensate for this deficit.

Moreover, the options were very limited, particularly given the constraints of German unification, the need to respect the Maastricht criteria, a sluggish economy, and an unreformed welfare state. Germany's weaknesses on the EU level are mainly grounded in its internal weakness. After four years under the Red–Green government, Germany is still not a model for socioeconomic success and has shifted far from its former image as a model pupil (*Musterschüler*). However, if Germany's politicians and policy-makers want to continue successfully with shaping the development of the EU they " . . . must try to influence and convince others and must be familiar not only with their interests, but also with their perceptions and beliefs—if only to avoid misperceptions when trying to establish European initiatives or when making policy suggestions" (Jopp 2002: 11). Here German foreign policy is in a transitory phase of learning to cope with a new environment, while the EU is learning to cope with a new Germany.

Moreover, Germany today is more inward looking, and the reflex to go down the "German path" (Schröder 2002a) with regard to labor market and social policy is strong. But for third countries and EU partners, it is not really an attractive model. This narrows the impact of Germany as a structural (Markovits and Reich 1997: 2) or soft power (Nye 2002) that gets others to want what it wants. Given its aforementioned constraints and deficits in coalition-building, the Red–Green government could not exert real leadership inside the EU although it was indeed a motor of deepening and widening and, as a result of its geographical centrality, an important player. Fischer, in particular, succeeded in opening avenues for both pragmatic and strategic innovations within the EU political system. Chancellor Schröder and his party followed suit, despite their initial preference for policy over polity issues. The Schröder/Fischer team strategically allocated roles in EU policy-making, with Schröder appearing as the "modern chancellor" (one of his campaign slogans in September 2002) of a normal and grown-up Germany that values the EU as an arena for problem-solving, while Fischer appeared as a "neo classic" (Ross 2002) in the footsteps of Chancellor Kohl, sensitive to German history and holding a vision for an integrated Europe in the twenty-first century.

Germany under the next government will remain an institutionally "tamed power" (Katzenstein 1997) that must seek a new balance of power with France as the twin engines of European integration. Germany must overcome its internal economic and social weaknesses to make other EU partners join their course of European integration. Germany will increasingly act as a normal "post-classic nation state" (Winkler 2002: 232) and will try out what this means when confronted with policy choices as well as strategic decisions. Both the government and the political class must work together to upgrade the economic and material resources available for Germany's leadership capacities, but also create a viable foreign and European policy that combines "prudent self restraint" with assertiveness and normal practices of *Realpolitik* (Hellmann 2002). Any German government will witness greater benefits within an increasingly integrated EU and embedded Germany than in an increasingly intergovernmental EU of twenty-five and more members. Trends in post-Wall Europe and in the world seem to indicate that Germany's role in the EU will and must change toward comprehensive cooperative leadership.

Notes

1. I do not deal with issues like European employment policy, CFSP/ESDP, Justice and Home Affairs, etc., which are covered in other contributions to this book. This chapter benefits from a research project of the Institue of European Politics in Berlin (IEP) on Germany's new EU politics in the period 1989/2001 that resulted in two publications: Schneider et al. 2001 and Jopp et al. 2002.

2. A comparison of party programs highlights the broad consensus and the evolution of the *Bündnis '90/Die Grünen* toward mainstream positions on EU politics, cf. Korte and Maurer 2001.

3. See: P. Norman, "Integration drive set to continue," *Financial Times* (10 November 1998); also Jopp et al. 2002; Korte 1998.

4. He used this formula throughout the election campaign (also P. Norman, "Integration drive set to continue," *Financial Times* (10 November 1998).

5. For example, he took up the notion of gravitation center from the "Quermonne-report" (Quermonne 2000), and the notion of Federation of Nation States from Jacques Delors (Interview with Le Monde), Schneider 1998: 113.

6. P. Norman (1998) "Integration drive set to continue," *Financial Times* (10 November 1998).

7. Schröder shares the school of thought propagating "normalization" of German foreign policy and Germany as a nation state: Schröder 1998b; also Bahr 1999. For a critical appraisal see: Hellmann 1999; P. Bahners, "Total Normal. Vorsicht Falle: Die unbefangene Nation," *Frankfurter Allgemeine Zeitung* (3 November 1998). For a critical position also Fischer 2002.

Bibliography

Adam, H. (1972) *Die Konzertierte Aktion in der Bundesrepublik* (Cologne: Bund-Verlag).

Alamir, F.M. (2000) "Blaupause für das 21. Jahrhundert? Das strategische Konzept der NATO," *Blätter für deutsche und internationale Politik* no. 4: 436–44.

Alber, J. (2001) *Recent Developments of the German Welfare State: Basic Continuity or Paradigm Shift?* (Bremen: University Bremen).

Algieri, F. (2002) "Die gemeinsame Europäische Sicherheits- und Verteidigungspolitik," in W. Weidenfeld (ed.), *Europa-Handbuch* (Gütersloh: Verlag Bertelsmann Stiftung), 586–601.

Andersen, M.S. and D. Liefferink (1997) "Introduction: The Impact of the Pioneers on EU Environmental Policy," in M.S. Andersen and D. Liefferink (eds.), *European Environmental Policy. The Pioneers* (Manchester: Manchester University Press), 1–39.

Anderson, D.C. (1995) *Crime and the Politics of Hysteria. How the Willie Horton Story Changed American Justice* (New York: Random House).

Arnold, H. (2002) "Wege und Möglichkeiten künftiger europäischer Sicherheitspolitik," *Aus Politik und Zeitgeschichte*, B24, retrieved on 08/29/2002 at <http://www.das-parlament.de/2002/24/beilage/004.html>.

Auswärtiges Amt (2002) "Der finanzielle Beitrag Deutschlands für die Vereinten Nationen," retrieved on 08/29/2002 at <http://www.auswaertiges-amt.de/www/de/aussenpolitik/vn/vereinte_nationen/finanz-deutsch_html>.

Aznar, J.M. (2002) "Speech by the President of the European Council at St. Anthony's College in the University of Oxford, 20 May 2002," retrieved on 09/05/2002 at <http://www.ue2002.es>.

Bach, S., M. Kohlhaas, and B. Praetorius (2001) "Wirkungen der ökologischen Steuerreform in Deutschland," *DIW-Wochenbericht* no. 14: 202–25.

Bäcker, G., R. Bispinck, K. Hofemann, and G. Naegele (2000a) *Sozialpolitik und soziale Lage in Deutschland. Bd. 1: Ökonomische Grundlagen, Einkommen, Arbeit und Arbeitsmarkt, Arbeit und Gesundheitsschutz*, 3rd edition (Wiesbaden: Westdeutscher Verlag).

Bäcker, G., (2000b) *Sozialpolitik und soziale Lage in Deutschland. Bd. 2: Gesundheit und Gesundheitssystem, Familie, Alter, Soziale Dienste*, 3rd edition (Wiesbaden: Westdeutscher Verlag).

Bahr, E. (1999) "Die 'Normalisierung' der deutschen Außenpolitik. Mündige Partnerschaft statt bequemer Vormundschaft," *Internationale Politik* 54 (1): 41–52.

Baker, K.L., R.J. Dalton, and K. Hildebrandt (1981) *Germany Transformed. Political Culture and the New Politics* (Cambridge, Mass.: Harvard University Press).

Barbieri Jr., W.A. (1998) *Ethics of Citizenship. Immigration and Group Rights in Germany* (Durham, N.C.: Duke University Press).

Bastian, T. (2002) *55 Gründe, mit den USA nicht solidarisch zu sein—und schon gar nicht bedingungslos* (Zürich: Pendo).

Beck, U. (1986) *Risikogesellschaft. Auf dem Weg in eine andere Moderne* (Frankfurt am Main: Suhrkamp).

Becker, P. (2000) "Die Reformbereitschaft der Europäischen Union auf dem Prüfstand—die Agenda 2000," in B. Lippert (ed.), *Osterweiterung der Europäischen Union—die doppelte Reifeprüfung* (Bonn: Europa Union Verlag), 61–104.

Benz, A. (1995) "Verhandlungssysteme und Mehrebenenverflechtung im kooperativen Staat," in W. Seibel and A. Benz (eds.), *Regierungssystem und Verwaltungspolitik. Beiträge zu Ehren von Thomas Ellwein* (Opladen: Westdeutscher Verlag), 83–102.

Berger, C. (2000) "Beschäftigungspakt Bayern—Das bayerische Bündnis für Arbeit," *WSI-Mitteilungen* 53 (7): 458–62.

Betz, H.G. (1994) *Radical Right-Wing Populism in Western Europe* (New York: St. Martin's Press).

Bispinck, R. (1997) "The Chequered History of the Alliance for Jobs," in G. Fajertag and P. Pochet (eds.), *Social Pacts in Europe* (Brussels: European Trade Union Institute), 63–78.

BKA (Bundeskriminalamt) (2002) "The *Bundeskriminalamt's* Concept of Its Tasks," retrieved on 06/24/2002 at <http://www.bka.de/lageberichte/ps/psb_kurzfassung_eng.pdf>.

Blair, T. and G. Schröder (1999) *The Third Way—Die Neue Mitte* (London: Labour Party).

Blanke, B. (1994) "Zuwanderung und Asyl. Zur Kommunikationsstruktur der Asyldebatte," *Leviathan* 21 (1): 13–22.

Bleses, P. and E. Rose (1998) *Deutungswandel der Sozialpolitik—Die Arbeitsmarkt- und Familienpolitik im parlamentarischen Diskurs* (Frankfurt am Main: Campus).

Bleses, P. and M. Seeleib-Kaiser (1999) "Zum Wandel wohlfahrtsstaatlicher Sicherung in der Bundesrepublik Deutschland: Zwischen Lohnarbeit und Familie," *Zeitschrift für Soziologie* 28 (2): 114–35.

Blumenwitz, D. (1994) "Abstammungsgrundsatz und Territorialprinzip. Zur Frage der Hinnahme doppelter Staatsangehörigkeit in Deutschland," *Zeitschrift für Politik* 41 (3): 246–60.

Blyth, M. (2001) "The Transformation of the Swedish Model. Economic Ideas, Distributional Conflict, and Institutional Change," *World Politics* 54 (1): 1–26.

BMAS (Bundesminister für Arbeit und Sozialordnung) (1986) *Statistisches Taschenbuch 1986. Arbeits- und Sozialstatistik* (Bonn: BMAS).

—— (1998) *Sozialbericht 1997.* Deutscher Bundestag. 13. Wahlperiode (BT-Drs. 13/10142).

—— (2002a) "Für ein soziales und wirtschaftlich starkes Europa. Bericht über die Ergebnisse der deutschen EU-Präsidentschaft im 1. Halbjahr 1999 im Bereich der Arbeits- und Sozialpolitik," retrieved on 06/05/2002 at <http://www.bma.bund.de/download/broschueren/a223.htm>.

—— (2002b) *Sozialbericht 2001,* retrieved on 07/30/2002 at <http://www.bma.de>.

—— (2002c) *Materialband zum Sozialbericht 2001,* retrieved on 07/30/2002 at <http://www.bma.de>.

—— (2002d) *Statistisches Taschenbuch 2002—Arbeits- und Sozialstatistik* (Bonn: BMAS).

BMBF (Bundesministerium für Bildung und Forschung) (2002a) *Faktenbericht Forschung 2002* (Bonn: BMBF).

—— (2002b) *Zur technologischen Leistungsfähigkeit Deutschlands 2001* (Bonn: BMBF).

BMF (Bundesminister der Finanzen) (2002) "Die Ökosteuer—Ein Plus für Arbeit und Umwelt," September 2002, retrieved on 11/18/2002 at <http://bmwi.de>.

BMFSFJ (Bundesministerium für Frauen, Senioren, Familie und Jugend) (2002) "Chronologie der familienpolitischen Entscheidungen seit Beginn der Legislaturperiode," retrieved on 05/16/2002 at <http:// www.bmfsfj.de>.

BMG (Bundesministerium für Gesundheit) (2002) "Bekanntmachung des durchschnittlichen allgemeinen Beitragssatzes der gesetzlichen Krankenversicherung zum Stichtag 1. Januar 2002 und des für versicherungspflichtige Studenten und Praktikanten maßgebenden Beitragssatzes," retreived on 11/01/2002 at <http://www.bmgesundheit.de>.

BMI (Bundesministerium des Innern) (2001) "Cornerstones of Germany's Second Anti-terror Package," retrieved on 11/05/2001 at <http://www. eng.bmi.bund.de/top/dokumente/Pressemitteilung/ix_64084.htm>.

BMU (Bundesministerium für Umwelt, Naturschutz und Reaktorsicherheit) (2000) "Germany's National Climate Protection Programme—Summary," retrieved on 08/19/2002 at <http://www.bmu.de/english/download/climate/files/climateprotection.pdf>.

—— (2002) "EEG und Biomasseverordnung auf Erfolgskurs—Bundesregierung legt Erfahrungsbericht vor," retrieved on 12/12/2002 at <http://www.bmu.de/download/dateien/eeg_erfahrungsbericht_hintergrund.pdf>.

BMWA (Bundesministerium für Wirtschaft und Arbeit) (2002) "Wirtschaftsdaten Neue Länder. Stand Oktober 2002," retrieved on 01/30/2002 at <http://www.bmwi.de/Homepage/download/wirtschaftspolitik/WirtschaftsdatenNBL.pdf>.

Böckem, A. (2000) "Die Umsetzung der deutschen Klimaschutzziele im Spannungsfeld gesellschaftlicher Interessen," *Zeitschrift für angewandte Umweltforschung* 13 (1–2): 170–85.

Böhning, W.R. (1984) *Studies in International Labour Migration* (London: Macmillan).

Boix, C. (1998) *Political Parties, Growth and Equality* (Cambridge: Cambridge University Press).

Bonß, W. (1995) *Vom Risiko. Unsicherheit und Ungewißheit in der Moderne* (Hamburg: Hamburger Edition).

Braunthal, G. (1990) *Political Loyalty and Public Service in West Germany. The 1972 Decree against Radicals and Its Consequences* (Amherst, Mass.: The University of Massachusetts Press).

Brettschneider, F. (2002) "Candidate-Voting. Die Bedeutung von Spitzenkandidaten für das Wählerverhalten in Deutschland, Großbritannien und den USA von 1960–1998," in H.-D. Klingemann and M. Kaase (eds.), *Wahlen und Wähler. Analysen aus Anlaß der Bundestagswahl 1998* (Opladen: Westdeutscher Verlag), 351–400.

Brouns, B. and M. Treber (2002) *Paradepferd mit bleiernen Füßen— Internationaler Klimaschutz und die Umsetzung in Deutschland* (Bonn: Forum Umwelt & Entwicklung).

Brubaker, R. (1992) *Citizenship and Nationhood in France and Germany* (Cambridge, Mass.: Harvard University Press).

Bruha, T. and M. Bortfeld (2001) "Terrorismus und Selbstverteidigung. Voraussetzungen und Umfang erlaubter Selbstverteidigungsmaßnahmen nach den Anschlägen vom 11. September 2001," *Vereinte Nationen* 49 (5): 161–62.

Buchheit, B. (2002) "Neue Impulse für die Arbeitsmarktpolitik," *Bundesarbeitsblatt* no. 2: 5–10.

Budge, I., H.-D. Klingemann, A. Volkens, J. Bara, and E. Tanenbaum (2001) *Mapping Policy Preferences: Estimates for Parties, Electors, and Governments 1945–1998* (Oxford: Oxford University Press).

Bull, H.-P. (1999) "Die Ein-Partei-Regierung: eine Koalition eigener Art. Beobachtungen eines Teilnehmers," in R. Sturm and S. Kropp (eds.), *Hinter den Kulissen von Regierungsbündnissen. Koalitionspolitik in Bund, Ländern und Gemeinden* (Baden-Baden: Nomos), 169–79.

Bulmer, S., C. Jeffery, and W.E. Paterson (2000) *Germany's European Diplomacy. Shaping the Regional Milieu* (Manchester: Manchester University Press).

Bulmer, S., A. Maurer, and W.E. Paterson (2001) "Das Entscheidungs- und Koordinationssystem deutscher Europapolitik: Hindernis für eine neue Politik?" in H. Schneider, M. Jopp, and U. Schmalz (eds.), *Eine neue deutsche Europapolitik? Rahmenbedingungen—Problemfelder—Optionen* (Bonn: Europa Union Verlag), 231–65.

Bulmer, S. and W. Wessels (1987) *The European Council. Decision-Making in European Politics* (Houndmills: Macmillan).

BUND (Bund für Umwelt und Naturschutz Deutschland) (2001a) "Atomstrom 2000: Sauber, sicher, alles im Griff? Aktuelle Probleme und Gefahren bei deutschen Atomkraftwerken," retrieved on 08/25/2002 at <http://www.bund.net/lab/reddot2/Energiepolitik_1148.htm>.

—— (2001b) *Die ökologische Steuerreform—eine Investition in die Zukunft* (Berlin: BUND).

—— (2002) "Vier Jahre Rot-Grün—eine umweltpolitische Bilanz," retrieved on 08/12/2002 at <http://www.bund.net>.

Bundesrat (2002) "Die Arbeit des Bundesrats im Spiegel der Zahlen. Statistische Angaben für die Zeit vom 07.09.1949 bis 17.10.2002," retrieved on 11/12/2002 at <http://www.bundesrat.de/PdundF/zahlenspiegel.html>.

Bundesregierung (1999) *Vor wichtigen Aufgaben. Das Arbeitsprogramm 1999 der Bundesregierung* (Bonn: Presse- und Informationsamt der Bundesregierung).

—— (2001) "Nuclear Energy Phase-out: Draft Bill Ending Nuclear Energy Use," retrieved on 08/31/2002 at <http://www.eng.bundesregierung.de>.

—— (2002a) "New Atomic Energy Act Enters into Force," retrieved on 08/12/2002 at <http://www.bmu.de/english/news/pressrelease020425.php>.

—— (2002b) "Bericht über den Stand der Markteinführung und der Kostenentwicklung von Anlagen zur Erzeugung von Strom aus erneuerbaren Energien (Erfahrungsbericht zum EEG)," retrieved on 12/12/2002 at <http://www.bmu.de/download/dateien/eeg_erfahrungsbericht.pdf>.

—— (2002c) "Bündnis für Arbeit," retrieved on 06/11/2002 at <http://www.bundesregierung.de/top/Schwerpunkte/Buendnis_fuer_Arbeit/ix7274_.htm>.

—— (2002d) "Climate Protection Creates Jobs and Export Opportunities," retrieved on 08/12/2002 at <http://www.bmu.de/english/news/pressrelease011210.php>.

—— (2002e) "The Ecological Tax Reform—Initiation and Continuation," retrieved on 08/15/2002 at <http://www.bmu.de/english/topics/oekosteuerreform_e.php>.

—— (2002f) "Fourth Phase of Ecological Tax Reform started on January 1, 2002," retrieved on 08/20/2002 at <http://eng.bundesregierung.de/dokumente/Background_Information/Environmental_P.html>.

—— (ed.) (2002g) *Perspektiven im Osten—Investitionen, Innovationen, Infrastruktur* (Berlin: Presse- und Informationsamt der Bundesregierung).

—— (2002h) "Perspektiven für Deutschland—Unsere Strategie für eine nachhaltige Entwicklung" [n.p.].

—— (2002i) "Zwischenbilanz der Ergebnisse des Bündnisses für Arbeit, Ausbildung und Wettbewerbsfähigkeit," retrieved on 05/24/2002 at <http://www.bundesregierung.de/doku...Arbeit/Ergebnisse/IX/29/_0/408.htm>.

Bundestagsfraktion Bündnis '90/Die Grünen (2002) "Hätten Sie's gewusst—Bilanz grüner Regierungsarbeit 1998–2002," [n.p.].

Bündnis '90/Die Grünen [1998] "Grün ist der Wechsel. Antrag des Bundesvorstandes an die BDK, Entwurf eines Bundestagswahlprogramms" [n.p., n.d.].

Bündnis '90/Die Grünen (2002) "Grün wirkt! Unser Wahlprogramm 2002–2006," retrieved on 07/30/2002 at <http://www.gruene-partei.de/rsvgn/rs_rubrik/ 0,,654,00. htm>.

Burger, A. and I. Hanhoff (2002) "Unterwegs in die nächste Dimension—Elemente und Handlungsfelder einer ökologischen Finanzreform," *Politische Ökologie* no. 77–78: 15–18.

BVerfGE (Entscheidungen des Bundesverfassungsgerichts) 65, 1–72. Urteil des Ersten Senats des Bundesverfassungsgerichts vom 15. Dezember 1983.

Caesar, R. and H.-E. Scharrer (eds.) (2000) *Die Zukunft Europas im Lichte der Agenda 2000* (Baden-Baden: Nomos-Verlagsgesellschaft).

CDU (Christlich Demokratische Union) (2002) "Leistung und Sicherheit. Zeit für Taten. Regierungsprogramm 2002–2006," retrieved on 06/24/2002 at <http://www.cdu.de/regierungsprogramm/regierungsprogramm-02-06-b.pdf>.

Chirac, J. (2002) "Discours prononcé dans le cadre de la campagne electorale pour l'election présidentielle à Strasbourg, 6 March 2002," retrieved on 09/05/2002 at <http://www.elysee.fr>.

Clement, W. (2001) "Rede zur Zukunft Europas an der Humboldt-Universität in Berlin," 12 February 2001 [n.p.].

Coalition Agreement (1998) "Coalition Agreement between the SPD and Alliance '90/The Greens, signed in Bonn, October 1998," retrieved on 02/02/2003 at <http://archiv.spd.de/English/politics/coalition11.html>.

Conradt, D., G.R. Kleinfeld, and C. Søe (eds.) (2000) *Power Shift in Germany. The 1998 Election and the End of the Kohl Era* (New York: Berghahn Books).

Cox, G.W. (1997) *Making Votes Count* (New York: Cambridge University Press).

Dahl, R. (1989) *Democracy and Its Critics* (New Haven, Conn.: Yale University Press).

Dalton, R.J. (2003) "Voter Choice and Electoral Politics," in G. Smith (ed.), *Developments in German Politics III* (London: Macmillan [forthcoming]).

Dalton, R.J. and W. Bürklin (1995) "The Two German Electorates: The Social Bases of the Vote in 1990 and 1994," *German Politics and Society* 13 (1): 79–99.

Dalton, R.J. and M.P. Wattenberg (2000) *Parties without Partisans: Political Change in Advanced Industrial Democracies* (Oxford: Oxford University Press).

Dautel, R. (2001) "Tax-Optimized Acquisitions in Germany after the Corporate Tax Reform," *Intertax* 29, issue 10: 348–52.

de Swaan, A. (1973) *Coalition Theories and Cabinet Formation* (Amsterdam: Elsevier/Jossey Bass).

Deutsche Bundesbank (2002a) "Öffentliche Finanzen," *Monatsbericht* (February): 50–63.

—— (2002b) "Staatliche Leistungen für die Förderung von Familien," *Monatsbericht* (April): 15–32.

—— (2002c) "Kapitalgedeckte Altersvorsorge und Finanzmärkte," *Monatsbericht* (July): 25–39.

Deutsche Shell (ed.) (2002) *Jugend 2002. 14. Shell Jugendstudie* (Frankfurt am Main: Fischer).

Deutscher Städtetag (2001) "Städte fordern strukturelle Veränderungen in der Arbeitsmarkt- und Sozialpolitik," Press Release 28 August 2001, retrieved on 10/30/2002 at <http://www.staedtetag.de>.

Dingeldey, I. (2001) "Familienbesteuerung in Deutschland. Kritische Bilanz und Reformperspektiven," in A. Truger (ed.), *Rot-grüne Steuerreform in Deutschland. Eine Zwischenbilanz* (Marburg: Metropolis), 201–27.

DIW (Deutsches Institut für Wirtschaftsforschung) (2000) "Klimaschutzpolitik auf dem richtigen Weg, aber weitere Schritte unabdingbar," *DIW-Wochenbericht* 32/00, retrieved on 08/02/2002 at <http://www.diw-berlin.de/deutsch/publikationen/wochenberichte/docs/00-32-1.html>.

—— (2001) "Wirkungen der ökologischen Steuerreform in Deutschland," *DIW Wochenbericht* 14/01, retrieved on 12/19/2002 at <http://www.foes-ev.de/downloads/DIWOESR.pdf>.

DIW et al. (2002a) *Fortschrittsbericht wirtschaftswissenschaftlicher Institute über die wirtschaftliche Entwicklung in Ostdeutschland. Forschungsauftrag des Bundesministerium der Finanzen*, Halle (Saale), 17 June 2002, retrieved on 05/07/2003 at <http://www.iab.de/ftproof/fortschrittsberichtost.pdf>.

—— (2002b) "Die Lage der Weltwirtschaft und der deutschen Wirtschaft im Herbst 2002. Beurteilung der Wirtschaftslage durch die Mitglieder der Arbeitsgemeinschaft deutscher wirtschaftswissenschaftlicher Forschungsinstitute e.V," *DIW-Wochenbericht*, no. 43: 703–57.

Druckman, J.N. (1996) "Party Factionalism and Cabinet Durability," *Party Politics* 2 (3): 397–407.

Dünn, S. and S. Faßhauer (2001) "Die Rentenreform 2000/2001—Ein Rückblick," *Deutsche Rentenversicherung* 56 (5): 266–75.

Earle, T.C. and G.T. Cvetkovich (1995) *Social Trust. Toward a Cosmopolitan Society* (Westport, Conn.: Praeger).

Edelman, M. (1976) *Politik als Ritual. Die symbolische Funktion staatlicher Institutionen und politischen Handelns* (Frankfurt am Main: Campus).

Eder, K., V. Rauer, and O. Schmidtke (eds.) (2003) *Die Einhegung des Anderen* [forthcoming].

Ehlermann, C., A. Kowallik, and P.T. Lee (2001) "Scope of the New Dual Consolidated Loss Rule for Tax Consolidations Introduced by the Recent German Business Tax Reform," *Intertax* 30 (5): 198–205.

Emmert, T., M. Jung, and D. Roth (2002) "Das Ende einer Ära. Die Bundestagswahl vom 27. September 1998," in H.-D. Klingemann and M. Kaase (eds.), *Wahlen und Wähler. Analysen aus Anlaß der Bundestagswahl 1998* (Opladen: Westdeutscher Verlag), 17–56.

Esping-Andersen, G. (1990) *Three Worlds of Welfare Capitalism* (New York: Polity Press).

Esser, J. (1982) *Gewerkschaften in der Krise* (Frankfurt am Main: Suhrkamp).

Esser, J. and W. Schroeder (1999) "Neues Leben für den Rheinischen Kapitalismus. Vom Bündnis für Arbeit zum Dritten Weg," *Blätter für deutsche und internationale Politik* no. 1: 51–61.

European Commission (1997) *Agenda 2000. For a Stronger and Wider Union,* COM(1997) 2000 final, Brussels, 15 July 1997.

—— (1998) *Communication from the Commission to the Council and the European Parliament on the Establishment of a New Financial Perspective for the Period 2000—2006,* COM(1998) 164 final, Brussels, 18 March 1998.

—— (2002) *Germany's Growth Performance in the 1990's. Directorate General for Economics and Financial Affairs,* Economic Papers No. 170, Brussels.

European Council (2001) *Laeken Declaration on the Future of the Europen Union,* SN 300/1/01 REV 1, Annex I to the Presidency Conclusions, Laeken, 14 and 15 December 2001.

Ewald, F. (1986) *L'Etat providence* (Paris: Bernard Grasset).

Faist, T. (1994) "How to Define a Foreigner? The Symbolic Politics of Immigration in German Partisan Discourse, 1978–1992," *German Politics and Society* 33 (3): 51–71.

FDP (Freie Demokratische Partei) (2002) "Bürgerprogramm—Programm der FDP zur Bundestagswahl 2002," retrieved on 06/24/2002 at <http://fdp-bundesverband.de/pdf/wahlprogramm_neu.pdf>.

Federal Government (2000) *The Alliance for Jobs 05: Results and Perspectives* (Berlin: Presse- und Informationsamt der Bundesregierung).

Fels, G., R.G. Heinze, H. Pfarr, and W. Streeck (1999) *Bericht der Wissenschaftlergruppe der Arbeitsgruppe Benchmarking über Möglichkeiten zur Verbesserung der Beschäftigungschancen gering qualifizierter Arbeitnehmer,* November 1999 (Online Version), retrieved on 06/11/2002 at <http:www.bundesregierung.de/Anlage255396/Bericht+der+Benchmarking-Gruppe.pdf>.

Fischer, J. (1994) *Risiko Deutschland. Krise und Zukunft der deutschen Politik* (Cologne: Kiepenheuer & Witsch).

—— (1998a) "Von der Macht und ihrer Verantwortung," in A.S. Markovits and S. Reich (eds.), *Das deutsche Dilemma. Die Berliner Republik zwischen Macht und Machtverzicht* (Berlin: Alexander Fest Verlag), 7–16.

—— (1998b) "Rede aus Anlaß der Übernahme der Amtsgeschäfte als Bundesaußenminister," Bonn, 28 Oktober 1998, retrieved on 09/05/2002 <http://www.auswaertiges-amt.de/www/de/infoservice/download/pdf/reden/1998/r981028b.pdf>.

—— (1998c) "Reply in the Plenary Session of the German Bundestag on 18 June 1998," quoted in B. Lippert (2001a) "Die EU-Erweiterungspolitik nach 1989—Konzeptionen und Praxis der Regierungen Kohl und Schröder," in H. Schneider, M. Jopp, U. Schmalz (eds.), *Eine neue deutsche Europapolitik? Rahmenbedingungen—Problemfelder—Optionen* (Bonn: Europa Union Verlag), 349–92.

Fischer, J. (1999a) "Speech at the European Parliament," Strasbourg, 12 January 1999, in German retrieved on 09/05/2002 at <http://www.auswaertiges-amt.de/www/de/infoservice/download/pdf/reden/1999/r990112a.pdf>.

—— (1999b) "Speech at the German Bundestag about the Results of the European Council in Helsinki," Berlin, 16 December 1999, retrieved on 09/05/2002 at <http://www.auswaertiges-amt.de/www/de/infoservice/download/pdf/reden/1999/r991216a.pdf>.

—— (1999c) "Speech on the Occasion of the Conference for Security Policy," Munich, 6 February 1999. Ms. [n.p.].

—— (2000a) "From Confederacy to Federation: Thoughts on the Finality of European Integration. Speech at the Humboldt University, Berlin, 12 May 2000," in The Federal Trust (ed.), *From Confederation to Federation: Thoughts on the Finality of European Integration*, European Essay No. 8, retrieved on 09/05/2002 at <http:www.policybrief.org/PPNdelors/Report/Joschka%20 Fischer.pdf>.

—— (2000b) "Speech of the Foreign Minister in the Belgian Parliament," Brussels, 14 November 2000, in German retrieved on 09/04/2002 at <http://www.auswaertiges-amt.de/www/de/infoservice/download/ pdf/reden/2000/r001114f.pdf>.

—— (2000c) "Vom Staatenverbund zur Föderation—Gedanken über die Finalität der europäischen Integration. Rede von Bundesaußenminister Joschka Fischer in der Humboldt-Universität zu Berlin am 12. Mai 2000," retrieved on 08/29/2002 at <http://www.zeit.de/reden/Europapolitik/ 200106_20000512_fischer.html>.

—— (2000d) "Vortrag des deutschen Außenministers vor den Mitgliedern der DGAP am 24. November 1999 in Berlin," *Internationale Politik* 55 (2): 58–64.

—— (2001a) "Die Architektur Europas." Speech of Foreign Minister Fischer at the Assemblée Nationale, Paris, 30 October 2001, retrieved on 09/05/2002 at <http://www.auswaertiges-amt.de/www/de/eu_politik/ausgabe_archiv? archiv_id=2271&type_id=3&bereich_id=4>.

—— (2001b) "Kontinuität, Verläßlichkeit, europäische Einbindung." Speech on 3 September 2001, retrieved on 08/29/2002 at <http://www.zeit.de/ reden/Deutsche%20Au%dfenpolitik/fischer_botschafterkonf_200137.html>.

—— (2002) "Ein unheimliches Gefühl," Interview with Foreign Minister Fischer, *Der Spiegel* no. 21 (18 May 2002): 32–38.

Flasbarth, J. and G. Billen (2002) "Bilanz und Ausblick—Die deutsche Umweltpolitik zwei Monate vor der Bundestagswahl 2002," *Natur heute* no. 3: 12–6.

Freeman, G.P. (1979) *Immigrant Labor and Racial Conflict in Industrial Societies: The French and British Experience, 1945–1975* (Princeton, N.J.: Princeton University Press).

Frerich, J. and M. Frey (1996) *Handbuch der Geschichte der Sozialpolitik in Deutschland—Band 3: Sozialpolitik in der Bundesrepublik Deutschland bis zur Herstellung der deutschen Einheit*, 2nd edition (Munich: Oldenbourg Verlag).

Fröhner, R., M. von Stackelberg, and W. Eser (1956) *Familie und Ehe. Probleme in den deutschen Familien der Gegenwart* (Bielefeld: Maria von Stackelberg Verlag).

Fuchs, D. (1997) "Wohin geht der Wandel der demokratischen Einstellungen in Deutschland?" in G. Göhler (ed.), *Institutionenwandel* (Opladen: Westdeutscher Verlag), 253–84.

—— (1999) "The Democratic Culture of Unified Germany," in P. Norris (ed.), *Critical Citizens: Global Support for Democratic Government* (Oxford: Oxford University Press), 123–45.

—— (2000) "Die demokratische Gemeinschaft in den USA und in Deutschland," in J. Gerhards (ed.), *Die Vermessung kultureller Unterschiede. USA und Deutschland im Vergleich* (Opladen: Westdeutscher Verlag), 33–72.

Fuchs, D. and H.-D. Klingemann (1990) "The Left-Right Schema," in M.K. Jennings, J.W. van Deth et al. (eds.), *Continuities in Political Action* (Berlin: de Gruyter), 203–34.

Fuchs, D. and R. Rohrschneider (2001) "Der Einfluß politischer Wertortientierungen auf Regimeunterstützung und Wahlverhalten," in H.-D. Klingemann and M. Kaase (eds.), *Wahlen und Wähler. Analysen aus Anlaß der Bundestagswahl 1998* (Wiesbaden: Westdeutscher Verlag), 245–82.

Fuhrmann, N. (2002) "Drei zu eins für Schröder. Bergmann muss im Hinspiel eine Niederlage einstecken," in K. Eicker-Wolf, H. Kindler, I. Schäfer, M. Wehrheim, and D. Wolf (eds.), *"Deutschland auf den Weg gebracht." Rotgrüne Wirtschafts- und Sozialpolitik zwischen Anspruch und Wirklichkeit* (Marburg: Metropolis Verlag), 187–212.

Garrett, G. (1998) *Partisan Politics in the Global Economy* (Cambridge: Cambridge University Press).

Gerlach, F. and A. Ziegler (2000) "Territoriale Beschäftigungspakte in Deutschland—neue Wege der Beschäftigungsförderung," *WSI-Mitteilungen* 53 (7): 430–37.

German Presidency of the European Union (1998) "Ziele und Schwerpunkte der deutschen Präsidentschaft im Rat der Europäischen Union," 2 December 1998 [n.p.].

Gibowski, W. (1999) "Social Change and the Electorate: An Analysis of the 1998 Bundestagswahl," *German Politics and Society* 17 (1): 10–32.

Giddens, A. (1998) *The Third Way. The Renewal of Social Democracy* (Cambrigde: Polity Press).

Giering, C. (2001) "Die institutionellen Reformen von Nizza—Anforderungen, Ergebnisse, Konsequenzen," in W. Weidenfeld (ed.), *Nizza in der Analyse. Strategien für Europa* (Gütersloh: Verlag Bertelsmann Stiftung), 51–144.

Giesen, B. (2001) "National Identity and Citizenship. The Cases of Germany and France," in K. Eder and B. Giesen (ed.), *European Citizenship. National Legacies and Postnational Projects* (Oxford: Oxford University Press), 36–60.

Gohr, A. (2001) "Eine Sozialstaatspartei in der Opposition: Die Sozialpolitik der SPD in den 80er Jahren," in M.G. Schmidt (ed.), *Wohlfahrtsstaatliche*

Politik. Institutionen, politischer Prozeß und Leistungsprofil (Opladen: Leske + Budrich), 262–93.

Goldberger, B. (1993) "Why Europe should not Fear the Germans," *German Politics* 2 (2): 288–310.

Göler, D. (2002) "Der Gipfel von Laeken: Erste Etappe auf dem Weg zu einer europäischen Verfassung?" *integration* 17 (2): 99–110.

Goodin, R.E. (1996) "Institutions and their Design," in R.E. Goodin (ed.), *The Theory of Institutional Design* (Cambridge: Cambridge University Press), 1–53.

Goodin, R.E., B. Headey, R. Muffels, and H.-J. Dirven (1999) *The Real Worlds of Welfare Capitalism* (Cambridge: Cambridge University Press).

Green, S. (2000) "Beyond Ethnoculturalism? German Citizenship in the New Millennium," *German Politics* 9 (3): 105–24.

Greenpeace (2002) "Positionspapier zur Bundestagswahl 2002," retrieved on 08/12/2002 at <http://www.greenpeace.de/GP_DOK_3P/HINTERGR/C11HI30.PDF>.

Gros, J. (2000) "Das Kanzleramt im Machtgeflecht von Bundesregierung, Regierungsparteien und Mehrheitsfraktionen," in K.-R. Korte and G. Hirscher (eds.), *Darstellungspolitik oder Entscheidungspolitik? Über den Wandel von Politikstilen in westlichen Demokratien* (Munich: Hanns-Seidel-Stiftung), 85–105.

Guérin-Sendelbach, V. and J. Schild (2002) "French Perceptions of Germany's Role in the EU and Europe," in M. Jopp, H. Schneider, and U. Schmalz (eds.), *Germany's European Policy: Perceptions in Key Partner Countries* (Bonn: Europa Union Verlag), 33–55.

Guérot, U. (2000) "Die Reform der Europäischen Union vor ihrer Osterweiterung," in Deutsche Gesellschaft für Auswärtige Politik (ed.), *Jahrbuch Internationale Politik 1999–2000* (Munich: Oldenbourg Verlag), 173–84.

Gurr, T.R. (ed.) (1989) *Violence in America. Vol.I: The History of Crime; Vol. II: Protests, Rebellion, Reform* (Newbury Park, Calif.: Sage).

Habermas, J. (1990) *Die nachholende Revolution* (Frankfurt am Main: Suhrkamp).

—— (1993) "A Kind of Settlement of Damages: The Apologetic Tendencies in German History Writing," in *Forever in the Shadow of Hitler. Original Documents of the Historikerstreit, the Controversy Concerning the Singularity of the Holocaust*, translated by James Knowlton and Truett Cates (Atlantic Highlands, N.J.: Humanities Press), 34–44.

—— (2001) *Zeit der Übergänge* (Frankfurt am Main: Suhrkamp).

Hailbronner, K. (1989) "Citizenship and Nationhood in Germany," in R. Brubaker (ed.), *Immigration and the Politics of Citizenship in Europe and North America* (Lanham, Md.: German Marshall Fund of the United States and University Press of America), 67–81.

Halfmann, J. (1997) "Immigration and Citizenship in Germany. Contemporary Dilemmas," *Political Studies* 45 (2): 60–274.

Hammar, T. (1990) *Democracy and the Nation-state. Aliens, Denizens, and Citizens in a World of International Migration* (Aldershot: Gower).

Harlen, C.M. (2002) "Schröder's Economic Reforms: The End of *Reformstau?*" *German Politics* 11 (1): 61–80.

Hartkopf, G. and E. Bohne (1983) *Umweltpolitik. Grundlagen, Analyse und Perspektiven* (Opladen: Westdeutscher Verlag).

Hartz-Kommission (Kommission Moderne Dienstleistungen am Arbeitsmarkt) (2002) *Bericht der Kommission zum Abbau der Arbeitslosigkeit und zur Umstrukturierung der Bundesanstalt für Arbeit* (Berlin: BMAS).

Hassel, A. (2000) "Bündnisse für Arbeit: Nationale Handlungsfähigkeit im europäischen Regimewettbewerb," *Politische Vierteljahresschrift* 41 (3): 498–524.

—— (2002) "Sozialpakte. Die deutschen Gewerkschaften im Bündnis für Arbeit," *Forschungsjournal Neue Soziale Bewegungen* 15 (2): 58–67.

Hassel, A. and R. Hoffmann (1999) "Nationale Bündnisse und Perspektiven eines europäischen Beschäftigungspakts," in H.-J. Arlt and S. Nehls (eds.), *Bündnis für Arbeit. Konstruktion, Kritik, Karriere* (Opladen: Westdeutscher Verlag), 213–29.

Heinze, R.G. (2002) *Die Berliner Räterepublik. Viel Tat—wenig Rat?* (Wiesbaden: Westdeutscher Verlag).

Heitmeyer, W. (1994) "Das Desintegrations-Theorem," in W. Heitmeyer (ed.), *Das Gewalt-Dilemma einer gelähmten Gesellschaft* (Frankfurt am Main: Suhrkamp), 29–72.

—— (ed.) (1997) *Was hält die Gesellschaft zusammen? Vol. 2: Bundesrepublik Deutschland—Auf dem Weg von der Konsens- zur Konfliktgesellschaft* (Frankfurt am Main: Suhrkamp).

Hellmann, G. (1999) "Nationale Normalität als Zukunft? Zur Außenpolitik der Berliner Republik," *Blätter für deutsche und internationale Politik* no. 7: 837–47.

—— (2002) "Der 'deutsche Weg'. Eine außenpolitische Gratwanderung," *Internationale Politik* 57 (9): 4–9.

Helms, L. (2000) " 'Politische Führung' als politikwissenschaftliches Problem," *Politische Vierteljahresschrift* 43 (3): 411–34.

—— (2001) "The Changing Chancellorship: Resources and Constraints Revisited," *German Politics* 10 (2): 155–68.

Hettich, F. and C. Schmidt (2001) "Die deutsche Steuerbelastung im internationalen Vergleich: warum Deutschland (k)eine Steuerreform braucht," *Perspektiven der Wirtschaftspolitik* 2 (1): 45–60.

Hibbs, D. (1977) "Political Parties and Macroeconomic Policy," *American Political Science Review* 71 (4): 1467–87.

Hinrichs, J. (2002) *Die Verschuldung des Bundes 1962–2001*, Arbeitspaper No. 77 (June 2002) (Sankt Augustin: Konrad-Adenauer-Stiftung).

Hippler, J. (1999) "Rückblick auf den Kosovokrieg—eine Zeitschriftenschau," *epd-Entwicklungspolitik* no. 22 (November): 71–73, retrieved on 08/29/2002

at <http://www.jochen-hippler.de/Aufsatze/Ruckblick_auf_den_ Kosovokrieg/
ruckblick_auf_den_kosovokrieg.html>.

Hirschl, B. and E. Hoffmann (2002) "Zwei Jahre EEG—eine Erfolgsbilanz!"
Ökologisches Wirtschaften no. 3–4: 8–9.

Hogwood, Patricia (1999) "Playing to Win. Adapting Concepts of Rationality
and Utility for the German Coalition Context," in R. Sturm and S. Kropp
(eds.), *Hinter den Kulissen von Regierungsbündnissen. Koalitionspolitik in Bund,
Ländern und Gemeinden* (Baden-Baden: Nomos), 15–43.

Holtmann, E. and H. Voelzkow (eds.) (2000) *Zwischen Wettbewerbs- und
Verhandlungsdemokratie. Analysen zum Regierungssystem der Bundesrepublik
Deutschland* (Wiesbaden: Westdeutscher Verlag).

Hrbek, R. (1972) *Die SPD—Deutschland und Europa* (Bonn: Europa Union
Verlag).

Huber, E. and J.D. Stephens (2001) *Development and Crisis of the Welfare
State—Parties and Policies in Global Markets* (Chicago: University of Chicago
Press).

Hübner, K. (1998) *Der Globalisierungskomplex* (Berlin: edition sigma).

—— (2002) *Reputation Failure: The Economic and Monetary Union and Its
Institutional Flaws*, Working Paper Series (Toronto: Canadian Centre for
German and European Studies).

Hübner, K. and U. Petschow (2001) *Spiel mit Grenzen. Ökonomische
Globalisierung und soziale Kohäsion* (Berlin: edition sigma).

Hundt, D. (1999) "Der Kampf gegen die Arbeitslosigkeit ist zu gewinnen," in
H.-J. Arlt and S. Nehls (eds.), *Bündnis für Arbeit. Konstruktion, Kritik,
Karriere* (Opladen: Westdeutscher Verlag), 57–68.

Hunger, U. (2000) *Party Competition and Inclusion of Immigrants in Germany*,
Paper presented at the Annual Meeting of the American Political Science
Association, Washington D.C., August 2000.

IG Metall (1995) *Bündnis für Arbeit*, 18. ordentlicher Gewerkschaftstag der IG
Metall vom 29.10. bis 04.11.1995 in Berlin. Materialien/Auszüge aus dem
Protokoll, ed. Industriegewerkschaft Metall—Vorstand [n.p.].

Ingenhorst, H. (1997) *Die Rußlanddeutschen. Aussiedler zwischen Tradition und
Moderne* (Frankfurt am Main: Campus).

Inglehart, R. (1977) *The Silent Revolution: Changing Values and Political Styles
among Western Publics* (Princeton, N.J.: Princeton University Press).

—— (1997) *Modernization and Postmodernization: Cultural, Economic, and
Political Change in 43 Societies* (Princeton, N.J.: Princeton University Press).

Isensee, J. (1983) *Das Grundrecht auf Sicherheit. Zu den Schutzpflichten des frei-
heitlichen Verfassungsstaates* (Berlin: de Gruyter).

Jäger, W. (1988) "Von der Kanzlerdemokratie zur Koordinationsdemokratie,"
Zeitschrift für Politik 35 (1): 15–33.

Jänicke, M. and H. Jörgens (1998) "National Environmental Policy Planning in
OECD Countries: Preliminary Lessons from Cross-National Comparisons,"
Environmental Politics 7 (2): 27–54.

Jänicke, M. and A. Volkery (2002) *Agenda 2002ff. Perspektiven und Zielvorgaben nachhaltiger Entwicklung für die nächste Legislaturperiode,* Kurzgutachten für die Friedrich-Ebert-Stiftung und die Heinrich-Böll-Stiftung (Berlin).

Jänicke, M. and H. Weidner (in collaboration with H. Jörgens) (1997) *National Environmental Policies. A Comparative Study of Capacity-Building* (Berlin: Springer).

Jänicke, M., P. Kunig, and M. Stitzel (1999) *Lern- und Arbeitsbuch Umweltpolitik. Politik, Recht und Management des Umweltschutzes in Staat und Unternehmen* (Bonn: Dietz).

Jänicke, M., D. Reiche, and A. Volkery (2002) "Rückkehr zur Vorreiterrolle?— Umweltpolitik unter Rot-Grün," *Vorgänge* 41 (1): 50–61.

Janning, J. (1999) "Bundesrepublik Deutschland," in W. Weidenfeld and W. Wessels (eds.), *Jahrbuch der Europäischen Integration 1998/99* (Bonn: Europa Union Verlag), 325–32.

—— (2001) "Bundesrepublik Deutschland," in W. Weidenfeld and W. Wessels (eds.), *Jahrbuch der Europäischen Integration 2000/2001* (Bonn: Europa Union Verlag), 317–24.

Janning, J. and P. Meyer (1998) "Deutsche Europapolitik—Vorschläge zur Effektivierung," in W. Weidenfeld (ed.), *Deutsche Europapolitik—Optionen wirksamer Interessenvertretung* (Bonn: Europa Union Verlag), 267–68.

Jeffery, C. (1999) "From Cooperative Federalism to a 'Sinatra Doctrine' of the Länder?" in C. Jeffery (ed.), *Recasting German Federalism. The Legacies of Unification* (London: Pinter), 329–42.

Joerges, C., Y. Mény, and J.H.H. Weiler (eds.) (2000) "What Kind of Constitution for What Kind of Polity? Responses to Joschka Fischer," retrieved on 09/05/2002 at <http://www.iue.it/RSC/pdf/j.%20Fischer%20text%20.pdf>.

Jopp, M. (2001) "Deutsche Europapolitik unter veränderten Rahmenbedingungen: Bilanz—Strategien—Optionen," in H. Schneider, M. Jopp, and U. Schmalz (eds.), *Eine neue deutsche Europapolitik? Rahmenbedingungen—Problemfelder— Optionen* (Bonn: Europa Union Verlag), 813–61.

—— (2002) "Perceptions of Germany's European Policy—An Introduction," in M. Jopp, H. Schneider, and U. Schmalz (eds.), *Germany's European Policy: Perceptions in Key Partner Countries* (Bonn: Europa Union Verlag), 9–19.

Jopp, M., B. Lippert, and H. Schneider (eds.) (2001) *Das Vertragswerk von Nizza und die Zukunft der Europäischen Union* (Bonn: Europa Union Verlag).

Jopp, M., H. Schneider, and U. Schmalz (eds.) (2002) *Germany's European Policy: Perceptions in Key Partner Countries* (Bonn: Europa Union Verlag).

Joppke, C. (1999) *Immigration and the Nation-State. The United States, Germany, and Britain* (Oxford: Oxford University Press).

Jun, U. (2000) "Die Transformation der Sozialdemokratie. Der Dritte Weg, New Labour und die SPD," *Zeitschrift für Politikwissenschaft* 10 (4): 1501–30.

Kaase, M. and H.-D. Klingemann (1994) "The Cumbersome Way to Partisan Orientations in a 'New' Democracy," in M.K. Jennings and T.E. Mann (eds.),

Elections at Home and Abroad (Ann Arbor, MI: University of Michigan Press), 123–56.

Kastoryano, R. (2002) *Negotiating Identities. States and Immigrants in France and Germany* [original: La France, l'Allemagne et leurs immigrés: négocier l'identité, 1997] (Princeton, N.J.: Princeton University Press).

Katsioulis, C. [n.d.] "Der Kosovo-Konflikt. Ablauf- und Verhaltensanalyse," retrieved on 08/16/2002 at <http://www.uni-trier.de/uni/fb3/politik/liba/pafe/docs/jugo/kosovo_verh.pdf>.

Katzenstein, P.J. (1987) *Policy and Politics in West Germany. The Growth of a Semisovereign State* (Philadelphia: Temple University Press).

—— (1990) *West Germany's Internal Security Policy: State and Violence in the 1970s and 1980s* (Ithaca, N.Y.: Cornell University, Center for International Studies).

—— (1997) "United Germany in an Integrating Europe," in P.J. Katzenstein (ed.), *Tamed Power. Germany in Europe* (Ithaca, N.Y.: Cornell University Press), 1–48.

Kaufmann, F.X. (1970) *Sicherheit als soziologisches und sozialpolitisches Problem. Untersuchungen zu einer Wertidee hochdifferenzierter Gesellschaften* (Stuttgart: Ferdinand Enke).

Kern, K. and S. Bratzel (1996) "Umweltpolitischer Erfolg im internationalen Vergleich," *Zeitschrift für Umweltpolitik und Umweltrecht* 19 (3): 277–312.

Kern, K., H. Jörgens, and M. Jänicke (2001a) *The Diffusion of Environmental Policy Innovations. A Contribution to the Globalisation of Environmental Policy*, Discussion Paper FS II 01-302 (Berlin: Wissenschaftszentrum Berlin für Sozialforschung).

Kern, K., I. Kissling-Näf, U. Landmann, and C. Mauch (in collaboration with T. Löffelsend) (2001b) *Policy Convergence and Policy Diffusion by Governmental and Non-Governmental Institutions. An International Comparison of Eco-labeling Systems*, Discussion Paper FS II 01-305 (Berlin: Wissenschaftszentrum Berlin für Sozialforschung).

Kern, M. (1973) *Konzertierte Aktion als Versuch einer Verhaltensabstimmung zwischen Regierung und Wirtschaftsverbänden* (Cologne: Institut für Wirtschaftspolitik).

Kersbergen, K. van (1995) *Social Capitalism—A Study of Christian Democracy and the Welfare State* (London: Routledge).

Kitschelt, H. (1999) "European Social Democracy Between Political Economy and Electoral Competition," in H. Kitschelt, P. Lange, G. Marks, and J.D. Stephens (eds.), *Continuity and Change in Contemporary Capitalism* (Cambridge: Cambridge University Press), 317–45.

Klingemann, H.-D. and B. Wessels (2001) "The Political Consequences of Germany's Mixed-Member System: Personalization at the Grass-Roots?" in M.S. Shugart and M.P. Wattenberg (eds.), *Mixed-Member Electoral Systems: The Best of Both Worlds?* (Oxford: Oxford University Press), 279–96.

Kohl, H. (1996) "Speech on the Occasion of the Granting of the Honorary Doctorate by the Catholic University of Leuwen/Belgium on 2 February 1996," *Bulletin* (Presse- und Informationsamt der Bundesregierung) no. 12 (Bonn, 8 February 1996): 129–31.

Kohl, J. (2001) "Die deutsche Rentenreform im europäischen Kontext," *Zeitschrift für Sozialreform* 47 (6), 619–43.

Koopmans, R. (1996) "Asyl. Die Karriere eines politischen Konflikts," in W. van den Daele and F. Neidhardt (eds.), *Kommunikation und Entscheidung. Politische Funktionen öffentlicher Meinungsbildung und diskursiver Verfahren (WZB-Jahrbuch 1996)* (Berlin: edition sigma), 167–92.

—— (1999) "Germany and its Immigrants: An Ambivalent Relationship," *Journal of Ethnic and Migration Studies* 25 (4): 624–47.

Koopmans, R. and P. Statham (1999) "Challenging the Liberal Nation-State? Postnationalism, Multiculturalism, and the Collective Claims Making of Migrants and Ethnic Minorities in Britain and Germany," *American Journal of Sociology* 105 (3): 652–96.

Korte, K.-R. (1998) "Unbefangen und gelassen. Über die außenpolitische Normalität der Berliner Republik," *Internationale Politik* 53 (12): 3–12.

—— (2000a) "Solutions for the Decision Dilemma: Political Styles of Germany's Chancellors," *German Politics* 9 (1): 1–22.

—— (2000b) "Veränderte Entscheidungskultur: Politikstile der deutschen Bundeskanzler," in K.-R. Korte and G. Hirscher (eds.), *Darstellungspolitik oder Entscheidungspolitik? Über den Wandel von Politikstilen in westlichen Demokratien* (Munich: Hanns-Seidel-Stiftung), 13–40.

Korte, K.-R. and A. Maurer (2001) "Innenpolitische Grundlagen der deutschen Europapolitik: Konturen der Kontinuität und des Wandels," in H. Schneider, M. Jopp, and U. Schmalz (eds.), *Eine neue deutsche Europapolitik? Rahmenbedingungen—Problemfelder—Optionen* (Bonn: Europa Union Verlag), 195–230.

Koskela, E., R. Schöb, and H.-W. Sinn (2001) "Green Tax Reform and Competitiveness," *German Economic Review* 2 (1): 19–30.

Krause, J. (2000) "Die deutsche Politik in der Kosovo-Krise," in J. Krause (ed.), *Kosovo. Humanitäre Intervention und kooperative Sicherheit in Europa* (Opladen: Leske + Budrich), 103–19.

Kreutz, D. (2002) "Neue Mitte im Wettbewerbsstaat. Zur sozialpolitischen Bilanz von Rot-Grün," *Blätter für deutsche und internationale Politik* no. 4: 463–72.

Kropp, S. (2001) *Regieren in Koalitionen. Handlungsmuster und Entscheidungsbildung in deutschen Länderregierungen* (Wiesbaden: Westdeutscher Verlag).

Kropp, S. and R. Sturm (1998) *Koalitionen und Koalitionsvereinbarungen. Theorie, Analyse und Dokumentation* (Opladen: Leske + Budrich).

Kultusministerium des Landes Baden Württemberg (2000) "Verlässliche Grundschule flächendeckend umgesetzt," Press Release 25 October 2000.

Kurthen, H. (1995) "Germany at the Crossroads: National Identity and the Challenges of Immigration," *International Migration Review* XXIX (4): 914–38.

Lafontaine, O. (1999) *Das Herz schlägt links* (Munich: Econ).

Lamping, W. and F.W. Rüb (2001) *From the Conservative Welfare State to "Something Uncertain Else": The New German Pension Politics*, Centre for Social and Public Policy, Discussion Paper No. 12 (Hannover: Universität Hannover).

Lane, J.-E. and S.O. Ersson (1994) *Politics and Society in Western Europe*, 3rd edition (London: Sage).

Lang, K. (2002) "Die Mitte gewinnen—die Mehrheit nicht verlieren," *Forschungsjournal Neue Soziale Bewegungen* 15 (2): 49–57.

Lees, C. (2000) *The Red-Green Coalition in Germany. Politics, Personalities and Power* (Manchester: Manchester University Press).

Leggewie, C. (1994) "Ethnizität, Nationalismus und multikulturelle Gesellschaft," in H. Berding (ed.), *Nationales Bewußtsein und kollektive Identität* (Frankfurt am Main: Suhrkamp), 46–64.

—— (1999) "Böcke zu Gärtnern? Das Bündnis für Arbeit im Politikprozeß," in H.-J. Arlt and S. Nehls (eds.), *Bündnis für Arbeit. Konstruktion, Kritik, Karriere* (Opladen: Westdeutscher Verlag), 13–24.

Lehmbruch, G. (2000) *Parteienwettbewerb im Bundesstaat. Regelsysteme und Spannungslagen im politischen System Deutschlands*, 3rd edition (Opladen: Westdeutscher Verlag).

Leinemann, J. (2002) "Gold im Kopf," *Der Spiegel*, no. 38 (16 September 2002): 40–43.

Lepsius, M.R. (1985) "The Nation and Nationalism in Germany," *Social Research* 52 (1): 3–64.

Levy, D. (1999) "The Future of the Past: Historiographical Disputes and Competing Memories in Germany and Israel," *History and Theory* 38 (1): 51–67.

Liefferink, D. and M.S. Andersen (1998) "Strategies of the 'Green' Member States in EU Environmental Policy-Making," *Journal of European Public Policy* 5 (2): 254–70.

Lightfoot, S. and D. Luckin (2000) "The 1999 German Ecological Tax Law," *Environmental Politics* 9 (2): 163–67.

Lijphart, A. (1999) *Patterns of Democracy. Government Forms and Performance in Thirty-Six Countries* (New Haven, Conn.: Yale University Press).

Link, W. (1986) "Außen- und Deutschlandpolitik in der Ära Brandt 1969–1974," in K.-D. Bracher, W. Jäger, and W. Link (eds.), *Republik im Wandel 1969–1974. Die Ära Brandt* (Geschichte der Bundesrepublik Deutschland, Vol. 5/I) (Stuttgart: Deutsche Verlags-Anstalt), 163–282.

Link, W. (1987) "Außen- und Deutschlandpolitik in der Ära Schmidt 1974–1982," in W. Jäger and W. Link (eds.), *Republik im Wandel 1974–1982.*

Die Ära Schmidt (Geschichte der Bundesrepublik Deutschland, Vol. 5/II) (Stuttgart: Deutsche Verlags-Anstalt), 275–432.

Link, W. (2001) "Der internationale Wandel und die Europapolitik des vereinten Deutschland," in H. Schneider, M. Jopp, and U. Schmalz (eds.), *Eine neue deutsche Europapolitik? Rahmenbedingungen—Problemfelder—Optionen* (Bonn: Europa Union Verlag), 153–69.

Lippert, B. (1999) "Erweiterung und Agenda 2000," in W. Weidenfeld and W. Wessels (eds.), *Jahrbuch der Europäischen Integration 1998/99* (Bonn: Europa Union Verlag), 37–48.

—— (2001a). "Die EU-Erweiterungspolitik nach 1989—Konzeptionen und Praxis der Regierungen Kohl und Schröder," in H. Schneider, M. Jopp, and U. Schmalz (eds.), *Eine neue deutsche Europapolitik? Rahmenbedingungen—Problemfelder—Optionen* (Bonn: Europa Union Verlag), 349–92.

—— (2001b). "Neue Zuversicht und alte Zweifel: die Europäische Union nach 'Nizza' und vor der Erweiterung," in M. Jopp, B. Lippert, and H. Schneider (eds.), *Das Vertragswerk von Nizza und die Zukunft der Europäischen Union* (Bonn: Europa Union Verlag), 143–57.

Lippert, B. and W. Bode (2001) "Die Erweiterung und das EU-Budget—Reformoptionen und ihre politische Durchsetzbarkeit," *Integration* 16 (4): 369–89.

Lipset, S.M. and S. Rokkan (1967) "Cleavage Structures, Party Systems, and Voter Alignments: an Introduction," in S.M. Lipset and S. Rokkan (eds.), *Party Systems and Voter Alignments* (New York: Free Press), 1–67.

Logeay, C. (2001) "Labour Market in Downturn," *Economic Bulletin* no. 12, retrieved on 05/05/2003 at <http://www.diw.de/english/publikationen/bulletin/docs/eb01/n01_12dez_1.html>.

Long, S. (1997) *Regression Models for Categorical and Limited Dependent Variables* (Thousand Oaks: Sage).

Loske, R. and F. Steffe (2001) "Ökonomische Anreize in der Umweltpolitik—Plädoyer für einen Policy-Mix aus Ökosteuern, Subventionsabbau und Emissionshandel," *Blätter für deutsche und internationale Politik* no. 9: 1082–90.

Lovelace Jr., D. and T.-D. Young (1998) "Defining U.S. Atlantic Command's Role in the Power Projection Strategy," retrieved on 08/30/2002 at <http://www.carlisle.army.mil/usassi/ssipubs/pubs98/atlantic/atlantic.htm>.

Luhmann, N. (1991) *Soziologie des Risikos* (Berlin: de Gruyter).

Lupia, A. and M.D. McCubbins (1994) "Who Controls? Information and the Structure of Legislative Decision Making," *Legislative Studies Quarterly* 19 (3): 361–84.

Machiavelli, N. (1983) *The Discourses*, edited with an Introduction by Bernard Crick using the Translation of L.J. Walker, S.J. with revisions by B. Richardson (Harmondsworth: Penguin Classics).

Malunat, B.M. (1994) "Die Umweltpolitik der Bundesrepublik Deutschland," *Aus Politik und Zeitgeschichte*, B49/94: 3–12.

Maor, M. (1998) *Parties, Conflicts and Coalitions in Western Europe. Organisational Determinants of Coalition Bargaining* (London/New York: Routledge and LSE).

Marhold, H. (ed.) (2001) *Die neue Europadebatte. Leitbilder für das Europa der Zukunft* (Bonn: Europa Union Verlag).

Markovits, A.S. (1982) "Introduction: Model Germany—A Cursory Overview of a Complex Construct," in A.S. Markovits (ed.), *The Political Economy of West Germany. Modell Deutschland* (New York: Praeger), 1–11.

Markovits, A.S. and P.S. Gorski (1993) *The German Left: Red, Green and Beyond* (New York: Oxford University Press).

Markovits, A.S. and S. Reich (1997) *The German Predicament: Memory and Power in the New Europe* (Ithaca: Cornell University Press).

Massarrat, M. (2000) "Ölpreise, Ökosteuern und das Konzept einer nachhaltigen Klimaschutzpolitik," *Blätter für deutsche und internationale Politik* no. 9: 1494–503.

Meier-Braun, K.-H. (1995) "40 Jahre 'Gastarbeiter' und Ausländerpolitik in Deutschland," *Aus Politik und Zeitgeschichte*, B35/95: 14–22.

Meng, R. (2002) *Der Medienkanzler—Was bleibt vom System Schröder?* (Frankfurt am Main: Suhrkamp).

Merkel, W. (2000) "Die Dritten Wege der Sozialdemokratie ins 21. Jahrhundert," *Berliner Journal für Soziologie* 10 (1): 99–124.

Merkl, P.H. (1965) *The Origins of the West German Republic* (New York: Oxford University Press).

—— (1999) "Introduction: Fifty Years of the German Republic," in P.H. Merkl (ed.), *The Federal Republic of Germany at Fifty. The End of a Century of Turmoil* (New York: University Press), 1–24.

Meyer, B. and K. Müller (2002) "Ökologische Steuerreform—Blick nach vorne," *punkt.um* no. 6: 19–20.

Meyer, T. (1998) "Retrenchment, Reproduction, Modernization: Pension Politics and the Decline of the German Breadwinner Model," *Journal of European Social Policy* 8 (3): 195–211.

Mez, L. (2001) "Der deutsche Weg zum Ausstieg aus der Atomenergie—im Konsens zu einer Quote für Atomstrom," in A. Gourd and T. Noetzel (eds.), *Zukunft der Demokratie in Deutschland* (Opladen: Leske + Budrich), 416–32.

Moene, K.O. and M. Wallerstein (1999) "Social Democratic Labor Market Institutions: A Retrospective Analysis," in H. Kitschelt, P. Lange, G. Marks, and J.D. Stephens (eds.), *Continuity and Change in Contemporary Capitalism* (Cambridge: Cambridge University Press), 231–60.

Mückenberger, U. (1999) "So viel Pull wie möglich—wo wenig Push wie nötig. Was zieht die Menschen zur Umverteilung der Arbeit?" in H.-J. Arlt and S. Nehls (eds.), *Bündnis für Arbeit. Konstruktion, Kritik, Karriere* (Wiesbaden: Westdeutscher Verlag), 181–92.

Müller, E. (1989) "Sozial-liberale Umweltpolitik. Von der Karriere eines neuen Politikbereichs," *Aus Politik und Zeitgeschichte*, B47-48/89: 3–15.

Müller-Rommel, F. (2002) "The Lifespan and Political Performance of Green Parties in Western Europe," *Environmental Politics* 11 (1): 1–16.

Müller-Roschach, H. (1980) *Die deutsche Europapolitik 1949–1977. Eine politische Chronik* (Bonn: Europa Union Verlag).

Münz, R. and R. Ohliger (1997) "Long-distance Citizens: Ethnic Germans and their Immigration to Germany," in P. Schuck and R. Münz (eds.), *Paths to Inclusion* (New York: Berghahn), 155–201.

Münz, R. and R. Ulrich (1997) "Changing Patterns of Immigration to Germany: 1945–1995: Ethnic Origins, Demographic Structure, Future Prospects," in K. Bade and M. Weiner (eds.), *Migration Past, Migration Future: Germany and the United States* (New York: Berghahn), 65–119.

Murray, L. (1994) "Einwanderungsland Bundesrepublik Deutschland? Explaining the Evolving Positions of German Political Parties on Citizenship Policy," *German Politics and Society* 33 (3): 23–56.

Murswieck, A. (2003) "Des Kanzlers Macht: Zum Regierungsstil Gerhard Schröders," in C. Egle, T. Ostheim, and R. Zohlnhöfer (eds.), *Das rot-grüne Projekt. Eine Bilanz der Bundesregierung Schröder 1998–2002* (Wiesbaden: Westdeutscher Verlag), 117–36.

Neidhardt, F. (1978) "The Federal Republic of Germany," in S.B. Kamerman and A.J. Kahn (eds.), *Family Policy—Government and Families in Fourteen Countries* (New York: Columbia University Press), 217–38.

Nettelstroth, W. and E. Hülsmann (2000) "Bündnis für Arbeit, Ausbildung und Wettbewerbsfähigkeit in NRW—Eine Bestandsaufnahme," *WSI-Mitteilungen* 53 (7): 462–68.

Neumann, G. (2000) "Bündnisse für Arbeit in Deutschland—Ein Überblick," *WSI-Mitteilungen* 53 (7): 419–29.

Niclauß, K. (1988) *Kanzlerdemokratie. Bonner Regierungsstile von Konrad Adenauer bis Helmut Kohl* (Stuttgart: Kohlhammer).

—— (1998) *Der Weg zum Grundgesetz* (Paderborn: Ferdinand Schöningh).

—— (1999) "Bestätigung der Kanzlerdemokratie? Kanzler und Regierungen zwischen Verfassung und politischen Konventionen," *Aus Politik und Zeitgeschichte*, B20/99: 27–38.

Niedermayer, O. (1997) "Das gesamtdeutsche Parteiensystem," in O.W. Gabriel, O. Niedermayer, and R. Stöss (eds.), *Parteiendemokratie in Deutschland* (Bonn: Bundeszentrale für politische Bildung), 106–30.

—— (2000) "Die Entwicklung des deutschen Parteiensystems: eine quantitative Analyse," in M. Klein, W. Jagodzinski, E. Mochmann, and D. Ohr (eds.), *50 Jahre empirische Wahlforschung in Deutschland* (Opladen: Westdeutscher Verlag), 106–25.

Niejahr, E. and C. Tenbrock (2002) "Bundesanstalt für Alles," *Die Zeit* no. 28 (4 July 2002): 15–16.

Nullmeier, F. (2001) "Sozialpolitik als marktregulierte Politik," *Zeitschrift für Sozialreform* 47 (6): 645–67.

Nye, J.S. (2002) *The Paradox of American Power. Why the World's Only Superpower Can't Do It Alone* (Oxford: Oxford University Press).

Ostrom, E. (1991) "Rational Choice Theory and Institutional Analysis: Toward Complementarity," *American Political Science Review* 85 (1): 237–43.

Padgett, S. and T. Saalfeld (eds.) (2000) Bundestagswahl '98. *End of an Era?* (London: Frank Cass).

Pappi, F.U. (1973) "Parteiensystem und Sozialstruktur in der Bundesrepublik," *Politische Vierteljahresschrift* 14 (2): 191–213.

—— (1977) "Sozialstruktur, gesellschaftliche Wertorientierungen und Wahlabsicht," in M. Kaase (ed.), *Wahlsoziologie heute—Analysen aus Anlaß der Bundestagswahl 1976* (Opladen: Westdeutscher Verlag), 195–229.

—— (1979) "Konstanz und Wandel der Hauptspannungslinien in der Bundesrepublik," in J. Matthes (ed.), *Sozialer Wandel in Westeuropa* (Frankfurt am Main: Campus), 465–79.

—— (1986) "Wahlverhalten sozialer Gruppen bei Bundestagswahlen im Zeitverlauf," in H.-D. Klingemann and M. Kaase (eds.), *Wahlen und politischer Prozeß* (Opladen: Westdeutscher Verlag), 369–84.

—— (1990) "Sozialstruktur und Wahlverhalten im sozialen Wandel," in M. Kaase and H.-D. Klingemann (eds.), *Wahlen und Wähler: Analysen aus Anlaß der Bundestagswahl 1987* (Opladen: Westdeutscher Verlag), 15–30.

Pappi, F.U. and S. Shikano (2001) "Personalisierung der Politik in Mehrparteiensystemen am Beispiel deutscher Bundestagswahlen seit 1980," *Politische Vierteljahresschrift* 42 (3): 355–85.

—— (2002) "Sachpolitik und Kompetenz als Beurteilungskriterien von großen und kleinen Wettbewerbern in deutschen Bundestagswahlkämpfen," in H.-D. Klingemann and M. Kaase (eds.), *Wahlen und Wähler. Analysen aus Anlaß der Bundestagswahl 1998* (Opladen: Westdeutscher Verlag), 309–50.

Parker, G. (2002) "France and UK Call for New Force at Top of EU," *Financial Times* (15 May 2002).

Paterson, W. and G. Smith (eds.) (1981) *The West German Model. Perspectives on a Stable State* (London: Frank Cass).

Patzelt, W.J. (1997) "German MPs and their Roles," in W.C. Müller, and T. Saalfeld (eds.), *Members of Parliament in Western Europe: Roles and Behaviour* (London: Frank Cass), 55–78.

—— (1998) "Ein latenter Verfassungskonflikt? Die Deutschen und ihr parlamentarisches Regierungssystem," *Politische Vierteljahresschrift* 39 (4): 725–57.

PDS (Partei des Demokratischen Sozialismus) (2002) "Es geht auch anders: Nur Gerechtigkeit sichert Zukunft! Programm der PDS zur Bundestagswahl 2002," retrieved 07/30/2002 at <http://www.pds-online.de>.

Pehle, H. (1997) "Germany: Domestic Obstacles to an International Forerunner," in M.S. Andersen and D. Liefferink (eds.), *European Environmental Policy. The Pioneers* (Manchester: Manchester University Press), 161–209.

Piepenschneider, M. (2001) "Deutsche Prioritäten bei der Reform der europäischen Institutionen und Verfahren," in H. Schneider, M. Jopp, and U. Schmalz (eds.), *Eine neue deutsche Europapolitik? Rahmenbedingungen—Problemfelder—Optionen* (Bonn: Europa Union Verlag), 325–48.

Poguntke, T. (2000) "Präsidiale Regierungschefs: Verändern sich die parlamentarischen Demokratien," in O. Niedermayer and B. Westle (eds.), *Demokratie und Partizipation. Festschrift für Max Kaase* (Wiesbaden: Westdeutscher Verlag), 356–71.

Pollack, D. (1997) "Das Bedürfnis nach sozialer Anerkennung," *Aus Politik und Zeitgeschichte* B13/97: 3–14.

Popper, K. (1988) "The Open Society and Its Enemies Revisited," *The Economist* (23 April 1988): 23–28.

Pradetto, A. (1998a) "Identitätssuche als Movens der Sicherheitspolitik. Die NATO-Osterweiterungsdebatte im Lichte der Herausbildung neuer Identitäten im postkommunistischen Ostmitteleuropa und in der Allianz," *Osteuropa. Zeitschrift für Gegenwartsfragen des Ostens* 48 (2): 134–47.

—— (1998b) *Konfliktmanagement durch militärische Intervention? Dilemmata westlicher Kosovo-Politik* (Hamburg: Institut für Internationale Politik an der Universität der Bundeswehr Hamburg).

—— (1999) "Zurück zu den Interessen. Das Strategische Konzept der NATO und die Lehren des Krieges," *Blätter für deutsche und internationale Politik* no. 7: 805–15.

—— (2002a) "Funktionen militärischer Konfliktregelung durch die NATO," *Aus Politik und Zeitgeschichte*, B 24/02: 12–21.

—— (2002b) "Internationale Gemeinschaft und Hegemonialmacht: UNO und USA nach dem 11. September 2001," in A. Schölzel (ed.), *Das Schweigekartell. Fragen und Widersprüche zum 11. September* (Berlin: Kai Homilius Verlag), 119–49.

—— (2002c) "Die Vereinten Nationen nach den Terroranschlägen vom 11. September 2001: Anhängsel der USA?" *S + F Vierteljahresschrift für Sicherheit und Frieden* no. 1: 9–18.

Pradetto, A. and M.F. Alamir (1997) *Osteuropa und die Erweiterung der NATO: Identitätssuche als Motiv für Sicherheitspolitik* (Hamburg: Institut für Internationale Politik an der Universität der Bundeswehr Hamburg).

Priewe, J., C. Scheuplein, and K. Schuldt (2002) *Ostdeutschland 2010—Perspektiven der Investitionstätigkeit* (Berlin: Otto-Brenner-Stiftung).

Pulzer, P. (1996) "Model or Exception—Germany as a Normal State?" in G. Smith, W.E. Paterson, and S. Padgett (eds.), *Developments in German Politics 2* (Durham, N.C.: Duke University Press), 303–16.

Quermonne, J.-L. (2000) "Die Europäische Union auf der Suche nach legitimen und effizienten Institutionen," *Integration* 15 (2): 81–88.

Radtke, F.-O. (1994) "The Formation of Ethnic Minorities and the Transformation of Social into Ethnic Conflicts in a So-Called Multi-Cultural Society—The Case of Germany," in J. Rex and B. Drury (eds.), *Ethnic Mobilization in a Multi-Cultural Europe* (Aldershot: Avebury), 30–37.

Raschke, J. (2001) *Die Zukunft der Grünen* (Frankfurt am Main: Campus).

Rattinger, H. and T. Faas (2002) "Wahrnehmungen der Wirtschaftslage und Wahlverhalten 1977 bis 1998," in H.-D. Klingemann and M. Kaase (eds.), *Wahlen und Wähler. Analysen aus Anlaß der Bundestagswahl 1998* (Opladen: Westdeutscher Verlag), 283–308.

Rau, J. (2001) "Die Quelle der Legitimation deutlich machen. Eine föderale Verfassung für Europa," in H. Marhold (ed.), *Die neue Europadebatte. Leitbilder für das Europa der Zukunft* (Bonn: Europa Union Verlag), 132–35.

Rauer, V. and O. Schmidtke (2001) "Integration als Exklusion? Zum medialen und alltagspraktischen Umgang mit einem umstrittenen Konzept," *Berliner Journal für Soziologie* 11 (3): 277–96.

Reiche, D. (2000) "Erneuerbare Energien im europäischen Vergleich," *Blätter für deutsche und internationale Politik* no. 12: 1504–08.

—— (2002) *Handbook of Renewable Energies in the European Union. Case Studies of all Member States* (Frankfurt am Main: Peter Lang).

Renzsch, W. (1989) "Föderale Finanzbeziehungen im Parteienstaat. Eine Fallstudie zum Verlust politischer Handlungsmöglichkeiten," *Zeitschrift für Parlamentsfragen* 20 (3): 330–45.

Reutter, W. (2001) "Deutschland. Verbände zwischen Pluralismus, Korporatismus und Lobbyismus," in W. Reutter and P. Rütters (eds.), *Verbände und Verbandssysteme in Westeuropa* (Opladen: Leske + Budrich), 75–101.

Riedmüller, B. and T. Olk (eds.) (1994) *Grenzen des Sozialversicherungsstaates* (Opladen: Westdeutscher Verlag).

Robbers, G. (1987) *Sicherheit als Menschenrecht* (Baden-Baden: Nomos).

Roberts, G.K. (1999) "Developments in the German Green Party: 1995–99," *Environmental Politics* 8 (3): 147–52.

Rohrschneider, R. (1999) *Learning Democracy: Democratic and Economic Values in Unified Germany* (Oxford: Oxford University Press).

Rohrschneider, R. and R.J. Dalton (eds.) (2003) *Judgment Day and Beyond: The 2002 Bundestagswahl,* Special issue of German Politics and Society 21 (1).

Rohrschneider, R. and D. Fuchs (1995) "A New Electorate? Economic Trends and Electoral Choice in the 1994 Federal Election in Germany," *German Politics and Society* 13 (1): 100–22.

—— (2003) "It Used to be the Economy. Issues and Party Support in the 2002 Election," *German Politics and Society* 21 (1): 76–94.

Rohrschneider, R. and R. Schmitt-Beck (2002) "Trust in Democratic Institutions in Germany: Theory and Evidence Ten Years after Unification," *German Politics* 11 (3): 35–57.

Roller, E. (1992) *Einstellungen der Bürger zum Wohlfahrtsstaat der Bundesrepublik Deutschland* (Opladen: Westdeutscher Verlag).

—— (1997) "Sozialpolitische Orientierungen nach der deutschen Vereinigung," in O.W. Gabriel (ed.), *Politische Orientierungen und Verhaltensweisen im vereinigten Deutschland* (Opladen: Leske + Budrich), 115–46.

Roller, E. (1998) "Positions- und performanzbasierte Sachfragenorientierungen und Wahlentscheidung: Eine theoretische und empirische Analyse aus Anlaß der Bundestagswahl 1994," in M. Kaase and H.-D. Klingemann (eds.), *Wahlen und Wähler. Analysen aus Anlaß der Bundestagswahl 1994* (Opladen: Westdeutscher Verlag), 173–202.

Roller, E. (1999a) "Shrinking the Welfare State: Citizens' Attitudes Towards Cuts in Social Spending in Germany in the 1990s," *German Politics* 18 (1): 21–39.

—— (1999b) "Sozialpolitik und demokratische Konsolidierung. Eine empirische Analyse für die neuen Bundesländer," in F. Plasser, O.W. Gabriel, J.W. Falter, and P.A. Ulram (eds.), *Wahlen und politische Einstellungen in Deutschland und Österreich* (New York: Peter Lang), 313–46.

Rometsch, D. (1994) "The Federal Republic of Germany," in D. Rometsch and W. Wessels (eds.), *The European Union and Member States: Towards Institutional Fusion?* (Manchester: Manchester University Press), 61–104.

Ross, J. (2002) "Fürstenerzieher und Bewährungshelfer," *Die Zeit* no. 33 (8 August 2002).

Rüdig, W. (2000) "Phasing out Nuclear Energy in Germany," *German Politics* 9 (1): 43–80.

—— (2002) "Germany," *Environmental Politics* 11 (1): 78–111.

Rudzio, W. (1991) "Informelle Entscheidungsmuster in Bonner Koalitionsregierungen," in H.-H. Hartwich and G. Wewer (eds.), *Regieren in der Bundesrepublik 2. Formale und informale Komponenten des Regierens* (Opladen: Leske + Budrich), 13–40.

—— (2000) *Das politische System der Bundesrepublik*, 4th edition (Opladen: Leske + Budrich).

Sartori, G. (1976) *Parties and Party Systems: A Framework for Analysis* (Cambridge: Cambridge University Press).

Schäfer, C. (2001) "Ungleichheiten politisch folgenlos? Zur aktuellen Einkommensverteilung," *WSI-Mitteilungen* 54 (11): 659–73.

Scharpf, F.W. (1997) *Games Real Actors Play. Actor-Centred Institutionalism in Policy Research* (Boulder, Colo.: Westview Press).

—— (2000) "Economic Changes, Vulnerabilities, and Institutional Capabilities," in F.W. Scharpf and V.A. Schmidt (eds.), *Welfare and Work in the Open Economy. From Vulnerability to Competitiveness* (Oxford: Oxford University Press), 21–124.

Scheich, J., W. Eichhammer, U. Boede, F. Gagelmann, E. Jochem, B. Schlomann, and H.-J. Ziesing (2001) "Greenhouse Gas Reductions in Germany—Lucky Strike or Hard Work?" *Climate Policy* 1 (3): 363–80.

Scheingold, S.A. (1984) *The Politics of Law and Order. Street Crime and Public Policy* (New York: Longman).

Schettkat, R. (2002) *Regulation in the Dutch and German Economies at the Root of Unemployment?* CEPA Working Paper 2002–05 [n.p.].

Schimmelfennig, F. (2001) "The Community Trap: Liberal Norms, Rhetorical Action and the Eastern Enlargement of the European Union," *International Organization* 55 (1): 47–80.

Schindler, P. (1999) *Datenhandbuch zur Geschichte des Deutschen Bundestages 1949 bis 1999*, 3 vols. (Baden-Baden: Nomos).

Schmähl, W. (1999) "Rentenversicherung in der Bewährung: Von der Nachkriegszeit bis an die Schwelle zum neuen Jahrhundert," in M. Kaase and G. Schmid (eds.), *Eine lernende Demokratie—50 Jahre Bundesrepublik Deutschland (WZB-Jahrbuch 1999)* (Berlin: edition sigma), 397–423.

Schmidt, M.G. (1987) "West Germany: The Policy of the Middle Way," *Journal of Public Policy* 7 (2): 139–77.

—— (1996) "The Grand Coalition State," in Josep M. Colomer (ed.), *Political Institutions in Europe* (London: Routledge), 62–98.

Schmidtke, O. (2001) "Trans-National Migration: A Challenge to European Citizenship Regimes," *World Affairs* 164 (1): 3–16.

—— (ed.) (2002) *The Third Way Transformation of Social Democracy* (Aldershot: Ashgate).

Schneider, H. (1998) "Ein Wandel europapolitischer Grundverständnisse? Grundsatzüberlegungen, Erklärungsansätze und Konsequenzen für die politische Bildungsarbeit," in M. Jopp, A. Maurer, and H. Schneider (eds.), *Europapolitische Grundverständnisse im Wandel. Analysen und Konsequenzen für die politische Bildung* (Bonn: Europa Union Verlag), 19–147.

Schneider, H., M. Jopp, and U. Schmalz (eds.) (2001) *Eine neue deutsche Europapolitik? Rahmenbedingungen—Problemfelder—Optionen* (Bonn: Europa Union Verlag).

Schoen, H. and J.W. Falter (2002) "It's Time for a Change! Wechselwähler bei der Bundestagswahl 1998," in H.-D. Klingemann and M. Kaase (eds.), *Wahlen und Wähler. Analysen aus Anlaß der Bundestagswahl 1998* (Opladen: Westdeutscher Verlag), 57–90.

Schröder, G. (1997) "Ich will Europäer sein," Interview with Gerhard Schröder, *Der Spiegel* no. 9 (24 February 1997): 43–45.

—— (1998a) "Speech at the SPD Congress in Saarbrücken," 8 December 1998 [n.p.].

—— (1998b) "Weil wir Deutschlands Kraft vertrauen. Government Declaration of 10 November 1998," retrieved on 10/24/2002 at <http://www.germany-info.org/relaunch/politics/speeches/111098.html>.

—— (1998c) *Weil wir Deutschlands Kraft vertrauen. Die Regierungserklärung von Bundeskanzler Gerhard Schröder* (10 November 1998) (Bonn: Presse- und Informationsamt der Bundesregierung).

—— (1999a) "Außenpolitische Verantwortung Deutschlands in der Welt," Speech at the Deutsche Gesellschaft für Auswärtige Politik (DGAP) in Berlin, 2 September 1999. *Bulletin der Bundesregierung*, no. 55 (20 September 1999): 573–77.

—— (1999b) "Rede des deutschen Bundeskanzlers, Gerhard Schröder, vor der französischen Nationalversammlung am 30. November 1999 in Paris über

Grundlagen für ein europäisches Krisenmanagement (extracts)," retrieved on 08/29/2002 at <http://www.dgap.org/IP/ip0004/schroeder301199.htm>.

Schröder, G. (1999c) "Speech at the French National Assembly," Paris, 30 November 1999, retrieved on 09/05/2002 at <http://www.assemblee-nationale.fr/international/reception-allemagne.asp>.

—— (2000) "EU-Osterweiterung. Speech at the Upper Palatinate Regional Conference 2000 in Weiden," 18 December 2000, retrieved on 08/29/2002 at <http://www.zeit.de/reden/Europapolitik/200106_20001218_Gerhard Schroder.html>.

—— (2001a) "Governmental Declaration at the German Bundestag about the Results of the European Council in Nice," 19 January 2001, retrieved on 09/05/2002 at <http://www.bundesregierung.de/Nachrichten/ Regierungserklaerungen-,8674.29210/Regierungserklaerungen-von-Bunde.htm>.

—— (2001b) "Verantwortung für Europa—Deutschland in Europa. Decision of the SPD Party Convention, Nuremberg," 22 November 2001, retrieved on 09/04/2002 at <http://parteitag.spd.de/servlet/PB/menu/1002021/index. html>.

—— (2002a) "Am Ende der ersten Halbzeit," Interview with Chancellor Schröder, *Die Zeit*, no. 34 (15 August 2002): 3–4.

—— (2002b) "Gerechtigkeit im Zeitalter der Globalisierung schaffen—für eine Partnerschaft in Verantwortung," Regierungserklärung vom 29. Oktober 2002, retrieved on 11/11/2002 at <http://www.bundeskanzler.de>.

—— (2002c) "Nation, Patriotismus, Interesse." Rede des SPD-Parteivorsitzenden und Bundeskanzlers bei der Diskussion "Nation, Patriotismus, Demokratische Kultur." 8 May 2002, retrieved on 08/29/2002 at <http://www.zeit.de/ reden/Gesellschaft/200220_schroeder_patriotismus.html>.

—— (2002d) "Rede von Bundeskanzler Gerhard Schröder zum Wahlkampfauftakt am Montag, 5 August 2002, in Hannover (Opernplatz)," retrieved on 12/05/2002 at <http://www.spd.de/servlet/PB/show/1017816/ btw2002_0805schroeder_rede.pdf>.

Schröder, G. and T. Blair (1999a) "Europe: The Third Way," 8 June 1999, retrieved on 07/29/1999 at <http://www.labour.org.uk/views/items/ 00000053.html>.

—— (1999b) "Der Weg nach vorn für Europas Sozialdemokraten. Ein Vorschlag von Gerhard Schröder und Tony Blair vom 8. Juni 1999," *Blätter für deutsche und internationale Politik* no. 44: 887–900.

—— (2002) "Joint Letter to Prime Minister Aznar of Spain," 25 February 2002 retrieved on 09/05/2002 at <http:www.number-10.gov.uk/output.uk/ output/page4498.asp>.

Schroeder, W. (2001) " 'Konzertierte Aktion' und 'Bündnis für Arbeit': Zwei Varianten des deutschen Korporatismus," in A. Zimmer and B. Weßels (eds.), *Verbände und Demokratie in Deutschland* (Opladen: Leske + Budrich), 29–54.

Seeleib-Kaiser, M. (1997) "Der Sozialstaat und die Ware Arbeitskraft," *Widersprüche* no. 64: 41–51.

—— (2001) *Globalisierung und Sozialpolitik. Ein Vergleich der Diskurse und Wohlfahrtssysteme in Deutschland, Japan und den USA* (Frankfurt am Main: Campus).

—— (2002a) "A Dual Transformation of the German Welfare State?" *West European Politics* 25 (4): 25–48.

—— (2002b) "Neubeginn oder Ende der Sozialdemokratie? Eine Untersuchung zur programmatischen Reform sozialdemokratischer Parteien und ihrer Auswirkung auf die Parteiendifferenzthese," *Politische Vierteljahresschrift* 43 (3): 478–96.

Shalev, M. (1983) "The Social Democratic Model and Beyond," *Comparative Social Research* vol. 6: 315–51.

Shepsle, K.A. (1988) "Representation and Governance," *Political Science Quarterly* 103 (3): 461–84.

Shugart, M.S. and M.P. Wattenberg (eds.) (2001) *Mixed-Member Electoral Systems: The Best of Both Worlds?* (Oxford: Oxford University Press).

Smith, G. (1991) "The Resources of a German Chancellor," in G.W. Jones (ed.), *West European Prime Ministers* (London: Frank Cass), 48–61.

—— (1994) "The Changing Parameters of the Chancellorship," in S. Padgett (ed.), *Adenauer to Kohl. The Development of the German Chancellorship* (London: Hurst), 178–97.

Sorensen, P.B. (2002) "The German Business Tax reform of 2000: A General Equilibrium Analysis," *German Economic Review* 3 (4): 347–78.

Soysal, Y.N. (1997) "Changing Parameters of Citizenship and Claims-making: Organized Islam in European Public Spheres," *Theory and Society* 26 (4): 509–27.

SPD (Sozialdemokratische Partei Deutschlands) (1998) *Arbeit, Innovation und Gerechtigkeit—SPD-Programm für die Bundestagswahl 1998*, Antrag 4 (in der Fassung der Antragskommission) (Berlin: SPD Parteivorstand).

—— (2001) *Sozialdemokratie heute: Sicherheit im Wandel* (Berlin: Sozialdemokratische Partei Deutschlands).

—— (2002) "Erneuerung und Zusammenhalt—Wir in Deutschland," retrieved on 07/30/2002 at <http://regierungsprogramm.spd.de/servlet/PB/show/1076396/spd-regierungsprogramm.pdf>.

SPD and Bündnis '90/Die Grünen (1998) *Aufbruch und Erneuerung. Deutschlands Weg ins 21. Jahrhundert. Koalitionsvereinbarung zwischen der Sozialdemokratischen Partei Deutschlands und Bündnis '90/Die Grünen, Bonn, 20. Oktober 1998* (Bonn: Vorstand der SPD).

—— (2002) *Erneuerung—Gerechtigkeit—Nachhaltigkeit. Für ein wirtschaftlich starkes, soziales und ökologisches Deutschland. Für eine lebendige Demokratie*, Koalitionsvertrag zwischen SPD und Bündnis '90/Die Grünen vom 16. Oktober 2002, ed. Vorstand der SPD (Berlin: SPD).

SRU (Rat von Sachverständigen für Umweltfragen) (2000) "Handlungsbedarf zur Umsetzung des Nachhaltigkeitskonzepts," *Zeitschrift für angewandte Umweltforschung* 13 (1–2): 84–93.

—— (2002) *Umweltgutachten 2002—Für eine neue Vorreiterrolle* (Berlin).

Steinmeier, F.-W. (2001a) "Abschied von den Machern," *Die Zeit*, no. 10 (01 March 2001): 9.

—— (2001b) "Konsens und Führung," in F. Müntefering and M. Machnig (eds.), *Sicherheit im Wandel. Neue Solidarität im 21. Jahrhundert* (Berlin: Berliner Vorwärts-Verlag), 273–70.

Stephan, P. (2001) *Die Welt auf dem Prüfstand—Nachhaltigkeitsindikatoren in Rio-Follow-up* (Bonn: Forum Umwelt & Entwicklung).

Sternberger, D. (1990) *Verfassungspatriotismus. Schriften Bd.X* (Frankfurt am Main: Suhrkamp).

Stinchcombe, A.L. (1975) "Social Structure and Politics," in F.I. Greenstein and N.W. Polsby (eds.), *Macropolitical Theory, Handbook of Political Science. Vol. 3* (Reading, Mass.: Addison-Wesley).

Streeck, W. (1999) *Korporatismus in Deutschland. Zwischen Nationalstaat und Europäischer Union* (Frankfurt am Main: Campus).

Streeck, W. and R.G. Heinze (1999) "Runderneuerung des deutschen Modells," in H.-J. Arlt and S. Nehls (eds.), *Bündnis für Arbeit. Konstruktion, Kritik, Karriere* (Wiesbaden: Westdeutscher Verlag), 147–66.

Sturm, R. (1999) "Party Competition and the Federal System: The Lehmbruch Hypothesis Revisited," in C. Jeffery (ed.), *Recasting German Federalism. The Legacies of Unification* (London: Pinter), 197–216.

SVR (Sachverständigenrat zur Begutachtung der gesamtwirtschaftlichen Entwicklung) (2001) *Für Stetigkeit—Gegen Aktionismus. Jahresgutachten 2001/02* (Stuttgart: Metzler-Poeschel).

—— (2002) *Jahresgutachten 2002/2003. Zwanzig Punkte für Beschäftigung und Wachstum* (Stuttgart: Metzler-Poeschel), retrieved on 11/18/2002 at <http://www.sachvestaendigenrat.org>.

Taagepera, R. (1997) "Effective Number of Parties for Incomplete Data," *Electoral Studies* 16 (2): 145–51.

Taagepera, R. and M.S. Shugart (1989) *Seats and Votes—The Effects and Determinants of Electoral Systems* (New Haven, Conn.: Yale University Press).

Tews, K. (2002) *Die Ausbreitung von Energie/CO$_2$–Steuern. Internationale Stimuli und nationale Restriktionen*, FFU-Report 08-2002 (Freie Universität Berlin: Forschungsstelle für Umweltpolitik).

Tews, K., P.-O. Busch, and H. Jörgens (2002) *The Diffusion of New Environmental Policy Instruments*, FFU-Report 01-2002 (Freie Universität Berlin: Forschungsstelle für Umweltpolitik).

Thränhardt, D. (1993) "Die Ursprünge von Rassismus und Fremdenfeindlichkeit im parteipolitischen Wettbewerb. Ein Vergleich der Entwicklungen in England, Frankreich und Deutschland," *Leviathan* 20 (3): 336–57.

Thränhardt, D. (1995) "Germany: An Undeclared Immigration Country," *New Community* 21 (1): 19–36.

—— (ed.) (1996) *Europe—A New Immigration Continent. Policies and Politics in Comparative Perspective* (Münster: Lit.).

Trittin, J. (2000) "Germany's New Climate Change Program. Speech of the German Minister on Environment in The Hague on November 22, 2000," retrieved on 08/12/02 at <http://www.bmu.de/english/fset1024.php>.

—— (2002) "Wirksamkeitstest bestanden—Positive Effekte der ökologischen Steuerreform," *Politische Ökologie* no. 77–78: 38–39.

Truger, A. (ed.) (2001a) *Rot-grüne Steuerreformen in Deutschland. Eine Zwischenbilanz* (Marburg: Metropolis).

—— (2001b) "Der deutsche Einstieg in die ökologische Steuerreform," in A. Truger (ed.), *Rot-grüne Steuerreformen in Deutschland. Eine Zwischenbilanz* (Marburg: Metropolis), 135–69.

Tsebelis, G. (1999) "Veto Players and Law Production in Parliamentary Democracies: An Empirical Analysis," *American Political Science Review* 93 (2): 591–608.

Umweltbundesamt (2002) *Nachhaltige Entwicklung in Deutschland—Die Zukunft dauerhaft umweltgerecht gestalten* (Berlin: Erich Schmidt Verlag).

Unterhinninghofen, H. (2002) "Rotgrünes Rentenprojekt. Umbau des Sozialsystems, Eigenvorsorge und Tarifpolitik," *Kritische Justiz* 35 (2): 213–27.

Van Roozendaal, P. (1992) "The Effect of Dominant and Central Parties on Cabinet Composition and Durability," *Legislative Studies Quarterly* 17 (1): 5–36.

Vobruba, G. (1990) "Lohnarbeitszentrierte Sozialpolitik in der Krise der Lohnarbeit," in G. Vobruba (ed.), *Strukturwandel der Sozialpolitik* (Frankfurt am Main: Suhrkamp), 11–80.

Volle, A. and W. Weidenfeld (eds.) (2000) *Europäische Sicherheitspolitik in der Bewährung* (Bielefeld: Bertelsmann).

Waddington, D. (1992) *Contemporary Issues in Public Disorder* (London: Routledge).

Walser, M. (1998) "Erfahrungen beim Verfassen einer Sonntagsrede," in F. Schirrmacher (ed.), *Die Walser-Bubis-Debatte. Eine Dokumentation* (Frankfurt am Main: Suhrkamp), 7–17.

Weidner, H. (1989) "Die Umweltpolitik der konservativ-liberalen Regierung— Eine vorläufige Bilanz," *Aus Politik und Zeitgeschichte*, B47–48/89: 16–28.

—— (1999) "Umweltpolitik: Entwicklungslinien, Kapazitäten und Effekte," in M. Kaase and G. Schmid (ed.), *Eine lernende Demokratie. 50 Jahre Bundesrepublik Deutschland (WZB-Jahrbuch 1999)* (Berlin: edition sigma), 425–60.

Weil, P. (1996) "Nationalities and Citizenship: The Lessons of the French Experience for Germany and Europe," in D. Cesarani and M. Fulbrook (eds.), *Citizenship, Nationality and Migration in Europe* (New York: Routledge), 74–87.

Wessels, B. (1991) "Vielfalt oder strukturierte Komplexität? Zur Institutionalisierung politischer Spannungslinien im Verbände- und Parteiensystem in der Bundesrepublik," *Kölner Zeitschrift für Soziologie und Sozialpsychologie* 43 (3): 454–75.

—— (1999) "Die deutsche Variante des Korporatismus," in M. Kaase and G. Schmid (eds.), *Eine lernende Demokratie. 50 Jahre Bundesrepublik Deutschland (WZB-Jahrbuch 1999)* (Berlin: edition sigma), 87–114.

—— (2000a) "Die Entwicklung des deutschen Korporatismus," *Aus Politik und Zeitgeschichte*, B26–27/00: 16–21.

—— (2000b) "Gruppenbindung und Wahlverhalten: 50 Jahre Wahlen in der Bundesrepublik," in M. Klein, W. Jagodzinski, E. Mochmann, and D. Ohr (eds.), *50 Jahre Empirische Wahlforschung in Deutschland* (Opladen: Westdeutscher Verlag), 129–55.

Wessels, W. (2002) "Der Konvent: Modelle für eine innovative Integrationsmethode," *Integration* 17 (2): 83–98.

Winkler, H.A. (2002) "Der lange Schatten des Reiches. Eine Bilanz deutscher Geschichte," *Merkur* 56 (3): 221–33.

Wollschläger, F. (2001) "Gesetz zur Reform der Renten wegen verminderter Erwerbsfähigkeit," *Deutsche Rentenversicherung* 56 (5): 276–94.

World Commission on Environment and Development (1987) *Our Common Future* (Oxford: Oxford University Press).

Zahrnt, A. (2001) "Was bringt Rot-Grün für die Umwelt?" *Blätter für deutsche und internationale Politik* no. 1: 70–76.

Zank, W. (1998) *The German Melting-Pot: Multiculturality in Historical Perspective* (New York: St. Martins Press).

Zitzelsberger, H. (2002) "Highlights of the German Tax Reform 2002," *Intertax* 30 (2): 78–81.

Index